MW00773186

KUDZU
ON THE
IVORY TOWER

From the Backwoods
to an Academic Career
in the Deep, Deep South

EVAN PEACOCK

Kudzu on the Ivory Tower

From the Backwoods
to an Academic Career
in the Deep, Deep South

Evan Peacock

© 2021 by Evan Peacock
ISBN 978-1734573077

BORGO
PUBLISHING

www.borgopublishing.com

Text and cover design: Borgo Publishing, Tuscaloosa, Alabama
Cover artwork: Judith Jeffrey
Author's photo: Agnes Ray

All rights reserved. This book or any portion thereof
may not be reproduced or used in any manner whatsoever
without the express written permission of the publisher
except for the use of brief quotations in a book review.

Printed in the USA

CONTENTS

To Peacocks and their progeny,
Diverse, and yet homogeny.
Through joy and pain, you still re-
main,
My favorite phylogeny.

…and most importantly…

To David, Laura, Sebastian, and Sara;
Nikki, Paul, and Marigold;
Rob, Sandy, and Nathaniel;
Judy and Clifford;
and to Janet, who connected us all.

FOREWORD

IN THE SUMMER OF 2020, I COMPOSED AN AUTOBIOGRAPHICAL ESSAY, "Archaeological Fieldwork" and sent it to various colleagues. Evan Peacock immediately responded. "Why, thank you, Ian. I'm glad you're writing this stuff down, and I enjoy reading it. I have been up to much the same thing, as you will see from the attached monstrosity of a manuscript. Don't share this around, please, as it still very much is in draft form, and as I haven't decided what, if anything, I want to try to do with it. But writing it all down was both cathartic and a whole lot of fun. Hope you like it." I did indeed like it. I could not fathom how an archaeologist like Evan who has spent a lifetime studying and writing about evolutionary processes in archaeology had managed so effectively to prove Darwin wrong? If life goes from point A to point Z, Evan's existence should have ended at B, at least according to natural selection. Instead, he lived to tell his tale. The more I read the more I gasped, alternating between laughter, disgust, and just plain awe.

What you are about to read is another version of *The Adventures of Huckleberry Finn*, with Evan Peacock serving as Twain's model for Huck. Born in Clarksdale, Mississippi in 1961, Evan was one of seven backwoods Delta boys. Their maternal Granddaddy referred to them simply as "the heathens." He used the term endearingly, but Evan always suspected he really didn't know their names. There were just too many of them, and all were equally wild. Evan himself was the second to the youngest, probably the worst position to be in; the last born at least has a fair chance of being spoiled. With Pop, their equally wild father, as a model, Evan and his brothers were free spirits. They were absolute geniuses in fashioning unique ways to blow themselves to bits, not to mention doing damage to any and all who ventured into their world. Although the family was poor, the kids did not know it. They moved twenty-nine times over a sixteen-year period. "The correlation between those moves and rent deadlines is a strong one," says Evan. When he was five the family finally moved into a permanent home in Choctaw County, a dogtrot cabin located in the boonies about five miles from the village of French Camp. "I remember Mom's words to Pop as we stood in the dirt yard looking at the house for the first time: 'Oh, Bill, it's beautiful!' Those were encouraging words. And it was beautiful, lying on a small plot of land nestled among pastures, fields, and lush hard-wood forests and within a good slingshot's pull of a lovely unspoiled creek." From there the adventures gush forth, as narrated in the very colorful prose of the author.

I say the family was poor, but that must be understood solely in economic terms. What this bevy of boys had were loving parents and, most importantly, a Mom who insisted that they read. The family budget couldn't support much in the buying of books, but that wasn't going to thwart their mother's goal. The bookmobile in French Camp became a common destination for a pick-up truck loaded with Peacock kids. In addition to reading, their mother encouraged them to look to the ground. "Mom taught us how to search for fossils in gravel after they finally put rock on the dirt road in front of our house, creating magic out of the mundane, which is what she did best. She had a hard life, but she never had a hard heart." Here indeed was the formula for success for seven "heathens" who could very easily have gone in unwholesome directions. All were successful in life because they did eventually mature, "There is a difference between growing older and maturing, of course. We are all doomed to the first, while some never manage the second, as often is evidenced by the way we treat one another." These are solid words of wisdom, but to get to a point where they could be realized and uttered, the first twenty years of life must occur—that was never a guarantee in Evan's story.

After reading Evan's manuscript, I said to Easty Lambert-Brown of Borgo Publishing and of Ernest & Hadley Booksellers, who also happens to be my beloved spouse, "This work of Evan's needs to be published. It is unique. It is good. It is very good." Thankfully, she agreed. As you read *Kudzu on the Ivory Tower* you will witness a life in transition, the course of which is anything but smooth. Part One deals with the family, life on the farm, getting the basics of an education, military service, the endless pursuit of menial jobs simply to feed the rats in his domicile so they wouldn't feed on him, and then the epiphany. Not content to spend his life as a night worker at a convenience store, or a roofer, or an electrician more likely to die from electrocution than to fix the problem at hand, Evan quite abruptly made the decision to go to college. While standing on a rooftop on a sweltering summer day amid the stench of tar, he decided that it was high time to become an archaeologist—enter Part Two.

Other than mentioning a single class visit to Mississippi State's Cobb Institute as a lad, we do not get much of an inkling as to why Evan suddenly decided to be an archaeologist. I really do believe it was an epiphany though and I'm wondering if this is the norm for many if not most archaeologists? Whereas Evan's decision was declared from a lofty perch, high on a rooftop, in my own life the exact same epiphany occurred while lying in a state of drunken stupor in the bilge of a boat. Both Evan and I knew from the moment we started to do actual fieldwork, however, that we had indeed made the right decision.

The second half of this book deals with the progress of maturity. Evan first became a student, then an archaeologist, then a husband and father, and finally a professor. At the center of all of this is Janet Rafferty, his teacher, his spouse, and eventually his colleague. Although much older than Evan, the chemistry between them existed right from the beginning. Until Janet's death in 2014, they shared thirty-four years of life together, a solid measure of a successful relationship. As Evan matured, he came to realize that there were parts of his life he wished he could do over. From studying anthropology he learned about race; what it was and, most importantly, what it was not. Growing up in the backwoods of Mississippi in the 1960s and 1970s was not so challenging because most folks of the period knew the difference. There was white and there was black, and never the twain shall meet. Of course, they did meet, daily, and it was Evan's generation that dealt directly with the forced conjunction, primarily in terms of schooling. To his surprise, he learned that kids of varying hues really were not all that different. Later he also came to learn that assigning people to races or artifacts to types were arbitrary distinctions. Variations are important to study, he says, as they can reflect on many matters, but when they become a means of separating things into groups, they take on a life of their own. And when the groupings involve people and social matters, they are dangerous, very dangerous indeed. In "Lessons Learned," the final essay, the tone of the book changes, the presentation stiffens, the teacher emerges. At this point the reader recognizes that the message has become very serious indeed.

The maturing process is complete and the book is a whole by virtue of the two women in Evan Peacock's life. In his youth he was inordinately lucky to have a loving Mom who encouraged him to read and to look for meaning in rocks. As an adult he was fortunate to love and be loved by a woman who was much older and much wiser, who taught him to be an archaeologist, a husband, and a father. I say, "much wiser" (as would he), but I suspect that Evan impacted his mother and spouse in ways that he himself has not realized, or else is too self-defacing to propose. We have the impression that his mother's ideas about race might have been changing in her later years because of Evan stirring the pot, and we also suspect that Janet's notions as to the positive worth of Red Bird Imitation Vienna Sausages might have improved at his urging. Nope—that did not happen. The Vienna Sausages tale is just too horrible to even imagine, and I'll leave it at that. Janet must have wondered at times if maybe there still was a bit of the heathen in the man with whom she shared a life. Had she raised the matter, I suspect that Evan would have nodded, winked, and responded with his usual refrain, "That's an excellent idea!" Let us proceed.

Ian W. Brown
Tuscaloosa, July 2021

PART ONE

OUT OF THE EGG

PEACOCK—WHAT KIND OF A NAME IS THAT? I CAN ONLY ASSUME THAT ONE of my ancestors was a snappy dresser, a strutting egotist, or both. I once visited a genealogy booth at a county fair in England, where the pleasant young lass tending the table obligingly looked up my family crest: sable three peacocks displayed, in their pride, argent. Her hand-drawn sketch looks a lot like three Thanksgiving turkeys forming rank against the village butcher. Another version shows a head of armor sporting a long, frilly, red plume draped theatrically down the back, with the head of a blue peacock, trying not to grin over the rose in its beak, rising out of the top of the helm. On a shield below, three peacock heads dexter whisper conspiratorially into the ears of their decapitated neighbors. Neither version was likely to strike much fear into the hearts of the foe, but I suppose one could have rammed one's beak into enemy hauberks while they were wiping tears of laughter from their eyes. One downside to my peculiar surname is that people seem to have a hard time spelling it. Anyone taking my name, on the phone or over a counter, or whatever, *always* starts by saying, in a voice designed to reach the outer moons of Jupiter, "OK, that's P-e-a...", followed by a pregnant pause. I then am obliged to spell out the remainder, so that any bystanders within earshot would be forgiven for thinking that I suffer from Tourette syndrome.

According to "A History of the Peacock Family," by George F. Peacock, our ancestors were of Scottish descent, the clan's American progenitor being one John Peacock, born in the Borderlands in the Yeare of our Lorde 1698. John had partnered with his uncle to be the more gullible half of a traveling bagpiping duo. Lured by sailors onto a ship one night, ostensibly to provide entertainment for the crew, the clever John lost consciousness in suspicious (if not unholy) circumstances and awoke the next day to find himself bound for America. Upon arrival, he was sold to John Gosling, a justice of the peace (!) who owned a milling operation near Medford, New Jersey. Lumber milling being in his new environs a more practical profession than squeezing a musical windbag, John eventually prospered as a miller in his own right. He wedded Elizabeth Prickitt in 1723, and we are descended from their son Alexander. A more famous relative was John and Elizabeth's son Adonijah, born on August 5, 1724, in Chairville, New Jersey. Adonijah met his end in tragic, if spectacular, fashion. A manufacturer of gunpowder for the Continental Army, he was hastening to fill a rush order by General Washington by the questionable expedient of drying damp powder in a pot over a fire when the whole affair exploded. According to WikiTree,[1] "The blast was heard and felt some 30 miles from the Peacock home...It is said that women's ironing tables in nearby homes trembled. The damage was extensive. The Peacock home and workshop were gone. The only sign that a house had existed was a blackened crater where the cellar once was." While such single-minded devotion to duty is not the best-known of our family traits, the careless handling of gunpowder remains a point of stubborn pride among contemporary clan members.

I was born in Clarksdale, Mississippi, on October 10, 1961. I weighed five pounds, fifteen ounces, which is a bit more than your average adult Chihuahua. I am the sixth of seven sons born to Dennis Lamar Peacock, Sr., called "Bill" for some reason, and Joye Ann Peacock, *nee* Peters. Pop was one of thirteen children, a number that seems astonishing these days but wasn't out of the ordinary at a time when: a) offspring were your old-age insurance policy; and b) devoting time to fleeing from natural disasters (tornadoes, floods, locusts, revenuers) was the only acceptable form of birth control. I have been given to understand that his father Charlie supported his enormous brood largely through trapping, a phenomenal feat during the Great Depression era, when Mississippi was wiped nearly clean of

---

1 https://www.wikitree.com/wiki/Peacock-348

wildlife (a condition to which Grandpa Charlie apparently was an earnest contributor). I never met Charlie, as he passed before I was born; neither did I meet my paternal grandmother, Dora, to ask her why she didn't make Grandpa Charlie sleep in the barn before the hand-me-downs wore out. Good thing for us she didn't though, as Pop was the youngest of the lot.

Pop was a real mixed bag. He never finished high school, but had an innate sense of geometry and form, coupled with an imaginative design sense and a proclivity for experiment that made him an excellent craftsman. While sheet metal work was his particular forte, Pop could build anything out of anything. He once obtained an old hand-cranked forge for which he built a firebox out of rusty chunks of ferruginous sandstone and some sort of slate-gray mortar mix, allowing him to melt down anything at hand that was even remotely meltable. Like the aluminum beer cans he liquefied to make strangely-textured pewter-colored handles for wickedly hooked machetes fashioned from old lawn mower blades. Those things saw a lot of use around the farm. Another project that stands out is a metal steeple and cross that to this day grace the top of the First Baptist Church in French Camp, Mississippi. He constructed this icon over a period of several weeks, using a homemade metal brake in his homemade shop, working from homemade plans that he sketched out at odd intervals, Leonardo-like, with a knife-sharpened pencil on whatever flat surface was handy. After some period of work, Pop would requisition further funds from the church officers, part of which went for supplies and part of which went for liquid refreshment. Thus was an object of "vineration" achieved, twelve fluid ounces at a time. Pop liked history, fisticuffs, and Ole Miss football, except when they lost. He had a short fuse and a flash temper. Once, when the Rebels blew a game, I became aware of the fact when the front screen door banged open and our cheesy little brown plastic radio sailed out over the yard, exhibiting a perfect spiral of which Archie Manning would have been proud before it crashed to bits in the gravel driveway. At least Pop didn't run out to spike the ball.

Mom was the most stubbornly idealistic person in the face of adversity I ever have known. She was the eldest of three girls born to Bennie and Inez Peters. I never met Inez either, which is a shame because Mom clearly held her in great esteem. Inez must have been a patient person to put up with Granddaddy, a lovable rogue with a penchant for hard drinking and shooting craps. By the time I knew him, he drove a succession of enormous Buicks and playfully referred to his many grandkids as "heathens" while puffing away on a cartoon-sized cigar. I'm not sure Granddaddy actually knew our names, but he said "Heathen" with such sparkling affection that it all was fine by us. Legend has it that as a young man he once ran from the police while wearing a shirt that had been bloodied in a fight, assuming they were after him because of the altercation. As he swam across the Tallahatchie River, they opened fire, thinking he was one of John Dillinger's gang, who apparently were in the area at the time. Fortunately, they missed, which might explain why Dillinger got away with things for as long as he did. By the time I was old enough to know that I was one of the heathens, Granddaddy, ironically enough, had become a guard at the state penitentiary near Parchman. He carried an enormous .45 pistol that he once let me shoot; it was a terribly inaccurate and astonishingly loud piece of hardware. Granddaddy once brought over a bunch of homemade weapons confiscated from the prisoners, including a terrifying variety of shivs and an enormous shuriken forged from bipointed metal spikes welded together, presumably while the shop trusty was looking the other way. Needless to say, we heathen were entranced.

Inez passed away from tuberculosis in 1959, after a twenty-year battle with the disease. We were on a first-name basis with Granddaddy's second wife, Jean, who was not so fond of little primates, heathen or otherwise. Jean had a habit of pinching one's cheeks hard. Really, really hard. I always fancied that Mom was more like Inez. And, like Inez, she had to be very patient with her husband, whom she married in 1950 when Pop was twenty-two and Mom was just seventeen. She was, in fact, remarkably patient with all her immediate family, loyal to our many faults and dedicated to raising too many kids as best she could with never enough resources. Mom liked to make up songs and to characterize life in storybook ways, even though her own life wasn't the happiest of stories. For example, she liked to name places where we kids played: "Monkey Land" for a stretch of bottomland festooned with wild grape vines; "Cowboy Land" for the eroded banks of a road cut that did, in fact, look rather like miniature buttes; the "Cliffs" for another road cut dividing a prominent hill, leaving clay-loam faces exposed for handhold digging, initial carving, and other pedological adventures. Mom taught us how to search for fossils in gravel after they finally put rock on the dirt road in front of our house, creating magic out of the mundane, which is what she did best. She had a hard life, but she never had a hard heart.

Brothers…what can I say? Dennis is the eldest, and it shows. He is smart, has a razor-sharp wit, and still carries a bit of the sternness that helped him help Mom raise all the rest of us during some really difficult times. He was a Hebrew interpreter, first in the Navy and later in other branches of the Department of Defense. He was out of the Navy for a while after having been given a medical discharge for contracting a serious case of adult-onset diabetes, the kind where you have to stick needles into your body on a daily basis. He got back into the Navy after seeing a TV documentary about a one-legged frogman. If that dude could swim adequately with one leg, Dennis reckoned he could translate adequately with one-point-five brains. He made the case and won, which didn't surprise me in the least. He currently lives in Israel, where he teaches English to an astonishing coterie of clients and brews some wicked-good beer.

Bennie is next in line, and I love him: nerdy, sincere, and brainy in a nerdy, sincere, and brainy kind of way; slow to anger; able to flout tradition even while embracing it; incredibly hard working. He introduced me to science fiction, chess, and Go; I think I once took him squirrel hunting in return. Clearly, I am the better barterer. After a stint in the Navy and years of blue-collar labor, Bennie turned his fine mind to education, becoming a really good public-school math teacher of the kind that our country could use in much greater number. I once read a "Rate My Teachers" page generated by high school students in Xenia, Ohio, where he taught. The 4.6 out of 5 stars were indicative of his performance. One of my favorite comments reads, "I like his class because he keeps me alert. I always feel like he's gonna backhand me if I go to sleep." Bennie was Old School before Old School was cool.

Hardy was, I'm pretty sure, a superhero by night; by day, he was a self-taught engineer on a riverboat. He was the most original of us all, a real swashbuckler. He, too, did a tour in the Navy, but it didn't take, which was to be expected: swashbucklers don't like rules. Hardy really should have been an alchemist in the Middle Ages. It was he who discovered that if you fill the pointed plastic caps on the larger sort of rocket with black powder, the resulting aerial explosions are correspondingly spectacular. He, Dennis, and Bennie once enlisted our aid in unraveling scores of firecrackers so that the silvery-gray gunpowder could be tightly packed into a baby food jar; the fuses were braided together and the resulting gray rope run through a perforation in the metal cap. For some reason, this homemade bomb was detonated on the hood of a pickup truck. The blast punched a hole right through to the engine compartment. Not content to rest on those impressive laurels, Hardy once cut the end off of a driveshaft with a hacksaw and drilled a fuse-hole at the other end to form a makeshift cannon, which he then charged liberally with black powder. It successfully, and quite loudly, pro-pelled a peach can full of gravel over the tree line on the other side of the creek, probably traumatizing any number of squirrels in the process. Although it wasn't exercised nearly enough, Hardy had real artistic talent and, like Pop, he could make anything from anything. He always saw the humor in life and was generous of spirit in that it didn't matter if it was someone else making the joke. Hardy was larger than life, and his untimely death from brain cancer at the age of fifty-eight still seems unreal, like a bad episode in what had been a really good, old-time movie serial. Avast, my brother: I hope you had some idea of how much we all loved and admired you.

Glenn is the middle sibling, sandwiched in between the "older boys" and the "little kids." He, too, is larger than life, although with him it always has been a visibly conscious effort, perhaps one geared toward keeping up with his older brothers. He was a magnet for trouble: some, like construction site mishaps and snakebite, ac-cidental; others, like perennial insolvency and brushes with the law, the result of poor lifestyle choices as he scrappily bulled his way into adulthood. Jocosity, loudness, and generally acting out were unnecessary facades overlying a truly gentle soul. The confidence that comes with survivorship, aided by long marriage to a very supportive spouse, has allowed him to mellow with age and be easy with who he really is: one of the nicest people in the world. If there were ten thousand more just like him, we all would be that much better for it.

Robert: dear Robert! Awfully skinny to be an Atlas, he nevertheless tried to shoulder the world from a very early age. Our world, anyway, which was heavy enough. A natural-born worrier, Robert took it upon himself to act as a surrogate dad during our teenage years, an unsolicited effort not appreciated at a time when we already were busy trying to circumvent actual parental oversight. From Day One, Robert had something that it took me decades to develop, something that he still has in admirable abundance: real courage. This trait was displayed in his efforts to keep us in line while we were growing up; in his refusal to back down from any challenge, which led to physical altercations I would have talked my way out of; and in his shouldering of responsibility for anyone: family members who need backup, his companions during his tour in the Air Force, the work crews in the dairy company where he currently occupies a managerial role. Robert was the youngest grownup I ever have known. He is also very smart and is possessed of a wicked sense of humor that comes out in truly original ways. To give just one example, he coined a term that I really, really wish I'd thought of first: "*nausea vu*," the "feeling that you've puked there before." One can only bow.

Andy is the youngest and, if there is any justice in the world, he will be the last to go. He's earned that, given what rolls downhill and his position at the base of the slope. He once broke his collarbone sliding down the Cliffs on a rubber dish-drying mat, a stroke of brilliance dreamed up by an older brother (probably Hardy) with Andy as the test subject. He milked the sympathy engendered by the resultant arm sling for weeks, until it was noticed that he was swapping arms as convenient to immediate tasks. Relentlessly corny, built like a rock and occasionally as stubborn, Andy is a tinkerer whose mind eventually became as open as his heart. He was comfortable in the traditional roles of the olden days with which we all were more-or-less imbued, but he has met the inevitable changes in the world stoically. Some sort of weird cross between Tom Sawyer and Dr. Moreau, he takes his science fiction personally and never heard a bad joke that he wasn't far too eager to share. Andy deals fairly with anyone who deals fairly with him, and who can ask for more than that?

In Clarksdale, we lived in an old house next to the Safeway grocery store. One of my earliest memories is of walking with Glenn through a grimy alley on the far side of the store and finding a metal Green Hornet pin, a small treasure that I wonderingly liberated from the dirt. A harbinger, perhaps, of a life that eventually would center on liberating treasures from the dirt. Other memories from those earliest days are few and patchy, which is just as well given that chickens occupied two rooms of the house just prior to our tenancy. One memory involves a heavy truck moving slowly down the streets at dusk, releasing a sweet-smelling cloud of white vapor. We called it "the Fog Machine" and ran behind it, skinny wraiths gamboling happily about in the fantastic, artificial mist. Much later in life, I found out that this was the DDT sprayer making its anti-mosquito rounds, which could explain why I'm so bad at math.

The family moved a lot in those days. A *lot*. In order to obtain a security clearance for the Navy, Dennis once compiled a list of no fewer than twenty-nine addresses inhabited from May 1951 to September 1967. The correlation between those moves and rent deadlines is a strong one. I have only limited memories of some of those domiciles. We occupied a house for a time in Jackson, where I remember Andy getting stung by a bee in our back yard. I cried more than he did, much to Mom's exasperation. I remember a cousin(?) of some remove, and of particularly ample girth, who patiently allowed us kids to help as she made huge piles of cookies, some of which bore little silver sugar spheres hard enough to push our protesting deciduous teeth to the limit but which were nonetheless exotic and delicious. I would hide behind the couch there when the opening sequence of the "Underdog" cartoon came on every Saturday, terrified of the lumbering giant that Underdog would defeat, as he did every week, but one never knew; that giant was scary! I remember Dennis ushering all of us out onto the tin roof of an abandoned gas station we occupied for a while in Arkansas, where we ate oatmeal sweetened with cheap corn syrup while angry red wasps indignantly challenged our limited airspace. Or maybe they were just interested in the syrup. Either way, it was a pretty precarious perch, and I can only assume in retrospect that our parents weren't home at the time. On another occasion of parental absence, Dennis and Bennie were experimenting with the sounds made by firecrackers set off in different containers. Coke bottles and such were ok, but the intriguing metal pipe sticking up out of the ground promised an interesting aural return on the experiment. Which it did, as well as providing an equally impressive visual and tactile display. The ground shook and flames shot several feet into the air, as the pipe led to the station's underground gasoline storage tank, which still held residual fumes. The learned Portuguese polymath Abbé Correa said that there is a special providence over the United States and little children. Such providence apparently was in play that day, as both our brood and a sizable chunk of the state of Arkansas were spared an ignominious immolation. Adonijah would have been proud.

We eventually moved to the outskirts of French Camp, a small village of fewer than two hundred souls located on the Natchez Trace Parkway in the gently rolling interior hill country of Choctaw County. We successively lived in three houses there or nearby, beginning with one on the very edge of town that stood across from an old silent-movie-era theatre. I have only the vaguest memories of that building, of a wall running down the center of the big main room. I learned only recently that this wall was built to keep blacks and whites separated back in the days when the theatre was operational. The second house was the "house on the hill," which still had a functional two-seater outhouse that we used when the pipes froze. That made for some very cold trips to the outhouse. In fact, everything I remember about that house has to do with the fact that it was cold. The single most amazing picture in our family's collection is from that house. It shows the family dog curled up on a chair; the family cat is curled up on top of the family dog, and a chicken is standing on top of the family cat. Harsh weather and body heat combine to make strange bedfellows. We continued to use the outhouse as necessary until the time when Mom, tired of waiting for her enormous clutch to finish using the single toilet in the house, retired to the outer facility just before dawn. It was only as the sun came up that she discovered that Pop had removed the back of the building as part of a characteristically lackadaisical repair job.

When I was five, we moved to what really became home, an old enclosed dogtrot cabin out in the boonies about four miles west of town. I remember Mom's words to Pop as we stood in the dirt yard looking at the house for the first time: "Oh, Bill, it's beautiful!" Those were encouraging words. And it was beautiful, lying on a small plot of land nestled among pastures, fields, and lush hardwood forests and within a good slingshot's pull of a lovely unspoiled creek. I would grow up poor, a fact I didn't notice for many years. I would grow up rich, a fact I reveled in, as there were no boundaries to hem in our youthful energies and imaginations. What freedom, to run unchecked over the hardwood bluffs, to swing on grape vines across the creek, to catch a stringer-full of blunt-headed bream with a cane fishing pole and freshly dug earthworms!

That creek was central to our world. Its name is Elkins Creek, probably after a Gollop Elkins who lived in French Camp way back in the day. "Gollop." Only in the Deep South. Its spring-fed waters were too cold for real swimming but worked just fine to water the adjacent garden, nine painful bucketsful at a time. At night it gave off the most fantastic richly-aromatic scent, a sultry zephyr that settled with us as we sat on the front porch at dusk, watching clumsy chickens knock each other squawking into the void as they competed for space on the lowest branches of the massive oak tree in front of the house. In the spring, the creek often flooded, jumping its banks to submerge the wooden bridge so that the school bus driver would have to take the long way around to complete her route. I can still close my eyes and bring up the oddly-comforting smell of creosote, testament to the untold hours I sat on the edge of that bridge, cane pole in hand, waiting for the red and white plastic bob-ber to signify a hungry fish. If they weren't biting, maple seeds could be helicoptered into the watery abyss, or brown gravel collected and winged at skittish minnows. The shallower stretches were warm enough that one could wade, overturning pieces of bottom detritus to reveal annoyed crawdads, tiny darters, or befuddled madtoms. That was living.

The house was remote in a way that not so many houses in this country are these days. That had its disadvantages, one being that there were no neighborhood kids with whom to play. Other prob-lems were related to the lack of amenities. I remember one summer when our well gave up the ghost. We had to take glass jars and plas-tic milk jugs some distance down to a fork in the road where an or-nate cast-iron hand pump stood lonely vigil on a low hill, testament to an otherwise vanished homestead. The pump still functioned, for-tunately; several brisk workings of the handle and a strong stream of clear, truly delicious water would come gushing out. We would fill our containers and haul them back home on a Red Flyer wag-on. Many years later, some reprobate stole that pump. I hope he dropped it on his toe on the way down the hill.

Dusk was special, as the stars began to come out and lightning bugs wrote their mystical incantations in the warm summer air. Those insects were easily snatched up and stowed in canning jars, to be let loose in the house later, after the lights were out. It was bottled magic. Once, just as night fell, I had the great good fortune to be standing out in the yard as two massive thunderheads sidled up to one another, all bluff and gruff and rumbling. Of a sudden, ball lightning began jumping from one cloud to another. I counted forty-seven of those spectacular events before the bottom fell out and I had to take shelter. I only later learned what a rare spectacle it had been my privilege to observe. It could be pretty spooky, way out there in the boonies at night. Early one summer evening around 1970 we heard a panther scream. I didn't know enough at the time to make a formal report of that equally rare event, alas, but there is no doubt about what it was; it is a sound that will shred your soul from your bones. It sounds just like a terrified woman screaming at impossibly loud volume, a horrific wrenching shriek that must carry for miles. "Go close the chicken house door!" Mom ordered. Aghast, I hung around the back of the house for a bit, in the protective penumbra of the porch light, then cravenly slunk back inside. She found the chicken house door still open the next day, but had the kindness not to press me on the matter. What a mom; I really didn't deserve her.

Dusk was special for another reason; that's when "Lost in Space" came on. We loved television (especially Lost in Space!), although we only got three channels and mostly watched only two. The aerial was affixed to a tall metal pole on the east side of the house. Pop hammered a hole through the pole with a screwdriver (a process for which he apparently had a predilection, considering that he once cut a used sedan in half, one screwdriver blade-width at a time, in order to add a homemade wooden bed and convert it into an El Camino-style ride). Through the hole he emplaced another, larger screwdriver so that the pole could be turned, rotating the aerial to pick up Channel 9 (which came in well) or Channel 4 (which didn't). One of us would stand outside and twist the pole like a periscope operator until someone in the house yelled, "That's good!" The reception for Channel 2, PBS, was OK, but we weren't allowed to watch it much because there were too many shows featuring little black kids playing happily with little white kids, often with some scrawny, bearded Yankee in the background earnestly singing socialist propaganda over the plinking protestations of an overworked ukulele. There were exceptions to the public television moratorium, though. I remember the entire family gathering to watch episodes of Wodehouse Playhouse, which we all loved. Those actors were all white, of course. Really, really white, as: a) they were English, of Anglo-Saxon descent; and b) it was a black and white TV.

Most of our TV time came on Saturday mornings. I have to admit that cartoons of the time stank; the atrocious "Emergency +4" is a typical example (don't bother to Google™ it up). The live-action kids' shows were, if possible, even more awful: "Sigmund the Sea Monster," "H. R. Pufnstuf," "Electra Woman and Dyna Girl": they made the phrase "production value" oxymoronic in the extreme.

Sid and Marty Krofft inflicted a great deal of pain on my generation. We seldom missed an episode. We did at least have "Schoolhouse Rock," which definitely was not a misnomer: that stuff *rocked*! And, as education went, it worked. I remember taking a test at school for which we had to write out the preamble to the Constitution by memory. There was not a still leg in the room as all of the kids unconsciously kept time to the tune we'd heard hundreds of times on the TV: "We the people, in order to form a more perfect union…". The teacher must have been astonished by the high quality of the results. Maybe we should set all civics lessons to music. "Art for a Day" was another wonderful bit of programming, with its captivating harpsichord music and engaging historical vignettes. Where else would we rural ragamuffins have learned about the gripping drama of Rembrandt's *The Night Watch*? Or longed to join the ice skaters in Bruegel's *The Hunters in the Snow*? Or marveled at how van Eyck used the magic of oils to forever capture a bourgeois social climber and his trophy wife in "*Arnolfini and his Bride*"? Believe me, after "Electra Woman and Dyna Girl," it was nice to see some real art, even if none of us ever actually had been ice skating or had the faintest idea what "bourgeois'" meant.

When we weren't watching TV, we read. And read. And read. Somewhere Mom found a motto embroidered on cloth that was framed on our wall for many years: "Any child who has a houseful of books and two parents who love him isn't poor." By that standard, we resided comfortably within at least the *petit bourgeoisie*, even if we still didn't know what that meant. Our library was an eclectic mix, to be sure, as it was obtained mostly from small-town library giveaways and volumes salvaged from the public dump. It contained everything from fragile late-nineteenth-century printings of Jules Verne to a pretty full run of "Reader's Digest Condensed Books" (one of the worst ideas ever). Library giveaways not being as common as a country boy could wish, favored tomes were reread with studious regularity. I must have devoured *Journey to the Centre of the Earth* twenty times. Less genteel but endlessly satisfying were multitudinous Edgar Rice Burroughs and other pulp novels, many of which boasted those legendary Frazetta covers. One look at the over-muscled protagonists grappling with giant snakes or howling ape hordes and you definitely were not in Kansas—or Mississippi—anymore. And speaking of Kansas, L. Frank Baum was a wonder, as was C. S. Lewis. Tolkien was another perennial favorite, and H. G. Wells certainly was in the top ten. Felleman's *Best Loved Poems of the American People* was well thumbed. I still can recite numbers of the more maudlin or rollicking offerings from heart, and while Service couldn't be passed up, Frost's "Stopping by Woods on a Snowy Evening" was a revelation. Plus, we had the collected works of Edgar Allen Poe! Edith Hamilton's *Mythology* was another work that never grew old: poor Prometheus! *Boy's Life* magazine, taken by our grade school, wasn't much of a read, but it carried reprints of *Tintin*, which I happily discovered while "Children of the Sun" was being run. I've been a fan ever since. Our other main supply of literature came from the bookmobile. We'd pile into the pick-up truck (kids rode in back, like so much corn bound for market), head into French Camp, and come back home, arms laden with as much treasure as the kindly driver cum librarian would allow us to abscond with at any single time. That brought Dr. Seuss and Roald Dahl deep into the woods of Choctaw County. I think they would have liked our creek, and I'm sure that Dahl, for one, would have bottled his share of fireflies.

We had an enormous old travel chest full of comic books, mostly the product of my older brothers' efforts at hauling hay, hauling wood, or doing anything else they could to earn a dollar, which at the time would buy ten (!) comic books that were freely shared with us younger kids. If three older brothers earn four dollars each four times a year, that pretty quickly adds up to a lot of comic books. There also was a deal for a while where Mom got to bring home, for free, damaged issues from a grocery store where she worked. Those Silver Age comic books were terrific. We read them till they started falling apart; Mom would stitch them back together on her foot-operated Singer sewing machine and we'd read them to pieces again. One of the more unexpected, but eminently gratifying, phenomena of my adulthood has been to see the characters and stories I obsessed over as a child hitting the big screen to overwhelming popular, and even critical, acclaim. How weird is that? Had we saved those comic books in mint condition they now would be worth a small fortune. A few years back I looked up the going price on "Zzutak! The Thing that Shouldn't Exist!"(Marvel Comics, Strange Tales #88). Zzutak (a bizarre sort of Aztecky-looking monster that came to life from an image created with magical paints, ultimately to duke it out with another such impasto monstrosity) wasn't one of Marvel's better offerings, especially considering that it was the combined product of Stan Lee, Jack Kirby, and Steve Ditko (long may their glory reign!). But for some reason it stuck in my head. A good copy now goes for over a hundred bucks. If three brothers buy forty comic books each four times a year, and if you invest a few dollars in some shrink wrap...

Oh, well. There's more to life than money. If I remember correctly, Zzutak's battle turned out, appropriately enough, to be a "draw."

When Pop got tired of stepping over his comic-book-entranced progeny, he would kick us out of the house, proclaiming loudly (as was his wont) that life was a-wastin' (though not in such polite terms, as was also his wont). As often as not, we would smuggle some Robert E. Howard into our shorts (we rarely wore shirts— or shoes) and hit the woods, where we could read uninterrupted except for bookworm-feeding insects. When we did abandon the written page, entertainment was mostly self-manufactured and seemed to focus a great deal on the administering of physical pain. We had at hand a lot to work with, including potential targets (a.k.a. brothers). Dirt-clod wars were a perennial favorite, since a ready supply of ammunition was turned up in the fields every year. Gall flies turned goldenrod stems into water tower-shaped wands that, upon drying in the fall, were fairly flexible, gratifyingly hard, and serviceably durable for use as "beeter-boppers," a.k.a. brother-cranium-knocking devices. Our favorite group sport was a ritualistic melee called "Pitch Up and Smear." We gathered into a pack, someone tossed a football high up into the air, and whoever was lucky(?) enough to make the catch got "smeared" as the rest of us piled on once the tackle was made. You don't really appreciate how many brothers six is until you've been the football recipient in Pitch Up and Smear.

As we grew older, we engaged in activities so bellicose that in retrospect I scarcely can believe that our parents granted sanction. Christmas, a time when "Peace on Earth" supposedly is the official mantra, was in practice the Season of Fratricidal Intent. A huge stock of fireworks (again courtesy of my older brothers' manual labor; thanks, guys!) would be evenly divided amongst the seven of us. Then, *while our parents sat on the porch and watched*, we would take stations at more or less even intervals around the field adjacent to our house and, on cue, light our punk sticks and commence unloading Roman candles, bottle rockets, and other fairly powerful explosives at one another with gleeful abandon. That annual fireworks war had some truly memorable moments, like the time when Hardy lit the end of a yard-long ribbon of firecrackers and circumnavigated the field while spinning the explosive lacework over his head. As he ran, small sizzling bombs flew from the disintegrating filigree and arced like sparking meteorites in random directions while we all ducked, laughing hysterically. My most vivid memory of that peculiar incendiary bacchanalia is of the year when Glenn, in some inexplicable fit of madness, took mind to sprint across the middle of the firing range, becoming in the process the immediate focus of six pairs of raptorial eyes. While others would like to claim the honor, I hereby avow in no uncertain terms that it was *my* well-aimed Roman candle fusillade that ignited the fireworks ingeniously couched in the back pocket of his nylon coveralls. His desperate shucking of the blazing sacrificial garb did nothing to diminish the vigor with which we, his beloved siblings, poured it on in an eager attempt to complete the immolation. With astonishing rapidity, Glenn managed to shed his flaming cocoon and escape, near naked, into the night. Sociobiology purports to explain kin-based altruism by reference to genes. Appropriately enough, Glenn wasn't wearing any.

Our violent tendencies had targets other than bipeds, as plenty of alternative denizens of the natural world were readily available for abuse. If you've never seen tiger beetle larvae, you don't want to. They take the form of humpbacked worms with flat armored faceplates protected by two vicious sickle-shaped pincers. As the worms mature, they change from a pallid, semi-translucent white to a ghastly opaque yellow. The hump is placed well back on the squidgy body, perhaps to help hold this infernal death machine in place as it waits, hungrily, at the top of the perfectly cylindrical hole where it resides. Should an insect be unfortunate enough as to wander by, the carnivorous cutie jackknifes explosively out of its lair, flipping over backward using its hump as a pivot point; it pierces its victim with lethally pointed death sickles and drags it back down into the cold ground to be devoured at gruesome leisure. We knew nothing of the biological niceties of the organism or its life cycle at the time, of course; to us, they were "chicken chokers," so called because of a typically misinformed bit of folk knowledge holding that any barnyard fowl foolish enough to try to ingest one of the little monsters would die a slow, horrible death by internal strangulation. But here's the fun part: pluck a wild chive; slide it gently down the hole, stopping when resistance indicates that a satanic faceplate has been encountered; sit back and watch. After a few seconds the pungent exploratory instrument will begin to rise rapidly into the air! Grab it and yank and, with the lightest of pneumatic sighs, as though a miniature portal to hell has instantaneously opened and shut, the devilish creature comes flying up out of its lair, preferably not landing in your hair *en route*. We became quite practiced at that bizarre enterprise, especially after some genius in second grade deconstructed an individual-sized milk carton to create an arena where demon-jawed champions engaged in mortal combat at each recess period.

Almost as enthralling as the gladiatorial chicken choker extravaganzas was doodlebug feeding. More properly known as antlions, these cool creatures look sort of like trilobites with vicious, piercing mandibles. If you've ever seen "Star Trek II: The Wrath of Khan," that gross thing they stuck in Chekov's ear is basically a giant doodlebug. They live at the bottom of little conical holes excavated in loose dirt. Should an ant be so unlucky as to fall in, its motion triggers the doodlebug to start flipping little payloads of sediment up into the air, causing the madly-scrabbling insect to lose its footing and fall deeper into the trap. Sometimes the ant gets away, but should it be brought too close to the bottom, the industrious doodlebug snatches it up and drags it below for supper. We had a lot of doodlebug funnels around our place, especially in the dry dirt underneath the house, and I helpfully steered many an ant to an untimely end in order to watch the ensuing nature documentary. A few years ago, I had the extraordinary privilege of introducing two of my grandkids to this questionable sport. *Hakuna metata*, baby.

Another bizarre sport featuring insect life involved horse flies, which in Mississippi grow to be the size of small pterosaurs. If one was quick, one could capture one of those creatures as it futilely banged its ugly little head against the windowpane, presumably because it belatedly had discovered that we didn't live in a barn. A long thread was then loosely tied on behind the head, and presto! One had a flying dipterid on a leash!

Did I mention that times could be slow in Choctaw County?

When we weren't abusing other life forms, we were quick to make use of any alternative entertainment devices with which Fortune favored us. We once obtained from somewhere a batch of small plastic skeletons. I think it was our cousin Jeff who discovered that the things would sink if placed in liquid, whereupon we eagerly awaited the summons from a parent to bring them a cup of coffee, a stimulant consumed day or night regardless of season. The look on their faces when they got near the bottom of the cup and found themselves nose to ribcage with the boney frames was priceless. Nowadays I wonder how many phthalates were ingested; back then, I just thought it was hilarious. Back then, I also could run a lot faster.

True to Southern form, my siblings and I now nostalgically refer to "the old home place." If more people were fortunate enough to have that sort of connection, the world would be a much more stable place.

2

LIFE ON THE FARM

As we matured into adolescence, our diversions became, if any-thing, even *more* irresponsible. We were allowed, even encouraged, to graduate from BB-guns to the kind that can kill people at an age that people in other countries find simply unbelievable. There were material benefits to this practice; it takes a lot of meat to feed nine people, and there were many times when kinfolk of questionable lineage stayed with us for extended periods, so there always was a crowd. I never was too sure about who those people were in terms of their relation to us; kinship terms in the region are nothing if not confusing. All relatives of middle age or older are called "Aunt" or "Uncle" so-and-so, regardless of biological or marital nearness to one's parents. Cousins are equally vaguely defined, perhaps to discourage courtship, as consanguineal relationships tend to be a little too consanguineal in the Deep South. Folk categories further muddy the waters. Of what relation to Ego is a "Pawpaw," which plant biologists disdainfully would have us believe is a fruit-bearing tree? "Poppy/Papaw" and "Meemaw/Mammaw/Mimi/Meemee" refer usually, but not exclusively, to one's grandparents. One of my sisters-in-law is referred to by her grandchildren as 'Yetta," which surely must be the term for a female sasquatch? And so on. Pity the alien xenologist who lands its spaceship in that neck of the woods. Such confusion aside, kinship bonds are strong in the South, and if a relative of whatever remove is on hard times and comes to you for succor, they have to be fed as well as boarded. Accordingly, when we shot something, we ate it, whether it was obtained legally or not. Deer, squirrels, rabbits, doves, quail, raccoons, beaver: we ate them all, stopping only at the possum line, which separates your everyday yokels from the true hicks. Guns were everywhere; in Pop's home-made gun cabinets, on racks in whatever pickup truck was running at the time, stacked like umbrellas in one corner of the front hall-way. That was standard in a culture where men were men and any Y-chromosome who confessed at school to liking Robert Frost was apt to find the ball coming his way during "Pitch Up and Smear" a little too often.

We had a great many dogs over the years, but we never hunted with them, which I was glad of, since running deer always struck me as a particularly cruel enterprise, while sitting in an air-conditioned pickup truck with a high-powered rifle waiting for the dogs to chase a deer across the road seems anything but sporting. Our dogs were just pets and porch-warmers, each with its own unique personality. I remember a few in particular: Snuffy, a clever and beautiful part-Spitz; Loper, a good-natured, long-legged hound who could snap up a running rabbit without breaking stride; Biscuit, so named because, as repeated experiments demonstrated, he would literally climb a tree to devour one of his namesake breadstuffs; Chico, the first and by far the finest of a string of Chihuahuas that subsequently spread like plague-carrying rodents throughout the family; and Ripple. Ripple was bitten hard on the head by another dog as a young pup and never was "quite right" after that. He happily chased butter-flies and airplanes and frequently got stuck halfway across logs over the creek when his courage gave out, so that someone would have to go out into the woods and fetch him where he sat, howling piteously. Ripple's most intriguing trait was an apparently irresist-ible impulse to defecate on top of stumps, large rocks, or any other elevated, exposed platform where lucky passersby could best ap-preciate his intricately-sculpted artistic achievements. His crown-ing installation was a fecal payload that he somehow managed to deposit in the green interstices of an extremely sharp-leaved yucca plant, at a height considerably greater than that of his own rear end. He must have backed his way up one hind leg at a time, notwithstanding the sharp spikes that stood between him and his canvas. It's good to know that we are not the only species to suffer for art's sake.

Besides hunting, we shot guns for sport all the time, gangs of us clustered together, demolishing some makeshift target with chemically-propelled lead ballistae while shoeless urchins ran to and fro, more-or-less behind us, eagerly dreaming of the day when they, too, could loudly obliterate an offending milk jug or coffee can with a large-bore firearm. Show me a road sign out in the country in the Deep South that isn't acned with shotgun pellet craters and I'll show you a road sign that hasn't been there very long. Every Christmas we acquired mistletoe by the supremely elegant method of blasting it with shotguns out of the oak trees surrounding our house. And this was the stuff that the adults *saw*. Unsupervised shooting went on whenever we could afford the ammo and were away from the house. Ear protection? Hardly. Hearing loss, consequently, is another family trait.

Not surprisingly, given this freewheeling attitude toward firearms, I know a number of folks who accidently have been shot: Pop, who put a .22 bullet through the length of his leg while practicing the quick-draw; a cousin who took a #8 shotgun pellet up the nose, courtesy of an excitable compatriot unloading at a squirrel on the bluff where said cousin was standing; a nephew who similarly took pellets to the face courtesy of another nephew whose finger was on the trigger when it shouldn't have been; a sheetrock contractor's helper who somehow managed to blow his own finger off; and a graduate student who received one in the leg when his father was cleaning a rifle that turned out, as they so often do, to be loaded. These all were people who grew up with guns, who *knew* that they were dangerous. The fact that I don't personally know anyone who has been killed with a firearm is quite astonishing, but the growing fear of such an event is what eventually led me to give up gunplay, an action that, if possible, raised even more eyebrows than my earnest collegiate declaration of vegetarianism.

Gun-related traumas aside, our unbridled backwoods existence led to constant cuts, punctures, scrapes, bruises, contusions, black eyes, pink eye, bloody noses, rashes, parasitic infestations, and assorted illnesses of the internal variety. When something really bad happened, like the time Glenn was bitten by a snake, the victim was taken to the doctor, but that was a course of last resort due to distance and expense. Instead, Mom took care of it, whether it was staunching blood flow with a washcloth, wrapping stripped cloth bandages around lacerations, or poking noxious schmears of Vicks Salve up our noses to combat congestion. By the time she got to the little kids, she'd pretty much seen it all, and didn't panic even when we thought some panic was due. "You'll live" was a surprisingly accurate appraisal as we came in oozing corpuscles or hacking up phlegm. I personally suffered a couple of pretty serious injuries. One evening I did a "Superman dive" into bed only to discover that, for some reason, there was a broken Coke bottle hiding in the bed-clothes. I discovered that interesting phenomenon by dint of having my side sliced open to the ribs. On that occasion, we did not go to the doctor because a tornado was brewing right above our heads. True to prediction, I lived, although I still bear a thick, irregular scar on my left side. Another episode took place when Andy and I were unloading wood from the pickup truck. Andy was chucking lengths of log out of the truck with unusual vigor while I was picking up the smaller pieces in the yard to put on the porch. Suddenly, there was a terrific impact on the side of my head. For a few seconds everything went black, which freaked me out; once my vision returned and I found my head still attached to my neck, I calmed down, although it hurt like Hell. Andy had whipped a log out of the truck without looking to see where it was going, which happened to be directly toward my right orbital torus. That time, I was taken to the doctor, where I proudly received my first-ever stitches. It was only a few years ago that Andy confessed to me that he'd been in a hurry to get the truck unloaded because he was supposed to go somewhere to meet a girl. Had I known that at the time, I'd have told him not to worry; I would keep an eye out for her.

We supplemented the game we shot with various wild offerings from the Kingdom Plantae, especially blackberries, which Mom canned in large quantities. Blackberry jam on hot buttered biscuits: that is the stuff of which dreams are made. The fact that our nether regions provided prized real estate for chiggers eager to move out of the low-rent district of the blackberry patches was not sufficient deterrent, given the reward. We also plucked muscadines, wild cherries, wild plums, and anything else that could be plucked and eaten, although the fruits of such labors tended as often as not to become raw materials for experimental oenology. Pop once blew the doors off a kitchen cabinet when an exceptionally robust incipient batch of scuppernong wine expressed its enthusiasm for the cause in no uncertain terms. This hunting-gathering fare augmented the front-line resources provided by our truck-farm existence. Ours was a small property, forty-nine acres of woods and fields. We managed the latter mostly with brute force and hoes, except for the use of a tiller that Pop would coax into cranking with a select lexicon and a great deal of arm action. We were able, with a lot of hard work, to gather and put up enough food to help get us through the year, a necessary undertaking given that Pop's work at that time was as an occasional handyman and Mom's was at whatever factory or store was hiring. How she managed that on top of everything else, I'll never know. But when things really got tough was, ironically, when they managed to scrape together resources sufficient to purchase a used tractor. It was a small red one of significant vintage that was later replaced by a big terrifying green thing that Pop let me drive only once, after which he wisely allowed me to go back to the comic books. If the tractor was running but no other vehicle was, it wasn't unknown for Pop or one of my elder siblings to drive it via the back roads to French Camp (especially if Pop was out of cigarette makings). It was a sign of the time and place that such a spectacle was nothing out of the ordinary for the town residents.

The reason the tractor was a problem was that, with such an engine, one can break a lot of ground. Let me repeat: a *lot* of ground. If Pop felt like the lord of all he surveyed, up there on his big green sod-busting machine, we felt like serfs bound to the pitiless steppe as we hoed, and hoed, and hoed down the long, long rows and picked, and picked, and picked the beans, peas, okra, corn, squash, tomatoes, potatoes, etc. On top of all the hoeing and picking there was the cutting and transport of river cane from Monkey Land for beanpoles. There was applying Sevin dust using one of Pop's many inventions, dust-filled coffee cans with nail-perforated bottoms attached to sticks so that a hearty shake would deposit a cloud of pesticide onto each waiting plant. (And onto bare feet; and into lungs, no doubt). There was hauling endless buckets of water from the creek during the not-uncommon droughts. (Rain could be either a blessing or a curse, depending on intensity and duration: "sprinkles" were OK, a "good, soakin' rain" was best, but Heaven help us if ever there should "come a gullywasher." Prepping and planting fields was hard; having to do it all over again when the floodwaters receded simply added insult to injury). There was manufacturing and emplacing hundreds of newspaper tents when frosts were threatening. There was shelling butterbeans and purple hull peas until one's thumbs were reddened and sore. There was husking and shucking dried corn from the previous season for animal feed, something that does one's palms no favors. And so on, and so on, and so on, *ad punctum desperandum*. An early and very popular misconception of anthropology was that the evolution of a farming lifestyle "led to enough leisure time so that civilization could be invented." Yeah. Right.

And then there were the livestock, which mostly consisted of chickens and pigs. The chickens weren't so bad, really; I always loved eggs, even if one had to dodge seriously vicious pecks from irate nesting hens while trying to pick up the more shit-smeared obloids with as few fingers as possible. Sometimes those fowl were turned loose to forage around the farm, at which time their admirable stupidity made them easy prey for a favorite game: propping up a plastic clothes basket with a stick, placing a shred of loaf bread underneath, and then, when temptation overcame exquisitely small-brained caution, yanking a rope to dislodge the stick, penning the squawking, outraged creature beneath the basket. That never got old. For us kids, at least; can't really speak for the chickens.

Newly-hatched chicks were really cute, especially when they ran to hide beneath the wing of their clucking, frowning mother when one of her sisters sounded the alarm after falling, yet again, for the baited clothes basket trick. One glorious summer one of our hens set on a clutch of brown eggs amidst which there was a massive abnormal monstrosity of a fetal case that looked like an atmosphere-warped alien entry pod from a bad 1950's horror movie. Chickens sometimes lay really oversized eggs, often containing multiple yolks, which never hatch. *This one did.* And the gallinaceous wonder that emerged, a truly ugly, awkward, yellow piece of Brobdingnagian fuzz, embarked immediately upon a growth spurt so tremendous that it soon towered far above its embarrassed clutch mates. They all would move in a busy phalanx across the yard, the Thunder Chick (as I came to regard him) stomping awkwardly amongst his siblings, occasionally knocking them airborne whilst flipping leaves in an impressively oblivious search for consumables. When Auntie Hen was caught (yet again) beneath the basket and gave vent (yet again) to squawks of outraged protest, and the phalanx raced (yet again) to the protective cover of their mother's outstretched wing, TC's entire, remarkably unappealing, hind end would remain exposed to the elements while his head disappeared, ostrich-like, into the feathery sanctuary while his mom pretended to look the other way. Eventually TC reached the point where his energetic efforts at seeking refuge would simply flip his parent over sideways, putting an ignominious end to the operation. Despite his colossal size, TC's development otherwise was oddly restricted. When the other males of his clutch reached the point where they began their first proud attempts at crowing—*eeh-ah-eeh-eeeee*!— TC persisted in giving vent to an extraordinarily loud basso-profundo *PEEEEEEP!* Thunder Chick eventually matured into Thunder Chicken, still without achieving the milestone of masculine yardbird vocalization. I am not sure of his ultimate fate, although visions of gargantuan drumsticks occasionally haunt my dreams.

Another essentially useless bit of Mississippiana: that little wiggly bit at the top of a chicken's rear end is called the "preacher's beak." Back in the day, the Lord's finest made frequent circuits of the outlying domiciles, ostensibly to tend to their flock. But their penchant for showing up just in time for Sunday dinner earned them the dubious honor of having one of the less aesthetically appealing parts of the yardbird "christened" in their honor. The fried chicken back, complete with eponymous wiggly bit, would be passed to the bibbed proselytizer with a knowing smile. Flocks know when they're being fleeced, but it all was taken in good spirit.

So chickens weren't that bad; a few even became valued companions, including a Dominecker named "Miss Priss" and a matronly Rhode Island Red named "Pet" who had the run of the farm and who would come into the kitchen to watch as Mom cooked. Even when she was cooking chicken, which always struck me as rather gruesome. Pet, at least, was not eaten, but was given full burial honors as befitted a near-family member.

But the hogs; oh Lord, the hogs! I simultaneously was fascinated and repelled by the things. Swine are interesting creatures in that they will eat absolutely anything, a trait that led to a lot of homegrown experiments in inductive science. Ragweed, acorns, crawdads, fish heads, charcoal, grasshoppers, snakes; you name it, a hog will eat it and wiggle its nasty little tail in sincere gratitude all the while. They even will eat chicken-chokers with no resultant asphyxiation. But our hogs stank, as only penned-up hogs can stink, and for a while it was my unfortunate lot in life to take them their morning meal. Here's how that joyful enterprise worked: any leftovers that didn't go to the dogs were mixed into a five-gallon bucket with "shorts," some sort of wheat-processing byproduct bought in bulk in big reinforced-paper bags. This yummy agglomeration was stirred with water into a soupy, goopy mix appropriately named "slop" that had to be carefully carried about one hundred meters down a dirt path to the hog pen. The heavy cornucopia then had to be manually lifted over the wire fence and the slop poured, splashing, into a homemade wooden trough. The process itself was labor enough, but the joy was compounded by two blissful factors: 1) the feeding had to be accomplished in the morning, right before the bus came; and 2) the hogs, being somewhat under-schooled in dining etiquette, didn't wait daintily for their semi-viscous provender to be dispensed, but urged on the proceedings with insistent thrusts of their thick snouts against the bucket. Hogs are *strong*. The custom-made, vomit-colored solution willingly shot forth from the jolted bucket like the good, non-Newtonian fluid that it was. The result was that, more mornings than I care to remember, I found myself trying to hose aromatic hog slop off my britches before the bus showed up, figuring that looking like I'd wet myself would be more socially acceptable than smelling like a twenty-four-hour porcine breakfast emporium. Given that one of the other kids on the bus would eat live moths for a nickel, my choice probably was the right one, but I can't say that it's the most pleasant way to start the school day. Of course, neither is watching a kid eat live moths on the bus for a nickel.

Not only are pigs strong; they also are smart, so that trying to keep them penned up was a constant trial. When they escaped, as they too often did, we had to fan out like a search party looking for lost souls on the moor until we managed to channel the recalcitrant porkers back into the pen. One never knew when the dreaded call, "The hogs are out!" would come, at which point down went the hoes, or the comic books, or the chicken-snaring basket-prop rope, or whatever, and off we flew on bare feet like so many Fridays trying to round up Christmas dinner for Mr. Crusoe. Once, when I was about seven, we erected a makeshift canvas tent over an outstretched limb of a large pecan tree in our backyard for a camping adventure. As one does in such circumstances, we listened, wide-eyed, as one of my older brothers told the obligatory ghost story, a single flashlight providing ghoulish illumination against the inquisitive night. Just as the story reached its gruesome climax, a large, shuffling, red-eyed creature came snuffling loudly *through the back of the tent*, initiating a panicked mass exodus of screaming kids. It was, of course, a hog. It was, of course, Hardy who'd turned the creature loose, just to freak us all out. It was, of course, Hardy who jabbed the beast in the butt to make it squeal. It was, of course, many years before I again deigned to sleep in a tent.

Processing meat in the backwoods was not a pretty sight. Wild game was bad enough; I could scale a fish or skin a squirrel without growing overly vertiginous, but deer…yuck! You cut holes through the skin of their hind feet just behind the tendons, threaded a rope or chain through the holes, and hoisted them up, tying off the rope or chain so that the carcass was suspended in the air, looking very much like something from a Bosch triptych. The hoisting was done by the simple expedient of bear-hugging and lifting, which is rather a challenge, especially if the deer is a big one, and it didn't help that you were getting very up-close and personal with the hairy body of a large dead animal. Then you opened the belly, trying not to pierce any internal organs in the process. Even if you succeeded in that effort, the gas thus released still stank like a tubful of rotting silage. And you then had to get all the glistening, revolting, wibbly-wobbly stuff out of there, much to the delight of the hovering pack of yard dogs. I was so phenomenally bad at the process that an impatient older brother usually shoved me aside and took over, a tactic that, as a married man, I later used to good effect on laundry day.

Hogs were far worse to deal with. In fact, they were awful. First, they had to be dispatched, a task accomplished by a single well-placed .22 slug to the forehead. Hopefully well placed, anyway. If the slug turns against the skull, the animal will burst through the wall of any pen, understandably terrified and extremely dangerous. An adult male can weigh hundreds of pounds and can bite the handle-end off of a baseball bat. The elder brothers once spent the better part of an unseasonably warm fall day in pursuit of just such a wounded boar, firing whenever they got a more-or-less clear shot (we little kids had been ordered into the hay loft by Pop). By the time they brought it down, hours later, the meat was ruined from the exertion and the heat, as my brothers nearly were. I have yet to suffer the same experience with a potato. In ordinary circumstances, once the beast was dispatched, the carcass was doused repeatedly with boiling water ladled out of a 55-gallon drum tilted and half-buried in a fire pit. As the water was applied, all of us scraped away at the grainy corrugated hide with knife blades held perpendicular to the skin to remove the thick, coarse hair. It was gross. Even more so on those soul-wrenching occasions when Pop took a notion to cut the skin into meaty ribbons that he deep-fried to make "cracklins." Cracklins are bad enough when they come out of a clean plastic bag from the store. Pop's homemade products were loathsomely thick, still boasted the occasional hair, and were sodden with cooking grease and pig fat, like some revolting gelifluction deposit oozing downslope on an alien Hell-planet. I remember Andy once puking up a vast stream of homemade cracklin ejecta. I remember wishing that I could follow suit.

(Other than the unspeakable cracklins, Pop didn't cook except when he was three sheets to the wind and the alchemical spirit took hold. One avoided the kitchen on such occasions, lest one be offered a bite. The base ingredient of those fell experiments always seemed to be either fried weenies or fried bologna, although Pop would cheerfully toss into the well-greased pan whatever was at hand as he swayed to and fro before the stove, one eye slightly open to provide a visual counter to his unsteady balance. The agglomerated charred mass then was inevitably bedded between two slices of cheap white loaf bread liberally smeared with cheap white mayonnaise. When Pop really was feeling it, he'd add some raw onion for extra zing. Bon appétit!)

Once the initial processing was accomplished, the meat, be it deer or pork or whatever, had to be dealt with. Some of the deer meat was just cut off the bone and put in the freezer. Some of what remained, and almost all of the pork, was laboriously converted into sausage using an antique hand-cranked grinder clamped onto the kitchen table. At far-too-frequent intervals, this Torquemadian device had to be dismantled so that stringy sinew could be teased out of its gunked-up internal mechanism. Pieces of meat would fit only if they were smaller than a man's fist, which is a pretty good safety feature unless you happen to fall into a different age/sex category, like those of us conducting the operation. The large mammals upon which we subsisted yielded many, many such pieces which had individually to be fed into the slippery metal maw of the device. One of us would cut slices from the carcass which rested on towels on the table and feed them in while another pushed and hauled at the grinder, which reluctantly disgorged sticky pinkish extrusions of unmitigated blech for a good ten or fifteen minutes until it had to be disassembled for another bout of sinew removal. Blech. Unmitigated. Yay, potatoes.

When we killed something, regardless of its size, everything—killing, dressing, cleaning, processing, packaging, stowing, and cleanup—had to be accomplished in one episode lest the already well-fed bacteria in our gory laboratorium become too chummy. It was exhausting work and the first sausage sandwich always carried a bit of the spice of vengeance, if by that time one hadn't lost one's appetite due to the unsavory nature of the whole operation. Pop clearly wasn't bothered, as he considered scrambled eggs and pig brains to be a delicacy. At his insistent urging, I once, and only once, tried that evil concoction. It was like French-kissing a waterlogged zombie. Likewise, I only once tried that other legendary southern delicacy, "chitlins." "Chitterlings" to the more upper-class sort of backwoods lunatic, these terrifying *hors d'oeuvre* are appreciable lengths of pig intestine from which the feces have been displaced by repeated lashing, or "slinging," against a tree stump or some other hard surface. During the Citizens' Band radio craze of the 1970s, Robert's "handle" was "Mississippi Chitlin Slinger," an appellation that created a certain amount of *nausea vu*. (My own handle was "Celestial Grubworm," chosen for no particularly good reason except to hear it returned in cloyingly thick accents by regional truckers who somehow reduced "Celestial" to something between two and three syllables. Once they shortened it to "Grubworm" for convenience's sake, the magic faded). Anyway, once the slinging is finished, the sternly-admonished intestinal tube looks a lot like an enormous tapeworm. Slinging is followed by desultory washing, division into bite-sized proglottids, and prolonged boiling, after which one holds one's nose and chokes down the rubbery things. Boiled chitterlings were a staple in Europe during the Middle Ages, a time when given names weren't bestowed upon children until they were too big to fit in the family cauldron. An alternative method of preparation following boiling is battering and deep-fat frying, the variety I was foolish enough to sample. If eating scrambled pig brains and eggs is like French kissing a zombie, eating deep-fried chitlins is like having that zombie slip you some reciprocal tongue. I think even Roald Dahl might have passed on that one.

Despite those gruesome labors, meat never was plentiful, even in a good year, so protein came mostly from legumes and government largesse. Once a month Mom would come home with a large load of "commodities" that we would fall upon like starving sled dogs. The processed "cheese," which came in squidgy units nominally constrained in thin metallic wrap inside a long rectangular paper box, was an especially favored comestible, although I'm pretty sure that nothing of that horrific orange-yellow color ever was meant to occur naturally in our solar system. I also particularly remember the peanut butter, which came in large metal cans, and the raisins, which no doubt gave us all some much-needed iron. Between meals, Mom would send us youngsters away with "peanut butter spoons," which were exactly what it sounds like: large spoons holding large gobs of peanut butter that we would slowly, sloppily ingest. Not exactly toothsome, but it got the job done. The government could do worse than to provide its less-fortunate citizens with peanut butter spoons, especially if the citizens provide the spoons. I am not sure what we would have done without those products of an entirely sensible system by means of which agricultural surplus actually went to feed poor people in our country while farmers got paid for the service. It hardly seems credible these days, when poverty is treated like a lifestyle choice. As of February 6, 2014, the commodities program has been restricted to low-income elderly persons; women, infants, and children have to apply elsewhere for help, and I guess younger guys just starve.

Another resource we sometimes could afford was the baked goods sold at the "used bread store." This was an outlet where products at the end of their shelf lives were sold at heavily-discounted prices. We ate a lot of "Wonder Bread" thus acquired, which I believe was an ingenious mixture of over-bleached flour, stale factory air, and kaolin clay. But of far greater interest to us kids were the residual sweet stuffs: Hostess "Ding Dongs," "Sno Balls," cupcakes, and some weird little Twinkie-like things blanketed with horrible, rubbery, yellowish-orange icing. The coconut shavings sprouting from one version of Sno Balls were dyed pink, as I remember, for what purpose I really can't imagine, unless it was part of an experiment on the cumulative toxicity of food dyes on the proletariat. Being that all of that stuff already was at, or just beyond, the formal expiration point, it had to be consumed with alacrity before life forms new to science were spawned by all the sugary catalysts within. We were only too willing to do our part in that regard, and on the rare occasions when mold sprouted before we could finish off the lot, the slop bucket stood ready and waiting. You haven't lived until you've seen pigs fighting over a mold-encrusted pink Sno Ball floating like a decomposing sea urchin in a choppy sea of vomit-colored slop. Ah, the formative years.

Other things we ate a lot of (or at least frequently): blackeye peas seasoned with a small hunk of salted meat; chicken and cornbread dressing; squirrel and dumplings; biscuits and gravy (yum!); biscuits and corn syrup; and cornbread in milk. That last item was not a complicated recipe: fill a large glass about three-quarters full with weighty chunks of cornbread, add milk, and scoop the soggy goodness out with a spoon. Many of the clan preferred that the combination be made with buttermilk, which I never could abide. For a time, some backwoods folks we knew—backwoods to *us*, mind—brought over gallon jars of milk fresh out of their cows' grimy udders, a gift that our parents accepted with gratitude as it reminded them of their own formative years. It reminded me of the caterpillar-like drawings of bacteria in our grade school textbooks. Store-bought sweet milk for me, please, the more stringently pasteurized, the better.

With the aid of such resources, we never went hungry, exactly, but there certainly were some lean times. One that holds a place of dubious honor in our family lore was a couple of weeks when we subsisted entirely upon waffles, as for some reason we had a stockpile of ready-made waffle mix available, and nothing else. I don't remember that episode, but I do remember long periods when breakfast consisted entirely of bowls of "cornmeal mush," a bland glop the delectability of which is pretty accurately conveyed by the title. When Washington and his officers at Valley Forge were reduced to the same expediency, they knew they truly had hit upon hard times.[2] We also relied on food stamps when they became available, bearing with surly fortitude the stigma of public display of little colored pieces of paper that proclaimed our challenged socioeconomic status as clearly as would a leper's sores. I honestly don't know what we'd have done without such help, which would not have been taken had it not been necessary. Mom was a proud woman.

---

2 Ron Chernow, *Alexander Hamilton*, p. 107. Penguin Books, 2004.

When I reached the age where I, too, could earn a dollar, as often as not I would spend it on "penny candy." The name was not false advertising, kids: this was candy that cost a penny. A *penny*. For a single dollar bill, one could obtain *one hundred pieces of candy*. Man, those were the days! The local store had at the time a prickly pavement of crown bottle caps out front; inside were wooden floors polished to a shiny caramel hue by generations of feet, shod or otherwise. There was a comforting aroma common to all such hamlet emporia, a warm, slightly sweet smell that draped its arms over your shoulders and said, "Y'all come on in." The counter bore large clear plastic bins full of Jack's sugar cookies and some other sort of corrugated, coconut kind that I liked a lot, although it left an aftertaste like a hobo's footwear. The candy was displayed in boxes kept behind glass counter walls. I'll always remember how patient the proprietor was as we agonized over how best to spread our limited wealth. Ten "Bit o' Honey's," or ten "Atomic Fireballs?" "Coconut Longboys," or "Mary Janes?" And so on. Luckily, our water was fluoridated, a benevolent government action that somehow failed to turn us all into little communists, lunatic predictions notwithstanding. I have had exactly one cavity in my entire life, peanut butter spoons and "Atomic Fireballs" notwithstanding. Thanks, Uncle Sam!

Halloween was a candy bonanza, when we little kids piled into some operable conveyance and were driven into French Camp, usually by a visibly bored older brother. In their studies of hunter-gatherers, anthropologists have employed a tool called the "catchment circle" as a means of quantifying the exploitation of resources within a given area of land. The local merchants must have rued the day that the internal combustion engine widened the circle, since we made it a point to hit town before the emporia closed their doors for the day. Once back home, most of the loot would be consumed rapidly but, driven by our competitive natures, a standard trick was to hide some portion of the evening's takings, to be pulled out later and *slooooowly* consumed, with much smacking of lips and rolling of eyes in ecstasy, in front of jealous siblings. Robert was the absolute master of that obnoxious practice. He was, in fact, the master of all obnoxious practices. On rare occasions, winter brought its own provender: snow, which Mom turned into sweet "snow cream" by means of some alchemical process the secret of which I never learned. It gave one awful brain-freeze, but it still was a divine treat.

All that sugar was needed, especially in the winter because that house, too, was darn cold. Nights were when things really got chilly. When I was still quite young, Robert, Andy, and I slept three in a bed, which helped, as did the blankets that Mom layered on until we literally could not turn over. We used to fight over who got Chico each night. A Great Dane would have generated more BTUs, but it might also have eaten our penny candy without asking. A fireplace on the west side of the house provided mostly light, because: 1) most of the heat went up the chimney; and 2) Pop's prone body after a drinking bout made a pretty effective firewall. We couldn't complain too much, as he was the one who got up in the cold to make the fire every morning. (We also did not complain lest he pitch a hissy fit.)[3], [4] Ever the inventor, Pop devised a short-cut method for successful combustion, using for kindling corncobs soaked in gasoline on the back porch overnight. These "corn flame," as we proudly referred to them, cannot in good conscience be recommended from a household safety standpoint, but firebugs, take note: they work! The fireplace on the other side of the house not being functional, we had there instead a succession of freestanding, wood-burning heaters, products of Pop's sheet metal wizardry. Those things definitely cranked out the heat, but they were terrifying contrivances in action. They would get so hot that the metal would glow red, at which point the heater literally would start to "breathe," the sides of the metal drum flexing in and out like an overworked dragon's gullet. How we didn't accidentally burn the place down, I'll never know.

---

3 "Hissy" is an ancient Scots Gaelic term for a farrow sow. Should a rival laird and his gang show up unexpectedly, livestock below a certain size (and the occasional wee bairn) were preserved from theft or destruction by the simple expedient of picking them up and "pitching" them over the settlement's defensive wall, where they usually survived landing in the squelchy, interior midden. This job, being quite physically demanding, was reserved for strapping young chields who were "fit" for such an undertaking; hence the origin of the phrase, "fit to pitch a hissy," which in modern times became "pitching a hissy fit."

4 I just made that up.

That heating regimen required a lot of wood, and one of my least favorite activities was the seemingly endless toting of logs to wherever we could get the pickup truck to in the forest, a task that was particularly brutal in winter when wood cut the day before was covered in a frozen rind of ice. What you are supposed to do, of course, is cut the wood months in advance to let it season, at which point it burns readily and produces heat far more efficiently. But that requires advance planning, a strategy Pop generally ignored. I never ran the chainsaw, which is just as well given that I am typing these words. At any rate, having twice seen the results of Glenn cutting himself badly with the implement, I was not inclined to volunteer. Splitting with an axe followed hauling the wood, after which came further transport and stacking; all very hard, very physical work. But compared to my oldest brothers, we had it easy; before I came of hauling age, they performed all such work without the aid of a chainsaw! With axes! And they still had the generosity to share their fireworks and comic books! One can only bow.

We were uncustomarily warm one year as a result of Pop taking a job in Florida. We had one running vehicle at the time, an old short-bed pickup truck. Pop built a camper top for the bed, and all of us piled in and headed south. This was in 1972, after my three oldest brothers had enlisted in the Navy. I remember the trip fairly clearly, which is not surprising given that three human beings were sharing the truck bed space underneath the camper shell with all of our luggage while three more, plus Chico, rode in the cab. We moved into a really nice little cottage nestled inside an orange grove outside of DeLand, until the owner showed up, demanding in very impolite terms to know who the heck we were and what the heck we were doing there. Turned out that the renter's sub-let deal had not been officially sanctioned. Subsequently we lived for a while in a large makeshift canvas tent in a KOA campground, eventually moving from there into another house I don't much recall except that it was right beside a trailer court, where we got to know some of the local kids. We were in the Sunshine State long enough to be enrolled in school, which was a real switch from the little white clapboard public schoolhouse at French Camp. My homeroom was

in a metal trailer, for one thing; for another, they had weird activities like soccer in which we were required to participate. The only
time the ball came my way I hit it with my hands, eliciting a harsh
outburst of scorn from my fellow students and the coach. I'd never
even *heard* of soccer. And what kind of crazy sport doesn't let you
use your hands?

While my actual memories of that time are pretty vague, there
is some interesting family lore to recount, such as the fact that Pop's
boss had a tightrope strung up in his backyard and willingly showed
his adeptness at that arcane skill. My personal favorite, though, is
the one about the cops being called on Pop while he was up working
on a roof. Pop "rolled his own," making cigarettes out of Prince Al-
bert tobacco and little white papers drawn from a boxed sheaf. An
observer evidently thought that he was rolling doobies.

It was at school in DeLand that I encountered my first bully, an
enormous lout named Richard who must have had a truly horrific
home life, given that he was a truly horrific human being. He is
probably a senator now. And while the other kids were more-or-
less normal, I did not make any true friends during that time, perhaps because: a) I won every weekly spelling bee for the few months
we were enrolled there, the much-coveted reward for which was
whatever spare change the teacher had in her pocket; and b) I was
insistent that, being a Choctaw County boy, I knew how to climb
trees better than any of my classmates. I wasn't really right about
that last one, because I was unfamiliar with the local flora. Turns
out that branches break off a lot easier in Florida, something to do
with the water content of the species involved. A big limb went out
from under me one day, dropping me onto a junked television set,
of all things, which caused some nasty gashes. Clearly, I was out of
my element in more ways than one. Whatever the reasons, I felt like
an outsider the whole time we were in Florida. That state of being
may have had to do with my burgeoning consciousness of our relative socioeconomic situation. As Robert once remarked to me, it
was one thing to be the poorest kids in a school replete with poor
kids; it was quite another to be the poorest kids in an essentially
middle-class enclave of an Orlando bedroom community. So I didn't

much like Florida except for a weekend trip we made to Daytona Beach, where the water was very cold and where we ate really cheap weenies washed down with really cheap pink lemonade. That was cool, even if the rest of the Florida experience had all of us, except for Pop, who loved the heat, ready to head back to our beloved old homestead in Choctaw County. Of all of us, I think Mom and I were the most homesick, and we were very, very glad when we pulled in beneath the cool shade of the old oak trees back home. Our joy was only momentarily dampened by Andy puking up a vast stream of "Beanie Weenie" ejecta just before Pop could bring the vehicle to a halt. Ah, memories.

THE FLEDGLING YEARS

JUNIOR HIGH SCHOOL WAS WHERE I BEGAN TO COME INTO MY OWN AS A clown, an evolution that my teachers viewed with considerable dismay even as my popularity among my peers skyrocketed. I picked up various skills along the way to increase my entertainment value. For example, we once had a "Fifties Day" at school, for which many lads donned blue-jean jackets and swept their hair back in ridiculous ducktails. ("Happy Days" was the most popular television show in the nation at the time). I was pretty sure I was "cool" in such garb, but I didn't want to take any chances on breaking character, so I elected to get through the day without ever once breaking a smile. That was hard to do, given all the ducktails perambulating around the grounds. I found that I could stifle smiles by directing the energy of my facial muscles backward, rather than upward. A completely unanticipated side effect was that I inadvertently learned how to wiggle my ears, a talent I continue to hone for the edification of grandchildren. Another skill was "gleeking," the voluntary triggering of the salivary glands under one's tongue that results in the ejection of "a concentrated jet of pure saliva."[5] I was quite accomplished at that arcane ability, which once earned me a paddling in the principal's office when I had the temerity to conduct a demonstration during study hall. Or at least I thought I was accomplished, until, while discussing the topic with an Air Force buddy some years later, he described a school mate who learned how to blow spit bubbles and who, following untold hours of diligent practice, succeeded in *gleeking one of his own spit bubbles out of the air.* Imagine *that* as an Olympic sport! (And imagine if he had spent that time study-

---

5 "4 ways to Gleek." www.wikihow.com/Gleek. I am not making this up.

ing). He, too, is probably a senator now. One can only bow. Or duck, whichever.

While growing up with multitudinous siblings out in the country was fine, I didn't realize how starved we were for other companionship until the Atkinses moved into an old house down the road, past the iconic water pump on the hill. There were three kids in their family, all girls, which was interesting enough to those of us just entering the hormonal stage, even if Pop did tease us about playing with them. I was still too young for romance of any kind, but we had a good time horsing around their place. Their parents were representative of a certain set of backwoods bedlamites who had a hard time distinguishing reality even as they negotiated their precarious way through it with duct tape, bailing wire, and wide-eyed astonishment at the enduring mystery of it all. To give one example, early one evening the entire family came tearing up into our driveway in their beat-up old pickup truck, absolutely convinced that a UFO had submerged itself in their little farm pond. I thought that was a pretty cool scenario, even as, considering the source, I gave it little credence. I fished in that pond for many years afterward, with ne'er a glowing tentacle or multifaceted alien eyeball to show for it, more's the pity. Maybe Antareans don't eat worms, even if they do travel through their holes.

Christmas always was a happy time, especially before I grew old enough to wonder how on Earth our parents managed to obtain even a modicum of loot for that many kids, given their perennially strained financial situation. I loved the glow of the lights in our hallway library and begged to be allowed to sleep under the tree, which Mom wisely never allowed. Among the traditional decorations were "icicles," little strips of aluminum that came in cardboard boxes like those used for spaghetti, with plastic windows that revealed the shiny treasure within. Although we all liked icicles on the tree, we had to quit using them because our cats would eat and then regurgitate them in twinkly little globs on the floor. Mistletoe leaves graced the mantel, light shining through the shotgun pellet holes to make festive little spots on the mirror behind. Family custom dictated that we were allowed to open one present on Christmas Eve.

Each year, the starting time for that longed-for event moved up a bit as Pop would crawl on his hands and knees, chosen present clamped between his teeth, to wherever Mom was sitting, shaking his head like a dog worrying a dead squirrel while we kids entered a state of hysteria at the performance. The two best presents I ever got were a chemistry set and a bicycle. The chemistry set was enhanced by a substantial number of beakers and other lab supplies liberated from the nearest junior college by one of my elder brothers, who shall remain nameless lest Santa still is keeping lists. I wasn't allowed to play with the set around the fire, which was a rare precautionary step on the part of the parental units. I tried to play with it in the kitchen, but it was so cold that I had to wait till spring to really get into it. I mostly ignored the boring experiments outlined in the manual and instead embarked upon a mission to see what combinations promoted the most exciting chemical reactions. Once, I made some foaming brown stuff that shot out of the beaker to land on my cousin Jeff's shoe, through which it quickly ate, followed by the sock. It got a good start on his flesh before he made it to the bathtub. Now, *that* was science!

The bike was wonderful. Andy and I each got a rugged red vehicle while Robert got a sleek blue racing bike. That Christmas morning, after the other presents had been opened, Mom told us to go look in the barn. We raced down the dirt pathway and there the bikes were. Andy and I entered into a competition to see who would first learn how to ride. I had a hard time in that regard, partly because gravel roads don't make the best starting surface and partly because I was watching my feet the whole time to make sure I was pedaling correctly. After a day or two of watching me fall over, Glenn helpfully said, "Look up!" I did and instantly found myself flying! It was glorious. Andy learned soon after that, and we put many, many miles on those bikes as we took them down the road, into the woods, and everywhere our sturdy legs could push them. Robert's bike wasn't as suited to the rustic surroundings, but that didn't deter him from challenging the bounds of reason in his own indomitable way. He once set up a wooden ramp at the edge of the field by the house, a field fronted by the gravel road. There was a good four-foot drop between the field's surface and the rocky byway below. Robert set the ramp up at an angle, the inspired plan being that he would hit the ramp at great speed, take flight with the airy grace of a frigate bird, sail out over the waiting roadway, and execute a running landing with the perfect timing of a circus performer. I knew with absolute certainty that disaster was imminent and tried my best to convince him to abandon the enterprise. That would have been chickening out, though, so he ignored me; Robert never chickened out of anything. He didn't break any bones, fortunately, but the crash was even more awful than I'd imagined. I didn't bother saying "I told you so," because I knew it wouldn't do any good and because, despite myself, I admired his derring-do. Andy and I came home from school one day, years later, to discover that Hardy had taken our bikes apart with a blowtorch and welded pieces back together into a three-wheeled motorized chopper, powered by a lawnmower engine, that never actually ran. We were devastated, even if we recognized that the idea was inherently pretty cool. Later in life, I ran Hardy's first car into a ditch while trying to eject an 8-track cassette from the player, so I guess we could call it even.

Other holidays had their charms as well. We always did a big Easter egg hunt and, with that many eggs to dye, the house smelled like vinegar for a week. Even the innocent act of hunting for the eggs carried a competitive element, of course, one that blended bull-headed manliness with my older brothers' penchant for mischief. When one cracked an egg, backwoods machismo code required that the egg be cracked upon the top of one's head. Why? Because, among the dozens of eggs hidden in the innumerable nooks, crannies, and tussocks around the farm, there always was one that was raw, dyed to blend in with its hard-boiled basket mates.

Did I mention that times could be slow in Choctaw County?

As happens, the innocent joys of early youth eventually begin to fade as other, more chemically-charged, interests awoke. My adolescence coincided with a period when our part of the country likewise was undergoing awkward changes. The Sixties—that tumultuous, glorious, consternating, stressful, exasperating, exhilarating mess of what was not really a decade—arrived in French Camp in 1976, the year I entered high school. It arrived in the form of a brother and sister from—gasp!—*New York City*, who moved down to live with some relatives in our little burg. Those urban waifs hit our school like a small nuclear bomb, especially the lad, the younger of the two, whose lank dirty-blonde hair *reached his shoulders*, an unheard-of affectation for males at that time and place. He was short, scrawny, and, with his long hair falling over the collar of his blue-jean jacket, looked (in retrospect) amazingly like a proto-Tom Petty. I had the enormous good fortune of having this exotic creature in my instructional cohort, where I watched him nonchalantly break just about every social norm with which we attendants of the local Christian boarding school were familiar. To give one example, many of us "local," i.e., non-boarding, kids worked for a certain number of hours a week at the school to help offset the cost of our attendance. Our exotic protagonist (I'll call him Vinny) worked in the Student Union, where he routinely filled his pockets with purloined candy. Literature class under the septuagenarian Miss Pilchuk (not her real name) immediately followed Vinny's work shift. Prayers were held at the beginning of each class. No sooner would her head go down than very loud "whispers" to the effect of, "Hey Vinny...over here!" would issue forth, followed by the "thwack!" of packets of M&Ms or some other sugary treat sailing across the room and impacting a hard surface when the intended recipient failed to make the catch. After a few such overtly audible salvos, Miss Pilchuk's tremulous voice would rise slightly with the heartfelt entreaty, "...and Lord... help us to be reverent."

As was customary for males of my age and socioeconomic set, I learned to drink early. The first buzz I ever copped was with a cousin who plied me with small "pony" bottles of American swill-lager in the school parking lot. After putting a number of ponies in the corral, I opened the door and fell out onto pavement, a denouement which seemed pretty funny at the time. Now, it's just embarrassing. Hard work on weekends—hauling hay for a nickel a bale, cutting enormously large lawns for two dollars, reading water meters for Mr. Wesley for a dollar an hour—provided funds for beer and cigarettes on the weekends, paraphernalia considered necessary for our earnest attempts to act "adult." Penny candy and comic books would have been far better investments. What little defense I could muster for such idiocy would involve the invocation of role models, those essentially being all of the older male relatives (and a number of the females) in our expansive kin network. To give one example, I remember one summer night when we were headed somewhere in the pickup truck; Mom and Aunt Jan were in the cab, while a number of us heathens shared the bed with Pop, our cousins Butch and Mike, and their dad Uncle Billy. Both Pop and Uncle Billy were smashed. Probably due to his smaller stature and consequent lower carrying capacity, Pop lay prone in the bed, eyes closed but with a satisfied grin on his face, demanding loudly at frequent intervals that we "Stop at the nearest phone booth!" so that he could change into Superman. Meanwhile Uncle Billy, whose carrying capacity was nothing short of awesome, stood in Falstaffian splendor at the back of the bed, bellowing out enthusiastic affirmations of Pop's civic-minded entreaties while arcing a seemingly endless stream of urine onto the whickering ribbon of blacktop below. Otto von Bismarck probably was right when he embellished Correa's dictum to include drunks. All I know is, there must have been some mighty impressed dogs in that part of the county the next day.

As marijuana culture, or a particularly silly variant thereof, slowly wafted into our corner of the nation, I found myself attracted to the notion, mostly, I think, because it was different and appeared to be associated with an admirably non-violent approach to life. Frisbee seemed a lot more genteel than Pitch Up and Smear, for example. Part of this reaction was a growing boredom with the conscribed world I inhabited, the limitations of which were becoming more apparent with every passing year. There wasn't a lot, outside of our overworked family library, mutual sibling abuse, and experiments to see which parts of Nature would consume which other parts, to stimulate the imagination, while interactions with the local populace ranged from quotidian to surreal. Let me give a few examples of what I mean. One day in high school I came into a classroom to discover one of French Camp's finest holding a National Geographic magazine open flat before his face, peering intently at its edge as though squinting through a telescope. When I asked my classmate what on Earth he was doing, he rather sheepishly showed me what the magazine was opened to: a beautiful photograph of a Central American street festival, complete with native musicians and women in colorful garb dancing in kaleidoscopic swirls. Braniac was trying to look up their dresses. On another occasion I was riding shotgun while a friend pushed his dad's Dodge to its absolute limit on a lonely blacktop road way out in the country late one summer night. When I inquired as to what the rush was, my buttocks involuntarily forming trace fossils in the vinyl seat as the whining engine reached suicidal pitch, he coyly replied that he was trying to "overrun the headlights." Apparently, this latter-day Einstein considered it within the realm of plausibility that an internal combustion engine could enable a wheeled vehicle to exceed a velocity of 671 million miles per hour. It's a pity he was wrong: I can only imagine the faces of the Antareans had a pickup truck popped out of the nearest wormhole, wide-eyed amateur cosmologist at the wheel.

Lest one think that such erudition was confined to my own, admittedly lost, generation, I offer the example of a high school teacher to whom fell the unlucky task of enlightening the boys when we were separated into opposing chromosomal groups for the purpose of sex education. He seemed to be as uncomfortable as we, which is cutting him at least a little bit of slack. To put us at ease, he let us know that it was normal to have questions, given that the whole human reproductive biology thing was complicated and mysterious. He himself, he solemnly informed us, had had lots of questions as a teenager: for example, how could girls urinate when they were virgins? (I confess that this was not a question I had pondered). He then proceeded to enlighten us by describing anatomical structures and processes that, as I later was to learn, simply do not exist in our particular sliver of the multiverse. He was married, I should note, to another faculty member who was busy in another room similarly enlightening students of the fairer sex. I can only imagine what sorts of arcane insider knowledge she provided to the girls. Perhaps the bulb in their bedroom was burned out. We came in confused; we left utterly confounded. It's a wonder any of us ever managed to breed.

And then there was the time when virtually the entire town of French Camp emptied out into an adjacent field to chase the first armadillo known to have entered Choctaw County in the last five thousand years. Good times.

There were outlets for one's attention other than the low-level mind-altering substances available at the time, of course. Sports played a very important role in southern small-town communities, then and now. There was intense peer pressure to participate, something that never, ever appealed to me. I participated nonetheless, learning a valuable lesson along the way: peer pressure is best ignored in the pursuit of happiness. I was very strong for my size, especially in terms of upper body strength, and I had good stamina. I might therefore have excelled at cross-country running or, as I always fancied, gymnastics. But such effete options didn't exist at the time. Instead, we had the big three: football, basketball, and track. Because it was expected, I briefly tried the lot, with truly pathetic results. I only weighed about a hundred pounds as a freshman, so I just bounced off the larger sort of simian on the gridiron. I stood about five-four at the time and was not particularly graceful, so I spent the basketball season sitting on the bench next to one of my best friends who, though well over six feet tall, was even more clumsy than I, so that he, too, seldom graced the court. His armpit and my nose were at the same level for the whole season, an olfactory experience I decided not to repeat. In track I was given the mile, at which I might have done OK, except that: 1) the other guys' legs topped out about where my elbows began; and 2) adrenaline never gave me strength, but rather sucked it straight out of my core, so that making four-point-something circuits around a football field left me gasping as though I had short-lined a sumo wrestler up Mons Olympus without an external oxygen supply. I only once came home with anything to show for my efforts: a pitiful little white fifth-place ribbon. There were six people in the race. Mom was proud. Dear, dear Mom.

There was one sport at which I made a decent showing, for which I had the potential to do quite well, and which, with great good fortune, I never really pursued with any gusto. That was boxing. I was lured into the activity thanks to Robert, who joined the Winona Boxing Club after we began attending high school there. Robert had a real flair for the sport. Quite gawky and awkward out of the ring, he had a peculiar grace within it, coupled with obstinate courage and a southpaw stance that made him a really difficult opponent. I had other qualities, two in particular: 1) I could hit really, really hard; and 2) I could take a punch. The first of those traits is useful insofar as the sport goes. The second is dangerous, especially if you have a coach who knows nothing about defense. Like ours. Actually, he knew nothing about offense, either. Robert had the dedication to study the situation and self-develop a fluid, dangerous style. I, on the other hand, basically just stood there and hammered away, taking far too many shots to the head in the process. If my opponent just stood there and hammered back, I generally won, thanks to my thick biceps and thicker cranium. Counting those that I had when I continued the practice after joining the military, I won more matches than I lost, at least. But for my efforts, minimal as they were, I gained eleven stitches across my right eyelid, at least one concussion, mild arthritis in my knuckles, and a permanently misaligned left nostril. And you should have seen the other guys.

While I didn't really like boxing, there was a core of dedicated supporters for whom we needed to at least put up a good fight. The girls we knew went out of their way to peddle raffle tickets to support trips to tournaments, often selling stuffed toys that Mom sat up all hours of the night making. Pop built a ring that was installed in our makeshift gym in Winona, and so on. And, more than anything, Pop loved it. He absolutely loved the whole idea of guys punching each other out. For his entire life he carried quite a large chip on his shoulder, and was himself as touchy and as feisty as a banty rooster. That meant rare moments of grudging respect when you won, acid criticism when you lost. One of the weirdest experiences of my life occurred when, due to a lack of participants, Robert and I wound up fighting each other at a tournament. It wasn't much of a fight, really: if described by a playwright, the script for all three rounds would look pretty much like this:

Robert: (swooshes in): Rat-a-tat! Rat-a-tat-tat!

Me: WHOP!

Robert: (flies back, shakes head, then swooshes in again): Rat-a-tat! Rat-a-tat-tat!

Me: WHOP!

Ultimately, my sporadic "whops" were insufficient to overcome Robert's determined "rat-a-tat-tats," and he quite deservedly won a unanimous decision. The most perilous part of the bout came when he spontaneously hugged me at the final bell. I came very, very close to bursting into tears as a weird mix of emotions—relief, frustration, confusion, love—came bubbling up all at once. I really don't know how Mom was able to stand it. Pop, on the other hand, thought it was great. "They're both men," he repeatedly said to anyone nearby who would listen, obviously moved by the spectacle of two of his offspring trying their best to do one another grievous bodily harm. Had he been equally generous when we lost, I might have liked the sport better. But I doubt it. Even when I won, I didn't like it, because I always felt sorry for my opponent. Clearly, competitive sports were not my thing.

Music might well have been, and I regret enormously that we were not made initiates at the larval stage. I never had a chance to play any instrument until my freshman year in high school, when I signed up for cello lessons. I can't remember why I made that particular choice, but it turned out to be a fortunate one. All musical instruments encourage transcendence;[6] cellos are bridges to the sublime. I took to it very well, sawing away enthusiastically on a nearly atonal instrument that I named "Clyde" for no particular reason. I progressed rapidly enough that I warmed the last chair as part of an evening concert with the Starkville Symphony Orchestra, an occasion for which we got paid (forty dollars!) and for which I had to purchase a cheap blue suit (forty dollars!). I'd like

---

6 Except, perhaps, for those that start with "B": banjo, bassoon, bagpipes, bongos, bombardino, botella de anís, bubble organ, bukkehorn…

to say, "Eat that, Pablo Casals," except that I faked my way badly through some of the enormously difficult position-shredding riffs in Schubert's "Unfinished Symphony." I'm sure I fooled no one, but at least I got through the evening without the conductor harpooning me with his baton. The other high schools I attended had no such longhair equipage, alas. I signed up for band during our year at Winona, where the teacher handed me a baritone horn, showed me a practice room, and told me to get back to him when I had mastered the thing. I was reasonably sure which end my mouth went on, but I didn't know what to do with my lips, let alone which clef I was supposed to be operating in. After a few weeks of sitting alone in my lonely monastic cell, dutifully producing doleful "spluts" like the labial aspirations of a dyspeptic sea cucumber, I bid farewell to the enterprise and spent the remaining band periods of the term smoking cigarettes in the parking lot. Astonishingly enough, I got a "B." Maybe the teacher had a thing for sea cucumbers. Later, in the military, I bought a middling-quality guitar and fell in love with the thing. In college I took piano lessons, which never felt natural and which were spoiled by a silly requirement that even non-majors had to perform in front of a visibly bored bevy of ill-paid music professors. Years later, I bought an electronic keyboard, quit trying to read music, and had a blast, especially after I purchased a teensy little recording deck and earnestly composed some of the worst songs you never have heard. I further discovered that I could play almost anything by ear: bass, fiddle, mandolin, harmonica, you name it. Not well, of course, but who cares? If music is food for the soul, who needs table manners? Eat that, Yo-Yo Ma.

And then, there were girls. I never was very accomplished along those lines, but I did have a couple of school-yard "girlfriends" over the high school years. My first lip-lock was an awkward affair, and my confidence was not boosted when the recipient so honored proclaimed loudly on the bus the next day that I "didn't know how to kiss." Well, duh. The second girl, Debbie, I met when I was older, which helped, even if my lips still were relatively unpracticed. She was astonishingly beautiful and one of the nicest people I ever have met. Despite those charms, while I liked her a great deal there was no real spark, and I wasn't even sure where the fuse was supposed to be. We never dated, as such, which might have been part of the problem. I think that growing up with no sisters contributes to a false impression of girls being members of a different species. Whatever the cause, I was basically hopeless in the romance department. I was fortunate enough to be friends with a number of girls, though, who helped make life interesting as we all bumbled and stumbled through adolescence, and some of whom wound up being my sisters-in-law. And thus, the Peacock phenotype was passed on to another generation, despite my own lack of contribution to the corporate gene pool. Just as well, really: in the South, the gene pool is so shallow that "Wade" is a common name for boys. Thank you; thank you very much.

But back to pot culture, if "culture" isn't too euphemistic a word for the strange syncretic practices that emerged in our particular space-time nexus. What happened was Willie Nelson. Willie was country, no doubt about that; yet he had long hair and made no bones about toking up. Now *that* was a paradigm shift. Next thing you knew, "head shops" began to appear in malls along the Coast, always the most proudly hedonistic area of the state. I think they called them "head shops" because of all the traditionalist crania that exploded as the counter-culture belatedly came calling in the Magnolia State. In an astonishingly short amount of time, virtually every one of my generation at least tried pot. (If anyone tries to tell you differently, it's probably the associated memory loss talking). I don't think it ever did any of us any real harm and, astonishingly enough, society didn't collapse, rapine and plunder remained infrequent, and crania eventually were glued back together with no apparent ill effects. There were, however, many strange incidents of the time. Pop once struck a deal to acquire the seats out of a county school bus, how and for what reason I have no idea. Not having a place to store them, they wound up in an unsightly pile over on the far side of our barn. That summer, an impressive crop of marijuana sprang up, courtesy of the seed bank provided by a lost generation of public-school kids. I always regretted that he spotted them before I did; my popularity at school could have experienced a major uptick.

I personally was, I believe, the fourth person in our little hamlet to get high, courtesy of the same cousin who'd set my liver down the path to perdition via the "pony beers" incident. He was insistent; I was willing, if understandably nervous. We drove out into the country in his grandmother's supremely uncool Pinto, where he produced a funny twisted cigarette that he referred to as a "joint." We smoked this; I felt nothing, except for a little embarrassment at the whole situation. We smoked another. Still nothing. He then produced a small metal pipe, packed the bowl, and we smoked that. Several times. No effect. He then produced a strange cylindrical plumbing fixture he called a "bong" that made a sound sort of like a coffee percolator when you sucked up on it, and with which we smoked three or four more "bowls." At that point, he gave up in exasperation. I was left wondering what all the fuss was about. Then I got a small itch on the right side of my face and blinked an eye in response, whereupon that side of my head melted and ran down into my lap. I had arrived.

All that sort of thing was fun for a while, especially after I discovered the "munchies." I bet even chitlins would be delicious if one had the munchies. I once got high on the Coast with some cousins who, when no funds were available because they'd blown everything on weed, addressed their pressing munchie needs by driving through a fried chicken place where a girl they knew would hook them up with copious amounts of deep-fried provender, *sans* payment. We were in a pickup truck that day and I was riding in the back, marveling at the unvarnished beauty of the world as only a stoned teenager can. They made the grievous mistake of passing the bucket of contraband chicken to me to hold until we returned to their apartment. The extra-large, family-sized bucket, I might add, out of which the most delectable aroma came calling. By the time we arrived at our destination, every single piece of the indescribably delicious fare was gone, the ends of the bones had been gnawed off and the marrow sucked out, and I had grease up to my elbows and plastering back my hair. I was in a state of bliss, if still feeling a little peckish. For some reason, that was the last time I was entrusted to be the holder of the chicken bucket.

Music was a very important part of that whole scene. Strange compositions, some of which were intricate and beautiful (e.g., Electric Light Orchestra, Alan Parsons Project), some of which were grating and cacophonic (e.g., Molly Hatchet, Uriah Heep) began to be heard echoing in the boxy sound chambers of dingy sedans in the school parking lot. By some fortuitous cosmic convergence, all of this was happening just at the time when one could express one's particular preferences by means of 8-track players in one's vehicle. Ah, 8-tracks; that most Freudian of music delivery devices. When you plunged a tape of Bob Seger, Queen, or Lynard Skynard into an 8-track player, you *felt* it go in, ker*chunk*. The tapes were large, plastic, and awkwardly-shaped; they tended to migrate to under the seats unless you had a fancy plastic caddy that would ride somewhere in the middle of the cab and hold all of six tapes at a time. If you made the mistake of leaving the tapes on the dash they curled up in the sun, making something sort of useful as an ashtray or a subject for still-life art but otherwise surrendering all functionality. And even if you took good care of them, the day inevitably would come when the tape would snarl in the inner mechanism of the player and stretch out like thin, brown entrails when the housing case was extracted. Cassette players came a little later; my cousin Butch had the first one I ever saw. He plugged a little cassette into the player in his Mustang and Queen's "Tie Your Mother Down" exploded out of the speakers, concussing all pine lizards within a twenty-meter radius. But the cassette itself looked so small and ridiculous compared to the sandwich-sized 8-tracks! I remember thinking, "Huh. Bet that'll never catch on."

While 8-tracks were cool, radio still was the mainstay. We were let more-or-less off-leash at an early age by the time Mom and Pop got down to raising the Little Kids. Even at the halting early stage of gettin' out there, our basic activities were like something from a Fifties nostalgia movie. Drive, smoke cigarettes, drink if we could get it, play the tunes, hoping desperately that we were cool while privately being pretty sure that we weren't. Occasionally we would bellow along, a heartfelt caterwauling in a variety of keys, assuring the universe at large that we *wouldn't* go breakin' your heart, that we *would* let 'em in, that we *would* go our own way, that *nobody* does it better, that WE WERE THE CHAMPIONS! And who could not but admire the Rubberband Man? Why, he had rhythm, grace, *and* debonair. Get down, Rubba! What is it about driving around on a warm summer night out in the country with too many of your teenage pals crammed into some dusty sedan of questionable vintage that makes music so especially awesome? The whole landscape felt like *ours*. Did you know that gravel roads have a smell? It would flow through the rolled-down windows, arid and cinnamony like the worm-spice of *Dune*. That smell is especially magnified after a rain, but it has a liquid quality then, as though the granular substrate turned out to be aquarium sand in some galactic overlord's punk kid's room. I don't think I've smelled that smell for a long time. Clearly, a field trip is in order.

They weren't all radio classics, of course. Even discounting disco, which was oozing like Twinkie filling through the walls of good taste, there were lots of sappy wonderments out there. "Heaven on the Seventh Floor," for example. And one could only hope that rabies was a poetic-justice consequence of "Muskrat Love." But even those awful earworms were sort of fun if one had pals with whom to sing along. I remember how excited we all were for a radio special on July 4th, 1976, which would play down the top two hundred songs of all time in recognition of the Bicentennial. It started off great; two or three excellent songs, followed by the usual commercial pap, then two or three more songs, etc. But as time progressed, they started rushing things, actually cutting off parts of songs higher up on the list as they got closer to the program cutoff point of midnight. That in itself was incredibly annoying: surely the radio overlords of north Mississippi had math skills sufficient to plan the programming? But we stuck with it, waiting with earnest teenage anticipation for the Number One song, arguing amongst ourselves about what it was likely to be. Finally, the moment arrived; we gripped each other's shoulders, ready to wolf-howl and fist pump in unbridled celebration the moment the ultimate, soul-shredding rock anthem came blaring out of the dashboard. And the song they'd chosen to be The One, The Song of Songs, the culmination of two hundred years of evolving Western minstrelsy, was none other than…

"You Light Up My Life," by Debbie Boone. To which nobody ever, anywhere, anytime, pumped a fist or howled like a wolf. Tragedy.

That also was the age when electronic home entertainment systems began to appear. I remember the summer of 1977 when, while staying with a host family during a chorus trip to the Coast, I beheld a stand-alone "Pong" console approximately the size of your average kitchen range. To be clear to today's younger readers, this magnificent contrivance had but one purpose: you stood there and played Pong on it. Pong was sort of a table tennis kind of game in which a little white square was bounced between two rectangular sticks which moved vertically with the twist of a dial until one player managed to get the "ball" past the other player's stick, scoring a goal and tallying a point with a satisfying electronic "*squernk*" sound. This chest-high device did not function as a phone; it did not operate via a touch screen; movies could not be downloaded; it would not heat up your leftover mac and cheese; there was no such thing as the "net" for it to connect to. You plugged it in, you stood there, and you played Pong. Nothing else; just Pong. I remember thinking, "Huh. Bet that'll never catch on."

But catch on it did, despite widespread fear among parents that the rays emanating from such devices would permanently fry their offspring's eyeballs. No one in French Camp had one of those consoles, of course, because they were expensive. But the times, they were a'changin'. A few years later, an acquaintance in the military produced the first home computer I'd ever seen, a RadioShack TRS-80. He allowed us to play games on it, including Pong (of course); a pre-Myst text game; a cool little 8-bit tank adventure that I lost with studious regularity; and a few more to boot. That stuff was *fun*. I remember thinking, "Huh. This just might catch on." And suddenly, affordable gaming consoles were everywhere, especially hooked up to TV's in people's houses, where offspring could more conveniently fry their eyeballs. There were really excellent little table versions in bars where you could sit, set your beer down right there beside the screen, and plunk quarters in with maniacal focus as though feeding the batteries in a coin-operated iron lung. I loved those things! I must have downed gallons of beer while zapping aliens in the dim recesses of various dives over the years. By the early eighties, I could pronounce with confidence that such things had indeed "caught on," not that anyone had been waiting on my sanction. I have remained behind the curve ever since. It's remarkable how archaic such things appear now, when I have watched my grandchildren confidently whipping their way around iPads by the age of two years. One can only wonder what their children will be whipping their ways around by the age of two months.

Whether fueled by beer, my minor dalliance with weed, or simple genetic contingency, I had a predilection for uppityness that led to some real misadventures while I was in high school. In retrospect, it's a good thing I didn't live in a place where more serious trouble easily could be had. Most of those exercises in ridiculousness—climbing up the outside of a fire tower during a thunderstorm, raiding watermelon patches, taking off running in downtown Winona when a cop drove by in order to initiate a night-time foot chase—are too dumb to warrant detailed description. When they involved alcohol, they were beyond dumb; they were downright stupid. When I was fifteen, I was arrested for DUI while carrying a learner's permit. An expired leaner's permit. *That* caused the arresting officer's eyebrows to rise. Not too long after, I was expelled for a semester from high school for drinking on a summer chorus trip. A Southern euphemism for getting one's act together is to "tighten up." Clearly, I needed to tighten up. My folks were unwilling to send us back to French Camp Academy after my expulsion, so Robert, Andy and I, the three still in school, had to change venues to a relatively large school at Winona. When that no longer could be afforded, Andy and I finished out school at the nearer, smaller, Weir Attendance Center (not a juvenile correction facility, despite the name). The negative impact of that teenage debacle on my brothers produced a lot of guilt, even though they were extraordinarily gracious about it. The only positive aspect of the whole affair was that, by going to a larger public school, we got to learn sex education from the real pros—our cigarette-smoking, bong-gurgling, pony-swilling peers out in the parking lots. It's a wonder any of us ever managed to breed.

OUT OF THE NEST

As high school graduation loomed, panic set in. Jobs, or at least jobs worth having, were virtually non-existent in our area at the time. There was a wooden-box factory where a lot of locals worked, but that was a grimy, low-paid existence that held no appeal even had they been hiring. College wasn't on my radar. Like so many poor kids in the Deep South, I began thinking about the military as an option, and for that course of action I did have some models to follow, given that my three eldest brothers all had enlisted in the Navy, while Robert was a Security Policeman (SP) in the Air Force, steadfastly standing night watch over rank upon rank of parked airplanes that no one had any intention of stealing. But which was the right branch for me?

The Army didn't seem romantic enough and, being a non-conformist, I wanted to choose something other than the Navy. I briefly considered the Marines due to a close encounter with a recruiter who came to our school. All students had taken the Armed Services Vocational Aptitude Battery, or ASVAB. This clever instrument supposedly can determine whether you are more cut out to be a cook, a computer programmer, a nuclear engineer, a gunnery specialist, or an expert filler of sand bags. I did well on the verbal and reasoning parts, but there was one section where lots of weirdly shaped boxes were shown unfolded, all rectangles and right angles poking out here and there, as though steam rollers had flattened so many excitedly gesticulating robots. The task was to pick the corresponding refolded box from a series that looked like airduct configurations on an alien space station. Pop would have aced that task. I, on the other hand, missed *every single question* in that section, a result that flies in the face of basic probability theory. At least that sad performance negated the possibility of my being encouraged to undertake a career in ductwork, alien space station or otherwise.

I signed up for a one-on-one meeting with the recruiter, mostly because it meant a break from study hall. He was a short, blocky, tank of a man, quite impressive in his impeccable uniform adorned with lots of colorful little ribboned bars. He growled at me for a while, chewing air and spitting syllables, very serious and truly daunting with his square head and prominent jaw. That was a *man's* jaw. Here was someone who doubtless could have punched his own brother out in businesslike manner without waterworks threatening his oculars. Sgt. Ironjaw praised my test scores and pushed hard to convince me that I was Jarhead material. He summed up his gruff sales pitch with a line that resonated strongly in my tremulous adolescent being: "Peacock, you'd make a *damn fine Marine.*"

Well, *that* certainly swelled my head. Who'd have known that I had the makings of a DFM, of all things? I sauntered through the rest of the school day, chest out, lording it over the hoi polloi and thinking seriously about whether I might not revisit Sgt. Ironjaw that afternoon and sign on the dotted line. Boot camp at Parris Island didn't sound like much fun, but surely, as manifestly superior DFM material, I could hack it. After all, Destiny had stamped me a DFM and who was I to argue with Destiny? Sometimes a DFM has to do what a DFM has to do. Fortunately, as I was on my way back to confer once more with Sgt. Ironjaw (a fellow DFM if ever I saw one), I ran into a schoolmate who was even lower on the societal food chain than I; a sallow, concave-chested, lank-haired fellow who might have weighed ninety-five pounds soaking wet; whose grades seldom escaped the platykurtic; and whose flair for physical activity was somewhat less than that of a lovelorn sea urchin. I noticed that this apparition was affecting something approximating a saunter and that his chest was rather less concave than usual. "Guess what?" he squeaked excitedly, as my impromptu visual inspection inadvertently allowed an instant of unsolicited eye contact. "I just saw the recruiter. He said I'd make a *damn fine Marine.*"

Despite the patent ludicrousness of that situation, options remained limited, so late in the spring I went to Grenada to talk to an

Air Force recruiter. The contrast with my previous experience could hardly have been more striking. The man slouching behind a desk in a rumpled sky blue uniform remarkably free of ribboned bars must have been pushing three hundred pounds. His massive, big-boned, gut-sprung frame seemed to create a palpable fold in the space-time continuum. One halfway expected to see doughnuts locked in greasy orbit around him. Whereas Sgt. Ironjaw had been tough and direct, a man on a mission to recruit as many concave-chested, lovelorn sea urchins as possible, Sgt. Lumpypants was carefree and seemed to have all day to talk about nothing in particular. Well, to be fair, the conversation wasn't actually about nothing in particular. Whereas Sgt. Ironjaw had talked service, honor, and duty to one's country, Sgt. Lumpypants talked about food, and little else.

"Wait'll you see the chow halls! All the food you want, and you can go back as many times as you like! I like the chipped beef on toast; it's made with dried beef cooked up in milk gravy. They call it 'shit on a shingle.' You can even get it on biscuits!"

"Um, that's nice. But tell me about technical school. Would I come out with something akin to a college degree, or is it more vocational-style training?"

"So, you grab a tray and go down the line, and just point at what you want. You want biscuits, you get biscuits. Sausage pizza, pepperoni pizza. They got chocolate milk dispensers, soft serve ice cream. And man, on cheeseburger night, they lay on the fries. All you can eat!"

"Uh, thanks, that's great. I like fries. But how much leeway does one have in choosing a duty station? Or does that depend upon training in any particular specialty field?"

"Eggs, bacon, sausage; all you can eat! Biscuits from here till morning. And hell, pour on the gravy! It's free!"

I found his dedication to the topic oddly endearing, and having been thus reassured that my next four years would not, at least, be calorically challenged, I signed on. With the die cast, a few nights later I attended my last high school function: that awful ritual known as the "Junior-Senior Prom." What kind of sadistic individual ever dreamed up such a torture-fest I cannot imagine, but it was painful in the extreme for all involved. The theme, embarrassingly enough, was "Disco Fever," which should have provided warning enough to skip the proceedings. Thankfully, I have forgotten most of the evening's goings-on, but two things I can't seem to forget are the awful, wide-lapelled, denim blue-jean suits that were all the rage for guys that year, and the fact that for "my" song, the student organizers (you know the type) chose the Village People's "In the Navy." Change "Navy" to "Gravy," and Lumpy would have been proud. As it was, the moment was simply incongruous on a cosmic scale, and I leave the scene of forty-five or so gawky, monumentally uncool, rural teenagers flailing around to the throbbing beat of a sweaty coterie of West Side cosplayers to the imagination of the reader. With apologies.

Three days after graduation, still just seventeen years old, I boarded a flight to San Antonio, Texas, to become an inmate—pardon me, inductee—at Lackland Air Force Base. It was my first time on a plane, which was cool. Texas was not. It was, in fact, brutally hot, even for a Mississippi boy. On particularly hellacious days they flew black "death flags" to signify the real likelihood of demise by heatstroke should one be foolhardy enough to march around in such conditions. We nevertheless were required to march around in such conditions. There is hot, there is damn hot, and there is central-Texas-in-mid-summer hot. How the inmates—pardon me, inductees—from the Northeast stood it, I really don't know.

My unit in boot camp was Flight 374, a motley squad of dubious specimens from across the country and a few assorted territories. We were an ungainly-looking lot upon arrival and the mandated uniformity had rather a leveling effect in that regard; to wit, we all turned out to be pretty ghastly when the wide variety of locks was shorn. We were required to be clean shaven, of course, except for some of the African-American guys who were allowed to keep short beards due to a skin condition called "pseudofolliculitis barbae," which is when stiff, tightly-curling hairs turn inward to pierce the skin. I never had heard of that condition before, and I couldn't help imagining Ken hanging out with Pseudofolliculitis Barbie, only to discover, once the alcohol wore off, that she had suspiciously large hands and a pronounced Adam's apple.

I remember some of my flight mates quite well: Barnhill, a large, personable bloke from Maryland who dreamed of motorcycle rides yet untaken; Booker, an African-American gentleman who fled the room should the frequently ribald conversation turn to oral sex; Lyle, a moon-faced lad from Sebastopol, Mississippi, who may or may not have faced me in high school football during the seven or so minutes I actually spent on the field; Martas, a short Chinese-American kid who fled the room should the frequently ribald conversation turn to sex of any kind; and Walton, another African-American who was immediately assigned to be Flight Leader, a role in which he was excellent: mature, serious, conscientious, and quietly commanding without being in the least bit dickish. I have to point out that Walton was not chosen to be Flight Leader because of those qualities, as there hadn't been time on the part of the Training Instructors for such critical assessment. Walton was chosen because Walton was the tallest of us all. It was our good fortune that physical stature and towering personality were reflective of one another in his case.

I saw some truly strange things at Lackland. For example, I once had the questionable pleasure of being assigned to Kitchen Patrol duty with Murray, one of the freer spirits in our group. "KP" was not an enviable task. Imaging being up to your elbows in stainless steel lasagna pans the size of small bathtubs, scrubbing futilely at crusty brown reefs of baked-on cheese while bloated ribbons of waterlogged pasta rippled by like albino Japanese pond carp. Murray didn't seem to mind, however; he apparently relished the work and the steamy, sauna-like atmosphere of the kitchen. In fact, he relished it so much that he decided to try the experience while wearing nothing but an ankle-length industrial rubber smock. I downloaded this astounding bit of data after he claimed my attention—and indeed, the attention of everyone whose ears lay within range of a very long shot—by shouting at the top of his impressive baritone voice, "A ROACH! A ROACH! A ROACH!" He held a large metal spatula aloft in his right hand, while with his left he thrust an accusing finger at the offending insect. *WHAAAAMMMMOOO!* The spatula came down like an Olympian thunderbolt. "NO MOOOOORE

ROACH!" Murray screamed triumphantly. The door to a saner world opened and a second lieutenant poked his head in.

"Is there a problem here?" he snapped.

"No problem, sir!" Murray bellowed enthusiastically, pleased beyond measure that his cookhouse operetta was attracting an audience. "There is NO MOOOOORE ROACH!" As a visual aid to this incontestable asseveration, he energetically brandished the bug-smeared utensil, Exhibit #1 in what should have been an immediate Section 8 discharge. Exhibit #2 would have been the smock, which had been spun halfway around Murray's ample, profusely sweating, disturbingly pallid body by the concentrated centrifugal force of his entomological *coup de grace*. The nonplussed lieutenant, showing admirable good sense, immediately disappeared and did not come back. Rank hath its privileges. I finished the shift with one eye on the exit and the other on the spatula. And/or the smock. Some things are hard to ignore.

And then there was Clarke. Clarke came to us from an inner borough of New York City, or perhaps it was some wispy fringe of the Outer Antares Nebula. Whichever, I suspect that they were happy to see him go. Clarke was about as suited for the military as I was for alien space station ductwork. His short, squarish body, enthusiastic hair (before they cut it all off), and enormous glasses unavoidably made one think of Elton John when that august personage still had a natural hairline but after his mid-life BMI increase. Clarke was completely hopeless at everything: no physical stamina, no ability to remember/follow orders, no concept of discipline, nothing. Early on, the TIs gave up chewing him out at morning inspection because he just stood there grinning disarmingly in his hopelessly unkempt uniform beside his hopelessly unkempt bed. Clarke was the first person I ever met who used the word "tool" as an invective, a routine example of why neither I nor anyone else usually had any idea of what he was talking about. Rather reassuringly, he did not make it through basic training. But before he was washed out, I was intrigued to discover that he was a savant of sorts, in a manner again reminiscent of Elton John. Toward the end of our training, we were allowed to do a little "R and R" in a large recreational complex on the base. In addition to the usual air hockey and pool tables, there were rooms holding musical instruments that were there for the playing. I happened to walk by while Clarke was at a piano cranking out an original number he'd composed about being in the Air Force, of all things. I still remember the words and tune; it was quite a good song (he rhymed "talking all about us" with "presidential palace"), to which he did full justice in a throaty, raspy voice. I am absolutely certain that he'd had no time to practice either the playing or the delivery of this piece; he just had it in his head, and he just sat down and did it. It was nothing short of amazing. Wherever Clarke is these days, I hope that he is still cranking them out. But I'm just as glad that he wasn't put in charge of anything munitions-related.

Our TIs were Sgt. Miller and Sgt. Belcher. Sgt. Belcher was rather a cold fish, austere and off-putting. I only once received a compliment from him, an epochal event that took place in the chow hall, of all places. Taking meals at Lackland involved a lot of silly little rituals and proscriptions designed to help develop us as front-line defenders of our country's precious freedom and/or to drive us all bat-shit crazy (the two are not mutually exclusive, of course). For example, if you absentmindedly popped a piece of food into your mouth before you sat at your table, you instantly would find yourself confronted by a red-faced TI whose outrage at your unspeakably gauche behavior could scarcely have been matched had you been found fomenting a communist cell over a shared bong in the ladies' room, in ladies' dress, at midnight while lighting said bong with a conflagrant American flag. Another example involved a full-length mirror placed just before the chow line, into which you were supposed to keep a straight face while executing a salute to your own bad self before fueling up. Now, due to some random roll of the genetic dice, I turned out to be a born saluter. Never mind that my boots might not be properly shined, that my gig line might be crooked, or that I might absent-mindedly toss a tater tot into my mouth before sitting at the table, thereby unwittingly inciting a cross-dressing Communist revolution; I can pop a salute with such electric vigor that my fingers snap together with an audible report, leaving my stinging hand quivering with the atomic aftershock. Many a torpid flock of Texas pigeons was startled into flight by the staccato crack when I acknowledged a passing officer. If the flap of a butterfly's wings can create a typhoon on the other side of the globe, my salute can breach the space-time continuum. Why the mirror didn't shatter like an overworked NBA backboard each time I saluted my own bad, bald-headed self in the chow hall, I'll never know. "Now, *that's* a salute," Sgt. Belcher was moved to remark upon witnessing my hand-snapping prowess on one particular occasion. I beamed proudly as I picked up my tray and began moving down the chow line. I may not have been a DFM but, buddy, I could *salute*! Oddly enough, this peculiar skill has proved to be of little practical benefit in the years since, except on those rare occasions when I needed to startle torpid flocks of pigeons into flight or to breach the space-time continuum.

Sgt. Miller was terrifying, even though he was no bigger than I. Built like a lean-waisted ninja, his sallow features were made all the more satanic by the black, wiry mustache standing guard over his sinister tooth-hole. He would have scared the pants off a banshee, if banshees wear pants. Yet I came to respect him, and would have jumped into a fire at his command, which of course is precisely the mindset they were trying to instill. One evening toward the end of my time at Lackland the scent of brimstone lifted briefly and Sgt. Miller was revealed as a human being, albeit a perennially daunting one. I overheard him discussing foosball with a fellow TI. Foosball is the table-soccer game with the little wooden or plastic players impaled on metal rods like anthropomorphic shish kebab cuts. Two players stand on either side of the table and try to look like they have girlfriends while twisting, spinning, and slamming the rods to and fro, trying to navigate a little round ball into a recessed hole at the end of the table, thereby scoring a goal. Not to brag, but my aptitude for foosball was only slightly less developed than that for saluting, and I had honed my skills through endless weekend hours at a skating rink in Winona. I wasn't the best, but I was damn good, with the liquid reflexes and extraordinary reaction time of a government-cheese-fed teenager with nothing better to do. I once read a short account of playing foosball, a.k.a. "little foot," by Calvin Trillin, who fancied himself an accomplished player. Trillin particularly stressed a shot he liked to execute by firing the ball down the table with his goalie. We socially-challenged ilk of the Winona skating rink had a ready response for that particular gambit, which was to return fire immediately with the center-most figure on the opposing pole. When properly executed, a matter of pure reflex and instant reaction, this "stuff shot" would fire the ball back into the opponent's goal with an immensely satisfying, gunshot-like report that could be heard clear across the rink. I lived for that moment, as I stood there swaying nonchalantly to "Undercover Angel" in my really cool beige tank top, one shoulder strap of which held down a pack of Marlboros in conspicuous fashion. I love Calvin Trillin's work, but had he been unfortunate enough to play foosball with me in my time-wasting, tank-top-wearing prime, I would have fed him stuff shots repeatedly with scornful abandon while second-hand Marlboro smoke sallied up his strangely beguiling nostrils. Having confessed this heretical fantasy, I doubt I'll be receiving an invitation to any receptions of the literati any time soon. Of course, if they read this book, that result already will have been achieved.

Anyhow, upon eavesdropping on Sgt. Miller's conversation, I mustered my courage to state that I wished I could have played him. "Get your shirt on," he ordered sharply, and shortly thereafter I found myself in the NCOs' hallowed rec room, opposite the game table from Sgt. Miller and the other TI, taking them both on simultaneously, flipping little wooden figures on metal bars as though the fate of the free world depended on it. A few balls in, it became apparent that I could, in fact, beat the both of them if they followed the rules; that is, if Sgt. Miller's colleague would let me move to the rear sticks before firing the ball toward the goal from his own forward position. He didn't; I lost; and all worked out for the best. Had I won, I might have found myself keeping a wary eye on Murray's smock again.

Being raised on a farm had its advantages during basic training. For one thing, I could shoot, and I greatly enjoyed popping away with the M-16 at the firing range, even if it had been modified to shoot .22-caliber shells as an eminently reasonable cost-saving measure. To rate Expert, one had to lie on one's stomach and place at least ninety-six out of one hundred shots into quite a small circle in a target set up a considerable distance away. I managed ninety-four, and had to wait until the next training session to make Expert and get a cool little ribbon on my uniform. My marksmanship seemed to pale in comparison to that of a flight mate at the other end of the line, however, who accomplished the remarkable feat of scoring one hundred thirty-six! Out of one hundred! Turned out that Clarke was lying next to him; Clarke, whose trembling hands had never before held a gun. Clarke, whose glasses could have focused the beams of a far-distant sun to laser intensity. Clarke managed to score four. Out of one hundred. And thus are legends made.

Another advantage I held over the majority of my flight mates was that basic training was far less physically demanding than the bean-hoeing, pig-chasing, wood-toting, tank top-sporting life I'd been leading. I actually gained seventeen pounds during those first six weeks in our nation's armed elite. That embarrassing pattern was to continue during my four-year enlistment, during most of which there was no daily exercise requirement at all. Instead, there was an annual "physical" that was anything but. Basically, we had to jog a mile and a half within a very generous amount of time. If that was too strenuous, we could choose to *walk* a mile and a half within an even more generous amount of time. It was quite the spectacle to see beer-gutted staff sergeants wallowing like walruses out of the burger and beer stations each year to lumber their way, gasping and blowing, around the track. I am sorry to say that I, too, was well on my way to sea-mammalhood by the time I got out. I think I weighed about one hundred and forty-five pounds when I went into the service; four years later, I weighed one hundred and eighty-three. Thanks, Lumpy.

Here's the weird thing about basic training: while you're there, it sucks; when it's time to leave, you don't want to. We had mastered various completely useless skills, such as making wrinkle-free beds with perfectly angled hospital corners, marching in step without ramming into the dip-shitted, slow-footed airman in front of us, saluting (some of us with particular élan), and generally having our shit together, at least as far as Lackland rules went. Outside the gates, the unknown again awaited. But as is true of all things military, we had no choice in the matter; orders were received and off we went. Upon leaving, they presented each of us with the equivalent of a high-school yearbook, written in the same faux-jocular type of prose as those annoying missives and full of pictures of buzz-headed recruits we didn't know doing various completely useless things we'd all just as soon have forgotten. Installing .22 magazines into M-16's is a wise cost-saving measure, the realization of which was completely squandered by the production of thousands of those ridiculous books each year. If any congressman is reading this volume, and if this particular waste of taxpayer money continues to this day, you might consider making a name for yourself by working to put a stop to it. Believe me, the bald-headed, acne-spotted subjects aren't photogenic enough to make the expenditure worthwhile.

Having managed to not wash out of basic, I was sent to complete a six-month training school in electronics. This training took place at Keesler Air Force Base in Biloxi, of all places, where I had some nearby family (those of purloined chicken-bucket fame) and which put me within driving distance of home, had I owned a car. At that time, I still was a "pinger," a bizarre pejorative applied to those of us so freshly out of basic training that we still couldn't get a part in our hair. The "pings" were the supposed sound of new hairs popping out on one's head. This should give the discerning reader a good sense of what passes for high humor in the military. I nevertheless was, I confess, proud when the day finally came that I was able to achieve a part, my gap-toothed visage gaping delightedly back at me in the mirror. Nowadays I listen nostalgically and in vain for pings.

The atmosphere in tech school certainly was more relaxed than in basic. We were required to do a whopping fifteen minutes of exercise once a day and to march in formation to our classrooms, which were a mile or so from the barracks. I had the unfortunate assignment of being a "road guard." Road guards marched along at the rear of the group. When nearing an intersection, the post-pinger in charge would yell, "Road guards, out!" at which point we had to run past the rest of the crew and stand in the intersection, left arm outstretched, hand palm out, as if to say, "Hit me first, please." Eventually I was moved into the more responsible position of Director of Flights. Basically, this meant that I stood in the middle of the largest intersection and held one flight up (using the same magical gesture I used to stop cars) while indicating to some other flight that they could proceed upon their way. While this task was not exactly intellectually stimulating, I could at least see the point of it, and I took the job seriously, a mistake I was to repeat many times during my military years. An Airman who was about to graduate from tech school trained me, showing me how to keep one flight standing and waiting until the flight before them had completely cleared the intersection. Once on my own, it didn't take long to realize that this procedure was stupid. Why keep people standing at attention in horrible heat any longer than necessary? Why not move them along and get everyone back to the barracks a little more quickly? The situation needed tightening up. I determined to do the tightening.

Accordingly, I exercised something that is anathema to many "lifers," as career military members are called: initiative! As one flight was beginning to move through the intersection, I boldly gestured for the waiting flight to come on. I could register the surprise on their faces from where I stood, but they obediently lumbered into action and, like clockwork, moved smartly in behind the first flight, saving a good ten or fifteen minutes of taxpayer-supported time and considerable human discomfort. I was pumped. My gestures grew snappier, my timing even more precise. If one were to sum up the person-hours saved, one would find that I saved a heck of a lot of person-hours that day. As the last flight moved through, I saw a Staff Sergeant approaching. I waited serenely for the commendation I knew was coming. Perhaps another little colored bar? Or invitation to a foosball table? Instead, I had to stand at attention in Tarzan-heat while being bawled out by the outraged, red-faced troglodyte, who vehemently forbade me to pull such an audacious stunt again. Accordingly, the next day a heck of a lot of person-hours were lost while flights of airmen again stood sweltering in the hot sun, waiting for the intersection to clear before I could wave them on. Staff Sergeant Dipstick looked on with the triumphant leer of the seriously in-bred. And thus was our nation served. From that point forward, I began to count the days until my enlistment was up. That was still a whoooooole lotta days.

The instructors at Keesler were civilians hired for the task, and they were quite good. I can still recite Ohm's Law ($E=IR$, as it was written in those days) and reel off the three requirements for sustained oscillation (forward bias, regenerative feedback, and a frequency determining device) without breaking a sweat. No fault of theirs that such feats of memorization were simply surface cover over a deep abyss of confusion. I had no, repeat no, aptitude for electronics (thanks, ASVAB!). I limped through tech school with minimal marks and remained generally unnoticed, except for the memorable occasion when a passing officer saw me sitting in the classroom with one of Mom's stuffed snake toys curled around my neck. I thought it was funny. He was not amused. I suspect that the phrase, "Airman, what's that around your neck?" has been one of the less common perorations in our country's military history. "A snake, sir!" presumably is even rarer as a response.

The only momentous thing that happened during my time at Keesler was that I inadvertently became engaged. I dated a woman for the last few months of my time there. She was slightly older than I, with a handsome toddling boy who lived back at home with her parents. Her name was Jewel. We had some good times that mostly involved the unregulated ingestion of cheap sangria. When my training was almost completed, she grew cross and despondent. Trying to find something to say to help alleviate the situation, all that came into my sun-addled, eighteen-year-old brain was, "How long can you wait?" To which she immediately replied, "Is that a proposal?" To which my sun-addled, eighteen-year-old brain replied, "Uh...yeah...I guess." The next day I was shocked when I showed up for classes and people started clapping me on the back, shaking my hand and otherwise offering their congratulations on the happy news. Apparently, I was engaged. I wanted to hide behind my stuffed snake. That situation lasted only for a month or so after our separate postings, which was a good thing, as neither of us really cared for the other. The sangria was nice, though.

As the end of tech school neared, we all filled out "dream sheets," forms on which we got to mark preferences for the next duty station. There were three bases, in particular, that scuttlebutt strongly suggested should be avoided: Incirlik, in Turkey; Thule, in Greenland; and Minot, in North Dakota. Accordingly, I steered clear of those potential destinations as I made my choices. Looking back, I regret not having been more adventurous: why not spend a part of my formative years in some truly exotic locale? Turkey! Greenland! North Dakota! As commonly happens, I did not receive posting to any of the destinations I checked on my dream sheet. I did, however, receive a posting to another country, to Lindsey Air Station in Germany, where I arrived in early 1980. The first thing encountered upon disembarking from the plane at the Frankfurt airport was "Doctor Mueller's Sex Shop." The giant rubbery things in the shop window looked like some sort of threatening alien life form, even if the basic shape left no doubt as to their intended function. Welcome to the big wide world, Airman Peacock.

PECKING ORDERS

MY ASSIGNMENT IN GERMANY WAS WITH THE 1836 ELECTRONIC INSTAL-lation Group. There, I had to attend another training school, Standard Installation Practices Technical Order, or something like that. We just called it SIPTO, in which Ohm's Law was set aside for hammer drills, cable lacing tools, conduit benders, and soldering irons. Upon completion of this practical training, our job was to install ranks of electronic communications equipment or, in a few cases, remove old equipment, at any base in Western Europe needing such work. Lindsey was a peculiar base in a number of ways. It was very, very small and was located right in the heart of downtown Wiesbaden, where it had been a German army base during World War II. The barracks were downright stately, with far more architectural flair than the boxy utilitarian architecture of home-side bases. There was an exquisite heavy wooden handrail running like an ebony snake down the stairs. I used to start on the top (fourth) floor, climb on, and whizz on my rear end down the entire length of the thing at breakneck speed. An enormous fluffle of rabbits lived underneath the building. They only came out late at night, when they emerged upon the drill field in front of the barracks to silflay on the well-trodden grass. I was one of three occupants of a second-floor room. The other two denizens were out on Temporary Duty Assignment (TDA) at some other base, so I had a few months of solitary existence during which my only company was one absentee roomie's enormous collection of music cassettes. Although the audio equipment wasn't mine, I would have gone mad without something to occupy my brain at night, so I worked my way systematically through the tapes. That was the first time I'd ever heard the White Album,

Dark Side of the Moon, Ziggy Stardust and the Spiders from Mars, and a host of other classic albums. "Helter Skelter" scared the shit out of me, and this was long before I knew anything about Charles Manson. I loved Pink Floyd so much that I went out and bought The Wall, which only recently had been released. I would put it in the deck, set the tape to auto loop, and leave it turned on very low while I slept, a practice that resulted in some very interesting dreams.

Discipline in the barracks was, for a while, practically non-existent, so that we all pretty much ran amok outside of the regular workday, drinking like fish in the NCO club, returning after closing time to drink like fish in someone's room until very late in the evening, getting up early the next morning to repeat the cycle all over again. As hard as it was to get up in the mornings, a dedicated group of us nonetheless struggled out of bed very early every Sunday, when vintage American cartoons were playing on the TV in the common room. Imagine a dozen or so bleary-eyed, seriously hung-over, desperately homesick teenagers lounging around on cheap sofas watching "Deputy Dawg" as the pale northern European sun came up, and you get the picture. Not that it's one that needs framing, unless it were rendered on black felt.

While alcohol was the drug of choice, hashish was a popular recreational aid for many enlistees at the time. That stronger things were available was evidenced in startling fashion late one evening while I was standing floor guard. It was my luck that Ziggy, a rather hard-bitten, taciturn lad from some northern industrial city, had chosen that night to ingest/smoke/snort/inject something far more potent than hash into his system. He came out of the communal bathroom in the center of the hallway, staggering strangely, a perplexed look on his pale face. There was something distinctly weird going on with his head. As he approached through the dim light, I suddenly realized that blood was literally pouring from his scalp down his face and onto his shirt. When I asked what was happening, he gave me a reply straight out of a Stephen King novel, saying in a sepulchral voice, "I can't get 'em off. *I can't get 'em off.*" Eventually I ascertained that Ziggy thought he had antennae coming out of his head. The poor sod had stood in front of the bathroom mirror employing a razor blade in an attempt to remove the offending appendages. When that impromptu surgery didn't work, he had tried buffing the wounds with a piece of steel wool. I have no idea what tertiary instrument he was *en route* to obtain when our encounter took place. I managed to keep him occupied until the SPs arrived, wondering nervously all the while what he had done with the razor blade.

The lack of discipline eventually resulted in such over-the-top behavior that the escapades were checked, and checked hard. One evening we had a toga party worthy of Delta House, with a bathtub-sized metal bin filled with "hunch punch," a ghastly mixture of whatever anyone decided to pour in, with some bloated fruit floating on top. Although I had phenomenal staying power at the time, eventually I realized I'd hit my limit and somehow found my way back to my room. That caused me to miss the highlight of the party, when several of the more testosterone-laden lads became overly excited and hurled a soda dispenser out the second-floor window, no doubt startling the leporine fluffle below. At that point the brass could no longer ignore the situation, and the next several months became a living hell. Strict curfews were imposed; alcohol was forbidden; surprise visits with drug dogs became frequent occurrences at any time of day or night. Inspections also could take place at any time, which meant that rooms had to be kept perennially spotless in case a pounding on the door awakened you to stand at attention in your tighty-whities at 3:00 a.m., when all of your carefully arranged belongings would be roughly sorted through and left in a shambles that immediately had to be set right, lest there be another surprise inspection that same morning. And I do mean spotless. To give an example, I failed one inspection when the maliciously grinning Master Sergeant opened the door to my mini-fridge, parted the rubber seam on top of the door, and found a few infinitesimal crumbs *inside the seam*. This tiresome trial seemed to go on forever, but I suppose we'd asked for it. At least the rabbits got some peace and quiet for a change. And they never put a drink dispenser in the building again.

It didn't take me long to start enjoying the perks of being stationed in another country. Germany has a lot to recommend it, including great beer and good food. For everyday fare, the *Wurst* stands on the side of the road were easily affordable, even on the salary of an Airman First Class such as myself. *Pommes frites* with that wonderful vinegary German mayonnaise are food for the gods. And there were some really excellent restaurants within easy walking distance of the base or, if one were feeling more adventurous, a short ride away on the equally excellent buses. My favorite dish was Jaeger schnitzel with a side of fries that could be swirled around in the rich mushroom gravy. I suspect that most of the many dozens of schnitzels I consumed were veal, which I now wouldn't touch with a ten-foot fork, but that they were delicious I cannot deny. To my astonishment, there was a startlingly large number of my fellow servicemen who never ate off-base except to go the nearest McDonalds. I can't imagine what idyllic destination those young adventurers put on their dream sheets. Poughkeepsie?

It was also during this time that I discovered one of humankind's greatest achievements: Kinder Eggs! These yummy chocolate eggs encase yellow plastic capsules inside of which are really intricate, astonishingly well-designed toys that sometimes take half an hour and a lot of brain power to put together. The same idea as Crackerjacks, but far superior in every way. You can't buy real Kinder Eggs in the United States because there are too many small parts; the wimpy Americanized version is a pale imitation of the real thing. Sometimes I think we don't give our kids (or their parents) nearly enough credit.

Those benighted souls too timid to stretch their comfort zones also missed out on one of the great cultural experiences of Germany, the fantastic outdoor excursions called Volksmarches. As a frequent participant, I trekked many a kilometer over the beautiful countryside, topping one hill to find a *Wurst* stand set up, a beer stand beckoning over the next, listening to the happy chatter of kids in a language I didn't really follow, and generally having a blast. I stumped along with the crowd, allowing my hangovers gradually to dissipate in the clear country air with the enviable recuperative powers of youth. It truly is regrettable that we don't have this custom in the United States; a good long walk in the country with our neighbors might do a lot to mend the overtly divisive politics that poison our country. Especially if there was a beer stand over every other hill.

If anything was better than the Volksmarches, it was the wine fests, where vendors would congregate in some small town and one could wander down the streets imbibing samples. For a nominal fee, one could obtain those samples in little glasses bearing a seal commemorating the event. I still have several of those quaint little souvenirs. I don't think I've ever had a happier buzz than those I acquired at wine fests, with one exception, which was the time I participated in the "*Rhine in Flammen*" celebration. Imagine hundreds of small boats in a loose flotilla drifting down the Rhine River as the sun slowly sets. Imagine really good beer and wine freely flowing from the well-stocked bars on such boats and the attendant good-hearted conversations that accordingly ensued on the crowded decks. Imagine anchoring at a spot upstream from two ancient castles facing one another on high bluffs on either side of the river. Imagine the spectacular visual effects of an extended fireworks war between those two castles. Then imagine the lights on all of the boats being lowered and a quiet descending over the whole scene, except for some lovely classical music softly performed live on one the boats, while those aboard the vessels stare out into the darkness. And then imagine, if you can, the amazing sight of thousands of burning candles on small floating dishes moving with the current through the flotilla and eventually vanishing in the distance along the dark ribbon of the storied river. There are times when it is a privilege to be a sentient primate. That night was one of the best.

Another real joy of the tour was getting to know a number of German citizens who worked for the U.S. military. We worked closely with a trio of guys who were great fun to be around. I remember Richard and Klaus with particular fondness. One night, at my Staff Sergeant's insistence, we all went out to a strip club, where a dubious creature executed unspeakable acts with a mechanical automaton up on stage. I moved to the back of the room, frankly terrified. Richard was made of sterner stuff and, as a consequence, wound up assisting in further unspeakable acts with said creature and a champagne bottle. Mississippi seemed very, very far away.

Klaus would never have been caught dead in such a place. He was conservative, solid, and avuncular, taking pains to correct my awful German and generally looking out for my best interests at all times. To our collective horror, we showed up at the hotel where they were staying one morning to find that Klaus had passed away during the night. He was only a few months away from retirement. His funeral was devastating. I wanted desperately to say something of comfort to his widow, but who has words in any language to assuage that kind of grief?

The German people in general were far friendlier and more polite than we representatives of a foreign military enclave might have had a right to expect. I learned a few tricks to help repay such kindness. For example, a *"Freundschaftfest"* (friendship festival) was held each year on base, to which basically anyone who wanted to come in was invited. A fleet of tanker trucks that literally were giant beer kegs on wheels parked in a line, with hoses running out the backs. A string of conjoined tents formed a continuous wall that hid the trucks, save for fire-hose-sized beer-dispensing umbilici. The fronts of the shelters were open to the thirsty crowd. I was one of the volunteers who stood behind a wooden table, filling glasses as fast as I could dispense them. After a while, I noticed that the Germans in the crowd were lining up in front of me, for the simple reason that I knew to pour with a head while my well-intentioned colleagues were topping things off at the rim. Poor Americans; we have been far too programmed to favor quantity over quality.

I was stationed in Germany for two years, during which time I made a number of other good friends. Billy Lee was as Southern as they come, in all the good ways and none of the bad. Perley was an insouciant swaggering Mainer who would have been the perfect voice for Garfield when that feline character was animated. Ron turned me on to Frank Zappa, the Fabulous Furry Freak Brothers, and other bits of counter-culture that probably still haven't made their way into Choctaw County. Ricky was another southerner, with a head like some sort of exotic melon and real talent for the guitar. He was patient enough to help me learn a few tricks on my first one, a Höfner I bought after seeing Billy Lee bludgeon his way through some traditional C&W favorites on the same model. Mac was a beefy, bawdy force of nature, all red hair and presence. And Danny was another country boy, from the Minnesota prairies, amiable, openhearted, slow-talking, and true. One of my fondest memories is of an incident that took place when he and I were on TDA at Aviano Air Base in northern Italy, during which time my limited horizons expanded quite a bit. That was the first time I ever had a cappuccino, for example, not to mention squid. (When I returned home, I found that some of my fellow inlanders considered noshing on multi-tentacled marine mollusks to be a rather repellant enterprise. Remember, these are the same people who devoured deep-fried pig intestines with gusto). It also was the first time I ever saw real mountains, with snow on top! But as firsts go, an incident with Danny tops the list. We took a weekend trip to Venice by train, during which we hopped a ferry to the Lido and rented bikes for a cycling trip around the island. About halfway around, Danny, who was ahead of me, suddenly crashed his bike into the low stone wall that ran along the bike path. He went down, hard; but I noticed, as I skidded to a halt, that even as he fell his eyes never turned from the right, toward the sea. I glanced over to see what was so attention-grabbing and beheld my (and his) first nude beach. Neither of us pedaled a particularly straight line from that point.

I saw things over the course of my many job assignments in Europe that would keep any good taxpayer up at night (if the Ziggy story hasn't done that for you already). I did a TDA on a base where nuclear weapons were stored (it shall remain nameless, as we were sternly enjoined not to reveal the locations of such facilities). A thickly-armored vehicle that looked kind of like a Mesozoic Suburban was driven around the base almost non-stop, twenty-four hours a day. This "Peacekeeper," as it was called, carried a crew of heavily-armed SPs to provide a mobile, unpredictable strike force in case of a base incursion by unfriendly invaders. Those elite warriors were under strict orders not to open the doors for anyone during their shift, not even a General, to prevent the possibility of enemy subterfuge. The more apt moniker applied to the vehicle by those young stalwarts was "Sleepkeeper": they piled in, the doors were shut and locked, and out came the recreational substances. When the doors were opened at the end of a shift, the bleary-eyed occupants practically fell out the back in a heady cloud of smoke and alcohol fumes. Dan Millman said, "A warrior does not give up what he loves, he finds the love in what he does." I think those kids had it cornered.

On another occasion, I was standing on an elevated metal scaffold using a hammer-drill to install anchors for steel conduit on the outside of a concrete munitions bunker. As I was drilling away, I caught a motion out of the corner of my eye and turned to see something bright and metallic go whizzing down a steep incline in the road. "Huh," I thought to myself. "I do believe that was a nuclear bomb." About the time I processed this interesting bit of data, a squad of airmen went tearing down the hill in hot pursuit, rifles clacking on their shoulders as they ran. Apparently, the heavy wheeled sled used to transport weapons had gotten away from its tenders and was headed for whatever greener pastures nuclear bombs dream of, there in the darkness of their cold concrete bunkers at night. "Huh," I thought to myself as this additional bit of interesting data fried my mental circuits, "that thing is headed for the electric fence." My options being limited, I counted ten and, when existence continued, went back to drilling my hole. I think I can be excused for getting bombed myself later that evening.

During a different TDA, a friend and I got called out to repair some gizmo up in the conning tower overlooking the base airfield. That was cool: I'd never been in a conning tower before. We quickly finished the job and were about to leave when the officer in charge asked if we'd take a look at a defunct radar unit while we were there. It never had worked properly, he explained, despite having cost many tens of thousands of dollars; instead, weird ghost signals flicked across the screen at unpredictable intervals, not a particularly useful characteristic for a radar unit at an active military airfield. Neither of us had any training in radar, but what the heck; it just meant more time in the conning tower. So we opened up the chassis and looked around at all the doodads inside, but didn't see anything obviously wrong. We opened things up a little more, and there, inside the very guts of that very expensive, very important machine, was a mummified cheeseburger and fries. I could only imagine someone shoving them inside when a surprise inspection team popped into the factory back in Poughkeepsie, or wherever. We removed those sacrificial offerings to the radar gods, closed the unit, fired it up, and presto! It worked like a charm. That's right: we made the world safe for democracy by vanquishing the zombie cheeseburger. You're welcome, America.

Two things of personal moment transpired during that tour. The first was that I fell in love with my best friend's wife. First loves might always be awkward; under the circumstances, mine was more so than most (although I'm sure Billy Lee had several songs in his repertoire about just such a scenario). Not surprisingly, things didn't end well; clearly, I could not yet claim much progress toward responsible adulthood. The second thing that happened was that I might have saved a life. I was visiting at a friend's apartment one evening, having a great time, when we heard a scream from outside. We rushed out to see another guest who had just left, clutching her baby and crying out that the child had stopped breathing. As we ran up, she held the little girl out to me. It was a seizure; her tiny frame was bowed and locked tight, her little face set in an awful grimace. And sure enough, she wasn't breathing. Her heart seemed to be beating, although I might have been feeling my own racing pulse in my fingertips. We were trained for such situations, of course, but I remain surprised to this day that the training actually kicked in, without thought, just like it was supposed to. I gave her CPR, a delicate prospect with an infant, because you have to administer oxygen via tiny puffs through the nose and mouth (or in this case, just the nose, as her mouth was clamped shut). After three or four such efforts, she suddenly shook, then relaxed and commenced breathing. And crying. And pooping. I felt like joining her on all fronts. The seizure might have been related to a heart condition with which she had been diagnosed, or it might have been something else altogether. I really don't know, and I never will be sure that my ministrations actually did any good. But I do know that, in the moment of crisis, I acted. Perhaps I wasn't so far from responsible adulthood after all.

Despite all of these experiences, I had long spells of considerable homesickness, so that my next dream sheet was populated with bases in the southeastern U.S. of A. I was happy when I opened the envelope and found that I was being posted to Eglin Air Force Base in the Florida Panhandle. Eglin is an enormous base where pilots train in A-10 Tank Killers and other nifty aircraft. Communications vital to this effort are maintained through a large number of small microwave repeater stations, basically little concrete block buildings out in the middle of the "range" that house ranks of equipment and hosts of angry little brown scorpions. We had to learn the equipment and make multiple rounds of those outposts every week for preventative maintenance. That would have been all right except that we were overstaffed, so that lots of time was spent sitting around our headquarters on the main base, training, swapping stories, and generally being bored to tears. Not that all of the time was wasted. Training turned out to be an experience different from any that I'd ever had, for the simple reason that, for the first time in my life, a real hunger to learn had evolved in my being. Not the usual penchant to glibly assimilate factoids for rote regurgitation; but to *learn*. After my rather pathetic showing at Keesler, I was determined to show that I could get my head around electronics, whether I cared for the subject or not. I studied my heart out and was rewarded by making the highest final score in my cohort.

The warm glow of that hard-earned victory was dimmed somewhat by the overt expression of a bias I'd noticed since Day One in the service, but to which I hadn't paid much attention until the point where I was getting serious about being taken seriously. That bias was one that kicked on like a switch whenever the conversation turned from random bullshit to issues of substance. It arose, I am quite sure, because of my Southern accent, which at the time was still as thick as five-minute grits cooked for an hour. Whenever anyone saw me open my mouth and heard the protesting groan of vowels pushed reluctantly across my laboring glottis, they instantly made three assumptions about me: I was racist, I was sexist, and I was ignorant. (One out of three, they had me, but ignorance is no sin unless one purposefully forgoes the cure). As long as we were clowning around, I could be in the thick of things. As soon as there was a problem to solve or something meaningful to discuss, I instantly became invisible. I could stand there, offering comments or suggestions, and be totally ignored while people literally talked around me. People who had been in the same class where I'd taken top honors, mind you. That was a weird feeling, and it led eventually to the conscious sacrifice of the corn syrup-soaked accent that marked my place of birth. Or most of it, anyway. Certain words still pass through my voice box like possums leaving the pouch backward. And run for the hills if you are within earshot should I attempt the future continuous tense for "all of you will," which inevitably comes out in Deep South form as the world's most awkward contraction: "y'all'll." It sounds like I'm gargling cracklins.

Combine that obnoxious bias against Southerners with the obstinate stupidity of some "superiors" described earlier, and you can understand why my determination to make Eglin my last assignment only grew with time. To give one example: about a week after topping another class on a new type of digital equipment, I got sent out alone to troubleshoot a problem. That was a big test, since I'd never before had to shoulder such responsibility solo. I stood before the rack of equipment, surveyed the blinking red lights, employed my hard-won knowledge, and diagnosed the problem as being either the "power and alarm board" (an eighty percent probability) or the "switching motherboard" (a twenty percent probability). I phoned the main base to tell them my diagnosis, expecting them to send out a P&A board, post haste. Instead, the insufferable Yankee Staff Sergeant on the other end of the line, no doubt reacting to my backwoods drawl, told me to pull the backup P&A board from the unit (there always were two of everything working, as a redundancy measure) and shove it into the problem spot to see if I was correct. To do this meant a violation of one of the sacred tenets of our specialty area: never, *ever* do anything to take a base off-line. Accordingly, I protested, pointing out rather defensively that I knew what I was talking about, having just completed training on exactly that kind of equipment. So he ordered me, of course, with the smug superiority that comes from knowing that your order must be obeyed, notwithstanding data, common sense, superior test scores, and laws of electro-physics. Short of a court martial, I was left with no option but to yank out the backup board, which I grudgingly did. The entire outpost instantly was plunged into communication darkness. A few minutes later, I was able to plug it back in, reestablishing links with the rest of what passed for reality and allowing me to report, angrily, that the problem was, in fact, the P&A board, as originally diagnosed. Go figure. About that time, a ranking NCO popped in demanding to know what the Hell I thought I was doing. Turns out he was talking to his wife on the phone when I cut off all communications to the base. His wife who was seriously ill in the hospital. As I was trying to explain myself, a Captain popped in demanding to know what the Hell I thought was doing. The Captain, who was sub-commander of that particular outpost. And so it went, until I found myself standing before a most irate Colonel. Sorry, sir; just following orders, sir; it's the one without the Southern accent who's the nimrod, sir. Staff Sergeant Nimrod never apologized, of course; he didn't have to. He outranked me, after all.

I was visiting another outpost with a fellow peon one day, on some routine mission, when, in a scene reminiscent of the zombie cheeseburger incident an officer pointed out another piece of very expensive equipment that never had worked properly. It was part of a communication link intended to carry both television and microwave radio signals. Neither came through well, especially the TV. This mattered because it was via this TV link that live missile launches were monitored. I wouldn't have touched that one with a ten-foot soldering iron, but my friend (who didn't have a Southern accent, although his Boston brogue was thick enough) was braver and leaped right in. I gamely did what I could to help, which mostly consisted of making vaguely affirmative noises while he whipped to and fro with a multimeter. In nothing flat he found and fixed the problem: in one spot on the metal frame supporting all of the apparatus a plastic washer had been used instead of a metal one, sporadically interrupting ground flow. With the amazingly simple and cheap fix of replacing it with a metal washer, a system that had cost the taxpayers hundreds of thousands of dollars began working like a charm. Officer Whozit didn't bother to say thanks, of course; he outranked us, after all. But he did take credit for the accomplishment, another characteristic of military life for which I had little fondness.

As had happened in Germany, I made some good friends during the Florida tour. Three who spring to mind are Mike, the blocky Bostonian of plastic washer fame who looked like a cross between Fred Flintstone and Tony Soprano; Paul, a clever, diminutive rogue from the Keystone State with a wry smile and a devilish sense of humor, who understood me better than most; and Andy, another mid-Westerner who split the rent on a house trailer with me for a while. Civilians with whom we worked and who were kind enough to befriend me included Gary, a razor-sharp iconoclast who was one half of a splendid hippie couple, the other half being his very cool wife Glenda; Mike, a huge fan of .38 Special (the band, not the gun) who had fish tanks half the size of my house trailer in his apartment; and Jimmy, a semi-redneck who loved nothing better than having us all over for oysters steamed on a piece of tin over a fire pit in his backyard, washed down with endless amounts of cheap beer. All were excellent guys who put up with my still-juvenile bullshit with enormous patience and great good humor. I always have had a penchant for making real friends from different age groups, and counted among them at this time Richard, a fellow Mississippian who understood as I did the simple joy of bream fishing, and Jimmy M., the soft-spoken epitome of a good leader who was able to command respect and productivity the way it should be done, via example. Among my list of acquaintances, I also must mention Ramón, a.k.a. "Gato," "the cat." Gato was from Puerto Rico, and to say that he hung out with a different crowd than I was putting it mildly. His main goal in life, and one at which he was extraordinarily successful, was sexual conquest. That was, in fact, his only goal in life. Gato painted the inside of his car's interior ceiling light with red fingernail polish to create a bordello-like atmosphere, generating who knows what kinds of toxic fumes as the small lamp heated the crimson slip. He was very macho, was Gato. As part of a routine psychological exam, we were asked what one word we thought best described us. I fumbled around, not really knowing what to say. Gato's immediate answer: "Fierce." Gato and I got along pretty well considering that we came from such different worlds. We split the rent on a townhouse for a while. He taught me some bad Spanish, and I'm not sure that I taught him much of anything in return.

I remember three things in particular about that townhouse. The first is that the landlady, who occupied one of the units near ours, was an elderly female relative of Bertie Higgins, a one-hit wonder who made it big that summer with "Key Largo." She made us come in and listen to it whenever we couldn't sneak past her. The second thing is the time when I woke up in the wee hours of the morning with Gato pounding on the door. The air was full of a greasy black smoke, forcing our evacuation. One of his friends had staggered in, popped a chicken into the oven, and then passed out. I cannot imagine a lousier epitaph. The third thing was that I approached the music director at my friend Richard's church about playing cello for them. They had one, and he let me take it home for some much-needed practice. I was unable to achieve that, however, because whenever I set bow to string, every dog in the neighborhood immediately went off like a banshee. Too bad; I might have learned the string section to "Key Largo" and gotten our rent lowered.

I mentioned living in a house trailer. That came during the latter part of my tour, perhaps presaging the horrible existence for which I would be heading. It was in a trailer court in the community of Niceville (I am not making up the name). Trailer court life wasn't too bad while Andy was there, except that: a) a short somewhere in the electrical system tended to pound voltage through one's body when one grasped the doorknob; and b) Andy and I tended to egg one another on where nightlife was concerned, especially after we discovered Barbee's Bar. Barbee's was a local dive with a country flavor that suited me far more than the coastal nightclubs that over-flowed with flashing lights, overloud music, bad dancing, and too many hormones, especially during Spring Break when the entire Panhandle turned into a nightmare scene. Barbee's definitely was not part of the Spring Break circuit. The proprietress was a boney middle-aged woman who was very kind to us military types. Heck, she was kind to everybody. Andy and I once "greeted the dawn" on the dock at her house, which is to say that we managed to stay up until the sun rose, pounding down warm brewskis long after everyone else who had headed over to her place after closing time had conked out. For something different, he and I for a while tried hitting hotel bars, operationalizing the obnoxious notion that two such eminently cool young dudes as our own bad selves would liven up what we imagined would be a pretty dismal scene. That venture was a complete bust: the "scene" was even more dismal than we'd imagined and we were not particularly cool to begin with.

When Andy and I weren't pounding down brewskis at Barbee's or cruising near-vacant hotel bars, we would be out on a fishing pier. Our more mature co-workers, perhaps pining for their own lost youths, envied us this irresponsible freedom, and upon occasion we could convince one of them to join us. One Sergeant we cajoled in this manner was a very strait-laced, upright kind of guy married to a young woman from the Philippines who spoke almost no English. He almost never socialized outside of work, but he accepted our invitation to hit the Valparaiso fishing pier early one weekend morning with pathetic eagerness, even going so far as to volunteer to bring the bait. We told him what to get, and where: a block of small, silvery "trash fish" sold by the frozen boxful at local bait shops. While not considered fit for human consumption, stinky chunks of this commercial bycatch were quite the alluring treat for the byproduct's larger, more sought-after brethren. We got there early and waited, impatiently, while more industrious fishermen passed us by to spread plastic filigrees of lines out from the choice stations at the end of the pier. The sun rose; the choice spots filled; still no Sarge. Finally, he showed up, but we could tell that something was wrong from the hangdog expression on his face as he trudged over. First, he apologized for being late. Then he apologized because— and I quote— "My wife ate the bait." Delighted to find a boxful of ready ocean bounty in the freezer, his missus had fried the little guys up and eaten the entire lot while her husband was at work. Consequently, we didn't get to fish that day, but my sides hurt for hours afterward. I don't think the poor guy ever accepted another invitation.

That was the time when MTV was taking the nation by storm, and it was glorious. The videos were good, as was much of the music. It was a revolution of sorts, and a pretty good one until the corporate decision-makers poked their collective head up their collective backside and decided they liked the smell so much that the rest of us would enjoy it as well, at which point the programming became all gunked up with insufferable, spoiled, narcissistic brats cohabiting some opulent manse whilst greatly embarrassing the rest of us by the fact that they were Americans. Anyway, one morning Andy and I came home from an all-night fishing trip during which we caught exactly 0.0 fish but consumed precisely 1.0 bottles of Canadian Mist whiskey, a relatively noxious but high-powered liquid that caused you not to be able to smell the fish on your hands if you'd drunk enough of it, and if you'd happened to have caught any fish. As soon as we made our way past the electric force field and shut the trailer door, Andy flipped on MTV. I forget what video was on, but it was one he liked, a lot; with a hearty bellow of approval and an impromptu fist pump, he cranked the volume. Neither of us made it to the end of the video, however, because the night's exertions finally caught up with us. I passed out on the couch, Andy on the rug in front of the TV. The next thing I knew, a cop was standing over me, very forcefully shaking me awake. Apparently, a neighbor had called to complain about the noise. Repeated hammering on the door of our trailer with the butt of his flashlight had failed to awaken us, so he let himself in. His entry was probably unlawful, but we meekly absorbed the well-deserved lecture given that he clearly was in no mood to argue niceties, a fact probably related to the amount of current that must have flowed through his flashlight as he pounded on the door. Set to music, that scene might have made a pretty good video.

Andy eventually moved out and, with no co-denizen in the trailer, I grew slovenly in the extreme. For example, I would wash my clothes, toss them into the adjacent dryer, and then fish the wrinkled items out one at a time over the ensuing week rather than fold them and put them away. My diet went completely to hell. *Haute cuisine* consisted of weenies boiled for five minutes, forked onto a plate, and covered with individual slices of American processed "cheese" that quickly melted into gooey funerary shrouds for the water-bloated tubules. Breakfast, when I bothered to eat it, was a bowl of sugary cereal. Lunch was something fried up at the bowling alley on base, washed down with a beer or two. Weenie-days excepted, supper always consisted of the same thing: two quarter-pounders with cheese and a side of fries picked up at the McDonalds drive-through, washed down with Canadian Mist picked up at a drive-through liquor barn and mixed about four to one with Sprite in a very large tumbler. That's four parts liquor, in case you were wondering. This ridiculous routine went on for months until a day when, in a rare moment of altruism, I decided to give blood. In those days they checked to see if your iron levels were acceptable by pricking your finger and pipetting a single red droplet into a test tube holding some sort of gray metallic liquid. If the droplet sank a certain distance into that mysterious substance, you were cleared to donate. I watched serenely from the reclining chair as the nurse dropped my sacrificial corpuscles into the glass tube. I calmly noted the perplexed expression on her face when the drop floated. Annoyed, she capped the test tube, shook it up, and looked again. A thin red line proudly capped the gray elixir, having spread to form a bright meniscus but otherwise touting its imperviousness to the demands of specific gravity or annoyed medical attendants. At that point the nurse set the tube down, leaned over me, put her face very close to mine, and said in measured, serious cadence as she stared me straight in the eye: "Go home...and eat some green vegetables... before you die." I thought that was pretty good advice, which I nonetheless didn't really follow very well. I did cut back on the whiskey, though.

Just for something to do, Paul and I enrolled in classes at a local community college. Paul took a writing course while I indulged my interest in history and signed up for Early Western Civilization. I can't remember the instructor's name, but I do remember thinking that he looked like the fifth Beatle. Because I read the massive textbook the first week, the class was pretty boring, though not for lack of effort on his part. I got either an A or a B as my grade; I don't know which because I never went in to find out. I do know that I went into the final exam with a solid A. But that test culminated in the following essay question: "Describe and discuss the factors leading to the decline and fall of the Roman Empire. Use the back of the sheet if necessary." The whole notion was so patently ludicrous that I decided to provide my answer in verse. While the other students studiously were regurgitating historical factoids in rote fashion, I whipped out a doggerel masterpiece in iambic pentameter: "Ah, Rome, the grandest dame of all, why did thy bastioned towers fall?" And so on, for about twelve stanzas. It was truly awful poetry, but I made sure to put in all the points of fact that I knew the professor was looking for, and I still managed to beat most of the other students in handing in my exam. I wish I could have seen the professor's face when he saw my answer; whatever score was assigned, I have to think that I provided him with a moment of weirdness in his academic career that he talks about still.

As I neared completion of my four-year enlistment, considerable pressure was put on me to stay in the military. Formally, that pressure consisted of a reenlistment bonus offer of five figures, an offer that would remain on the table for some months after my discharge. Informally, a lot of lifers in our squadron smugly pronounced, "You'll be back," an obnoxious attitude that only fed my determination to get out. And so, in May 1983, I tossed my luggage and honorable discharge papers into the back of my rattletrap pickup truck and, for the last time, waved at the SPs as I drove through the gate at Eglin. I was headed home.

FLUTTERING AIMLESSLY

Freedom is a toothsome bit, except that it tends to fall off the bone before you can get it to your mouth. Four years later, I wound up doing the very thing I had feared so much that I'd joined the military in the first place: living with my parents, with no job and no prospects for such. To their great credit, they never said a negative word, even as they watched me squander the small amount of money I'd managed to save, doing exactly the same sorts of stupid things I'd left behind: drinking, driving some place to drink some more, and drinking. Same old companions, same old gravel roads, even the same old vehicles, but it wasn't the same at all. It wasn't fun in the slightest. And, before I knew it, I was flat broke. Something had to give, and over the next year and some months that something was very nearly my will to live.

To find a job, I followed the usual paths available to the proletariat: I scanned the papers for relevant ads, to no avail; I went to the unemployment office, where the nice young lady behind the desk seemed very happy that I could say "Good morning," "Good day," "Good evening," "One quarter-pounder with cheese, please," and "A large beer" in German. For some reason, she was convinced that this extraordinary linguistic ability would sway United Parcel Service to snap me up, presumably to accommodate the enormous, historically underserved, and completely nonexistent population of monolingual, native *Deutsch* speakers of north-central Mississippi. Not surprisingly, UPS never called. *Schiesse*! Finally, I decided to offer my services to a cousin living near Nashville who ran a video business, thinking that perhaps my dubious electronics expertise might be of some use. A main attraction for this move was his son, my cousin Jeff, he of plastic skeletons in coffee and exploding acidic foam fame, whom I love dearly. Jeff is a supreme iconoclast who finds virtually everything in life to be highly amusing, an outlook he somehow manages to hold without being haughty, judgmental, or jaded. He is a marvelous and appreciative spectator of the comedy of human existence. Even the worst day is fun with Jeff. That assertion would be put to the test many times.

I met up with Jeff at the Parthenon in downtown Nashville. This building is an exact full-scale replica of the famous structure built in Greece in the year 447 BC to honor the pagan goddess Athena. Designed by a Confederate veteran, the replica in Nashville was built in 1897 in time for the Tennessee Centennial Exposition, at which I'm sure any number of pagans conveniently were in attendance. Why construct such an edifice? Because, historically, Nashville also has been known as the "Athens of the West," perhaps an affectation dating from the slave days, given that the ancient Greeks also kept human chattel. It certainly isn't a moniker reflecting similar acceptable sexual mores. To illustrate this point, in 2017 an escargatoire[7] of evangelical "leaders" released the "Nashville Statement," an uplifting document containing such enlightened gems as, "We affirm that it is sinful to approve of homosexual immorality or transgenderism and that such approval constitutes an essential departure from Christian faithfulness and witness," and "We deny that the approval of homosexual immorality or transgenderism is a matter of moral indifference about which otherwise faithful Christians should agree to disagree." In what could be considered an ironic touch by an annoyed Creator unappreciative of distraction from His unequivocal message of "Judge not," and "Love thy neighbor," the meeting where this repellent doctrinal statement was produced was the Gaylord Opryland Resort and Convention Center. The Gaylord. I only wish I was capable of making that up.

---

7 According to some authorities, this is the technical term for a group of slugs, spineless hermaphrodites that leave a trail of slime wherever they go. They also have anuses located very near their mouths, which seems an analogically appropriate phenotype for the life forms under discussion.

Jeff was filming a music video at the Parthenon that day. It took me a while to find him in the crowd, but as soon as I did, our completely nonsensical, traditional greeting rang out:

"The Ev...from Kiev!"

"The J...from Monterey!"

And with that bit of reciprocal idiocy, our excellent relationship instantly was reestablished. Jeff filled me in on the day's proceedings, which included his effort to get a drink at a nearby hotel where another scene had been shot. He'd had to work his way through a large crowd of women clustered around one end of the bar. The attraction, it turned out, was no one less than Hervé Villechaize, the little person made famous by his role as Tattoo on the excruciating television series, "Fantasy Island." Mr. Villechaize had been perched on his stool, swilling margaritas, king of all he could survey, which from his particular vantage point must have included a lot of lip gloss, up-thrust cleavage, and over-permed fe-mullets. I was sorry to have missed that spectacle, but spectacles enough would present themselves as I descended into the bizarre fantasy world that was showbiz Nashville in the early Eighties.

Jeff's dad, the elder cousin who ran the business, was a lovable rogue who could wheel and deal with the best of them but whose business skills only occasionally extended to providing a finished product to his exasperated clients. He preferred to operate well outside established norms, a strategy that unfortunately included having no formal payroll operations. On the other hand, being family, they took me in without question, and I quickly became one of a small crew who worked diligently in order not to be paid with anything like regularity. But always there was the allure of the next job, the next client, celebrities...fame! And we did indeed work for a few "names" during my time with the company, experiences which were alternately depressing and exciting. For example, we produced a television commercial touting the release of an album of standard covers by a once-popular country music star whose artificial light had long since dimmed. He had exactly one remaining sycophant, a lone, pock-faced leech sucking furiously at the withered, rhinestone-studded hide of his octogenarian dinosaur. At the other end of the spectrum of renown, we once filmed a massive outdoor concert for one of the true legends of the genre, a woman who somehow had managed to stay a person, a real person of dignity and grace, despite having trod the fetid cesspool of commercial entertainment for decades. True to form, we failed to provide a finished product in either case. In between, we failed to deliver finished products to a wide range of star-struck dreamers, grasping opportunists, and voracious toadies. Such was the situation in which I found myself in Music City, U.S.A.

Most of our off-location work was conducted from home, a townhouse in the Nashville suburb of Old Hickory for which rent payments followed the same irregular pattern as our pay. Why we weren't booted out on our rears, and how the utilities were kept switched on, I haven't a clue. Although it might have had something to do with the crew working mostly *gratis*, which made for a pretty light payroll deduction from the non-existent weekly ledgers. For a while, and by what kind of non-rent-paying deal I can't imagine, we operated inside the Tennessee Theatre, a large, Streamline Moderne "movie palace" housed in an earlier 1930s Art Deco structure in downtown Nashville. Although by that time it had been stripped of almost everything of value, it still was fantastic, a haunted cathedral from a lost opulent age. Tightly-wound spiral metal staircases led like Jefferies tubes to mysterious perches near the high ceiling. A small private screening room provided lonely sanctuary for the gluttonous Gilded Age spirits of the well-to-do. An astonishing bank of colored lights hanging over the stage was controlled from a monstrous switchboard that still more-or-less worked; it looked exactly like the sinister apparatus used to bring the monster to life in the classic Frankenstein movie of 1931. And I got to flip the switches! That exquisite building was torn down in the late 1980s, much to the loss of our collective American culture. That we had the run of the place for a while remains one of the few bright spots in an otherwise murky chapter of my life.

My boss-cousin's questionable M.O. led to association with a questionable set of characters, which in turn led to an endless series of debacles. The largest involved what otherwise might have been another positive life experience. We were contracted (by whom, I don't know, and I seriously doubt there actually was a contract) to film a fiddle competition in Dallas. We filmed for a solid three days, during which time we heard some pretty good music, although three nonstop days of even well-executed fiddle tunes can generate some rather radical thoughts of the antisocial variety. I was just learning how to operate one of the very large cameras and didn't know how tightly to screw in the stabilizing nuts, so that my back ached badly after the first day, but I caught on quickly, learning to frame shots so that Jeff, who ran the mixer, could cut to me at any time. Two things of note came out of this particular assignment. One was that Jeff fell in love with a fetching Latina lass who stopped to talk to us (they eventually married; they eventually divorced; Jeff should write his own book). The other was a check for $40,000 that was supposed to cover expenses while a world-beating documentary on three-day-long fiddle competitions was to be completed. While odds are high that the documentary never actually would have been produced, I can't say for sure, because a shady associate in the venture absconded with the cash. This scurrilous individual went by the moniker "Buzz," quite a fitting appellation given that his sleazy apartment was sanctuary to an amazing number of roaches. Not the scuttling arthropods, although I suspect that many of them led a happy communal existence on and under the greasy linoleum; but the soggy ends of joints, the mildly hallucinogenic properties of which apparently had clouded the face of Buzzard's moral compass with an opaque film of resinous, THC-laden scum. My own moral compass having failed to locate a worthy lodestone at that time, I would ordinarily have pocketed as many dozens of the things as I could in order to retrieve the leftover weedage for later reassembly into a smokable doobie. But roaches that had touched Buzzard's lips would never touch mine. Even I had my standards. Buzzard was never apprehended; accordingly, we never got paid. All par for the course in the City of Dreams.

Jeff and I edited videos in a small trailer parked beside the townhouse. There were some very, very long nights in that close space. For some reason, we worked on seemingly innumerable episodes of "The Ernest Tubb Show," for what client and for what reason I don't remember, although I seem to recall some sort of European television connection. Those shows were interesting mostly because Willie Nelson was a frequent guest "recording star." This was Willie before he let his hair down, both literally and figuratively; a clean-shaven Willie with swept-back hair, jacket, and tie. One suspects that even at that time he had better weedage than Buzzard; how else he could have faced the camera in that getup, I can't imagine. A weird aside: for some reason, the trailer was on loan from Barry Sadler, he of the "Ballad of the Green Berets" fame, also author of the "Eternal Mercenary" series of novels, which possibly were even more interminable than the Ernest Tubb episodes. I remember meeting Mr. Sadler only once. He seemed a very tired and worn individual, and much older than his mid-40s, which is about what he must have been at that time. He was a nice bloke, though, and I regret not talking to him more.

After a few months of this bizarre unpaid existence, I took a night job at a convenience store, the first job I'd ever had outside of the Air Force where I actually received a paycheck. The goal was clear, if rather a stretch given that I would be making the minimum wage ($3.35 an hour!): to buy a car, any car, and travel back to something approaching reality as fast as I could make the trip. I can't remember what happened to whatever vehicle I'd used to get to Nashville in the first place. It probably got passed along to some other family member: times were tough everywhere. But I was without wheels, which meant that I was trapped, and I saw no desirable future in collaborating with the Buzzards of the world. So when I saw the "help wanted" sign in a local convenience store window, in I walked, and out I walked again with an application in hand. That, as it transpired, was a massive mistake.

Dante's Inferno was an unforgiving place, which I suppose was the point, but a minor bolgia exists on this Earth for those souls unfortunate enough to spend some part of their corporeal existence as convenience store clerks. Where to start? Well, with the lie-detector test, I suppose. That's right; for the indescribable honor of working my tail to the bone, unaided, at all hours of the day or night in a dangerous part of town for minimum wage, I had to have my truthfulness vetted. That was unsettling for three reasons: 1) it was insulting; 2) I suspected it was illegal; and 3) I knew that I was going to lie. Why? Because, in those Reaganesque law-and-order days, the relatively minor offense of smoking marijuana was not considered a relatively minor offense at all. It could, in fact, land you in jail. As it happened, I actually had not smoked pot for quite a long while, primarily because I had been flat broke for so long (unlike Buzzard, who I imagine had immediately gone out and scored $40,000 worth of roach-makings). But I knew the question would be, "Have you now, or ever, partaken of an illegal substance?" or something along those lines. The truthful answer would be "Yes," especially if one were to factor in my underage drinking years with my sporadic experience with smokable plant products. I did not want to answer truthfully, because I had no idea what the ramifications would be. Would the polygraph operator be legally obligated to turn me in? Or, given that eighty percent of the poor working-class slobs like me desperate enough to apply for a convenience store clerk job doubtless had alleviated their mundane existences via a toke here and there, would my past transgressions be ignored? I mean, they had to hire somebody, right?

The experience was just as awful as I had imagined. Being hooked up to a polygraph machine is spooky and unsettling. It feels like you're about to be the unwilling subject of an experimental medical procedure designed to remove your conscience without the use of anesthetic. Then the questions began. After a few milquetoast openers, sure enough, there it was: "Have you ever used any illegal drugs?"

Popular folklore has it that superspies are trained to keep their pulse down in the face of professional interrogations. As a very small child, I had watched "Our Man Flint" at a drive-in theater in Arkansas. Flint was cool. So was Bond. I'd seen Bond, several versions of him, in fact. If Flint and Bond could handle it, so could I. I took deep breaths. Remain calm. Mind over matter. You can beat this thing.

"No," I ventured.

Skrtch, skrtch, skrtch! The machine's needle instantly committed my blatant falsehood to paper. My pulse skyrocketed; sweat burst out of my pores. The needle's path correspondingly increased both in frequency and amplitude, the arm whipping up and down like an amorous mantis trying desperately to get his wee little rocks off before his not-so-amorous mate chewed off his wee little head. I took more deep breaths, trying to steady my nerves. Slowly, the accusatory seismographic symphony began to wind down. Then my interrogator hit me with another question, one that took me completely off-guard.

"Have you ever stolen anything from an employer?"

That should have been an instant "no," except for the fact that I basically am an honest person, tactical denial of illegal drug use notwithstanding. A series of weird, spontaneously constructed faux-flashbacks flickered through my mind. Had I never stolen anything? I mean, like office supplies, or what? I didn't remember any such episode, but was I sure I'd never taken *anything*? Had I ever forgotten to drop a quarter into the coffee jar? Walked off with a government pen in my pocket? What about the two times I'd been late to work in the military? Did that count as "theft?"

"Uh...no?" I ventured.

Skrtch, skrtch, skrtch!

They hired me anyway. What all this just goes to show, I really couldn't say, except that we almost certainly are the weirdest species in the nearer regions of space. At least until the Alpha Centaurans show up to return my friend's pickup truck.

The job was awful; truly, soul-wrenchingly awful. Despite the fact that tens of thousands of dollars funneled through the store each day, my boss, a shrieking harridan whose grasping venality was matched only by an utter disdain for her fellow human beings, would only pony up for one peon per shift. For a while I had the day shift, which was the absolute worst, as customers would pile up at the counter, hurling verbal abuse at my minimum-wage-paid self while I tried unsuccessfully to do a gazillion things at once: man the register, work the controls for the gas pumps, stop everything to go out and scoop bait minnows out of a metal tank, keep the coffee brewed, inspect and sign for deliveries, keep the shelves and coolers stocked, sweep and mop the floors, keep the bathrooms clean and supplied, haul ice or other heavy items out to cars for elderly customers, compare checks to the list of people who previously had passed bad ones to us; on, and on, and on, and on, and on. And just when I thought things could not get more horrible, Frau Harridan had a lunch counter installed, which I had to operate, keep supplied, and keep clean on top of everything else I already was not managing to do.

Allow me to elaborate on this Daytime Deli of Death. The main "food" on offer was prepackaged weenies of the lowest possible grade. Large plastic bagsful of these rubbery items were dumped into a stainless-steel vat full of simmering water that quickly took on a ghastly rosé tinge. Into an adjacent vat would be dumped large chunks sawed from heavy, log-like tubes of rigidly congealed, prepackaged "chili." That stuff was gross beyond measure. Polypus animal bits would teasingly rise to the surface as the encasing matrix slowly melted into an odiferous brown glop, like macerated zombie carp nosing the surface of a horribly polluted pool. Visually cataloging such "chiblits" (chili giblits) became an irresistible pastime. I'm pretty sure I once saw a pair of lips float serenely by. Recessed containers in the counter held prepackaged minced onion, pickle relish, fibrous yellow strands of pre-grated "cheese," etc., while color-coded plastic squirt bottles of extremely low-grade ketchup, mustard, and mayonnaise were kept supplied out of industrial-scale condiment buckets with perennially encrusted nozzles. Upon the request of a discerning gourmet, one would harpoon a water-bloated hot dog from amidst the schooling pink tubules, slap it into a gluey bun of "bread," fling on a gobbet of soupy "chili," scatter a quick handful of designated additives as though sprinkling dirt on an open grave, then quickly wrap the offending comestible in a sheet of wax paper, ideally in such a way that chili didn't ooze out the end like noxious, leaky spigot drippings in the kitchen of Satan's summer home.

As horrific as that all was, there was an even more horrific follow-up action: people actually *ate* the stuff. Especially after Frau

Harpy conceived the stratagem of a "lunch-time special," a two-hour stretch during which the disgusting fare could be purchased, with all the trimmings, four dogs for a dollar. When I saw *that* sign in the window, my heart sank, for I knew what was coming. A lot of highway construction was taking place around Old Hickory, and the sun-addled asphalteers made daily stops at the store to purchase quart bottles of hideously overpriced beer with which to cool their desiccated palates on their way home from work. On a summer day that will forever remain dry-etched into my psyche, I was working the register when a grizzled bandana-wrapped head bone hove up in front of me. Its nominally toothed mandible yawed downward and slightly to the left so that words could fight their way past the sandpapery glottis.

"Them dawgs really four a buck?" the haggard apparition asked suspiciously, a horny tar-smeared index digit pointing like the accusing finger of Justice at the stainless-steel cauldrons, which obligingly hubble-bubbled up some willing chiblits in response.

Oh, God. "Uh...yes?"

And so it began. The next day, highway workers formed a line before the DDD that literally stretched out the door. They weren't there just to order for themselves, mind; they were there *to order for their entire crews.* "Gimme forty of them chili dogs with the works," was a typical order. The harpoon flashed down into the stainless-steel depths with Ahabian vigor. Chili flew in ropy strands from the ladle. Greasy packets of paper-encased offal were hastily shoved into white paper sacks that quickly grew their own stains, like perspiration blotches on the starched shirts of overworked Japanese salary men. And all the while the register line kept growing, angry horns and a beeping console signified irate motorists needing fuel, impatient fishermen loitered outside the minnow tank, impatient deliverymen thrust invoices in my direction, devious customers thrust bad checks into my hand, and so on, and so on, and so on. By the end of my shift, I literally was trembling with stress and exhaustion, but I couldn't leave until the DDD, which by that time looked like a leftover set from some B-grade schlock film, was properly cleaned. Dried chili splats resisted removal with a vigor indicative of an insensate desire to be timeless memorials for a lost generation. Intertwined filigrees of mustard and ketchup looked suspiciously like a Pollack masterwork. My clothes were no better, being drenched with sweat and pink weenie juice. Chiblits clung to my trunk like orphaned baby possums. All this, may I remind the reader, for minimum wage. After a couple weeks of this madness, I mustered enough courage to confront Frau Repugno and demand the midnight shift. Apparently, shuffling my schedule was more lucrative than paying for another sure-to-be-failed polygraph test, as she acceded, however ungraciously, to my terms. I could have kissed her, except that I'd sooner have kissed Buzzard. Or a chiblit, for that matter. At least the chiblits seemed to care.

While this move alleviated some stress, it brought with it a new corpus of problems. The suburbs of Nashville were, at the time, really dangerous places late at night. Convenience stores and other twenty-four-hour emporia were particularly desirable targets for criminals. Three such outlets in the near vicinity of the store where I worked had been hit in the wee hours of the morning just during the brief time I'd been employed. I held the fort alone, of course; Frau Frankengoober wasn't about to pay for any additional help just for the sake of a polygraph-failing peon's personal wellbeing. Fortunately, I never had to put my rusty boxing skills to the test. What I did have to contend with was a nightly parade of strange denizens of the night, feckless outcasts who were drawn to the glass doors of the illuminated store like moths to a flame. One young woman would loiter about for hours, assuring me with complete sincerity that each and every awful country music song that blasted out from the tinny speakers was her creation. Another offered herself to me if only I would give her one of the cheesy, overpriced tourist tee shirts occupying a seldom-perused rack in the middle of the store. A phone call in the early hours turned out to be the husband of someone who had been in the store and taken a fancy to me. He offered me serious cash to become intimate with her...while he watched. I gently declined, feeling at once oddly flattered and a strong urge to wash. Members of the homeless would wander in at odd hours, conspicuously hanging around the coolers where the sandwich meats were displayed. If left unmolested, an individual of that ilk eventually would disappear into a restroom, emerging sometime later with a triumphant leer on his/her begrimed face as he/she shuffled out the door with markedly more energy than had been displayed upon entry. I then would open the bathroom to find a dozen or so plastic sleeves emptied of their preservative-impregnated contents. I never had the heart to report this pathetic occurrence to Frau Soulwart. Her life was baloney enough.

Eventually I saved up $750, a sum that allowed me to buy a barely functioning, obscenely yellow, badly used Datsun B-210. I then had to save up some more to buy a used carburetor and some other necessary gizmos that had to be installed before I could trust the thing out on the open road. As a sign, perhaps, that I was making a good move, one day while I had my head under the dash working on some wiring, I removed the ash tray and an ancient yellowed joint fell out. Perhaps the car had belonged to Buzzard's hook-up. A dedicated search of the vehicle yielding no further recreational distractions, the next day I tossed my very, very few belongings into the hatch and headed home, to impose once more upon my poor long-suffering parents. After having lived in fantasyland, I was ready for things to get real again. I had no idea how real they were about to get.

Back at home, weeks passed with no job prospects, so that, once again, my miniscule funds rapidly disappeared. I finally found something vaguely resembling employment by banking on my shaky credentials as an electronicist. Given how weak my skills in that area actually were, it was fitting enough that the position was equally pathetic. I walked into a TV repair shop in Winona and offered my services to the proprietor. I knew nothing about repairing TVs, except for what to do should I find a zombie cheeseburger inside of one, but I figured I could wing it. The proprietor, Kenny, told me he wasn't hiring. Unwilling to be dissuaded, I persisted in my entreaty. Current, I assured him, could not flow without me, and unlike voltage, I would brook no resistance. Finally, Kenny offered me a deal: for anything in the shop that I could fix, he would give me half the labor charge, in cash. No actual position, no paycheck, no retirement, no insurance, no benefits, no pesky paperwork, no job security; but *work*. I was so desperate that this actually seemed like a good arrangement at the time. At least I could tell my folks I'd found *some*thing. We shook on it, and I immediately began looking for choice devices to resurrect.

I didn't have far to look. The building, which was quite large, was absolutely packed, floor to ceiling, with everything from televisions to radios to eight-track players to toasters to hair curlers. If it plugged in, we had untold scores of whatever it was lying in discordant piles. Turned out that Kenny, who was really very good at diagnosing and repairing electronic devices, was woefully lacking in business acumen. The shop was full not because he couldn't fix things; it was full because he rarely called people up to let them know that things had been fixed, and when he did call, he never called twice. He also never said no, so that there were hundreds of items, some of which had been there for months, that he never had gotten around to looking at. Despite the fact that I never had worked on any sort of domestic electrical impedimenta, I at least knew how to read a schematic and which end of a soldering iron you didn't want to hold onto when it was plugged in. So in I dove, relying on a combination of rudimentary knowledge, desperate intuition, and blind luck to begin resuscitating the orphaned discards of machine-kind.

It wasn't long before I began to focus almost exclusively on televisions, for the simple reason that the repair bills on smaller items were more than the items were worth, which is another reason why the shop looked like the graveyard of lost appliances. Upon seeing the bill, people simply turned around and walked out. While hair curlers and waffle irons apparently engendered little personal attachment, people tended to be quite loyal to their old TV sets, most of which at that time still operated via tubes. That was great, for me: identify the bad tube by the simple expedient of sticking new ones in until the set worked, write up a bill, call the customer, and eat. I especially liked the last part of the operation, since by that point, I literally had begun to starve. On a good week I might make twenty-five dollars, out of which I had to buy gas (it was a twenty-two-mile commute, one-way, from home to the shop) and other necessities. All the beer and burger weight I'd put on in the Air Force had long since melted away, along with any feelings of solidarity I'd held for my fellow human beings.

To say that I had no real knack for TV repair would be a charitable assessment. TVs in those days were big in multiple dimensions. One worked on them by placing a mirror in front of the screen, so that one could see the results as one tinkered around the innards of the things. On house calls, I always forgot my mirror, so I would crane my head around to try to watch the screen while groping inside the cabinet for the electronic equivalent of internal organs. Consequently, more times than I care to admit, I inadvertently laid my fingers across the power supply and quite literally blew my hand out of the set. The weird thing was that, about half the times that happened, the sets started working. Apparently, all that was necessary was to sacrifice a Peacock to the TV gods. I think the Aztecs would have approved.

Things improved a bit when we started installing home satellite systems, a brand-new technological innovation that few in the area could afford but which people bought anyway, with that curious fiscal abandon so readily expressed by society's lesser castes when times are hard. The dishes were enormous flying saucer-shaped things that had to be mounted on large-diameter sections of steel pipe set in deep holes filled with concrete. The best part was assembling the dish. It came in pre-cast curved sections like huge beige slices of orange peel that had to be bolted together to form the parabola. Even in the backyard of some cheesy ranch house in rural Mississippi, one couldn't help but feel like a NASA scientist when the dish went up. Kenny would then adjust the polar mount until the dish could track the very limited number of commercial communication satellites in orbit at the time (there were about eight or so, if I remember correctly, that we reliably could access from our point on the globe). Those who wanted to strain their credit to (or past) the limit could buy a motorized version of the system. By cranking a dial in their house to signal the actuator, the dish would slowly grind its way over to the optimum receiving point for the desired satellite.

Most folks opted for the hand-cranked version, having gone into hock to buy the basic setup in the first place. Running out to crank the dish to pick up the desired station: perhaps not that much had changed since my "Lost in Space" days.

All physical labor involved with the dish installation, from loading and unloading truckloads of sand with a shovel, mixing the mortar, digging a hole through the stiff clay substrate, setting the pipe and pouring the concrete, fell to me. I didn't mind, since I was better with a shovel than a soldering iron, and for a change I actually was getting paid: forty dollars per system, and sometimes we did two per week! I was so happy to have some actual bills in my wallet and so hungry that I celebrated my first dish installation windfall by going to the local pizza emporium and ordering an extra-large pie with the works. I ate *the entire thing* in that single sitting, by myself, a massive, carbohydrate-rich pig-out that left me feeling overwhelmingly bloated and grotesque, a feeling that quickly ripened into black depression when I got the bill and discovered that I had just consumed over half of my hard-won folding money. *Toujours gai.*

Business boomed, especially after we mounted a demonstration dish on the roof of the shop. Kenny tuned it to one of the main satellites, the one that carried HBO, MTV, and some other major channels (in those days, the number of channels available from any one satellite was in the low double-digits). The shop was right next door to an auto repair place, the owner of which would have looked and smelled like he'd been dipped in forty-weight Havoline even if car repair hadn't been his profession. He was, to put it charitably, an oaf. After putting up with his whiny haranguing for weeks, I finally agreed to come into town and open up the shop one night so that he and his mechanics could come in and watch some free, premium-grade TV. No sooner had I locked the door behind us than he started demanding that I tune it in to "that" satellite. The one carrying the Playboy Channel, which at the time carried porn that by today's sordid standards was very soft indeed. Kenny, in his infinite business wisdom, had not seen fit to install the motorized version of the system. In order to accommodate Mr. Oaf's juvenile request, I would have had to climb onto the roof and crank the dish around by hand until someone down below yelled, "Stop!" The only thing missing was the screwdriver through the pole! I refused, of course, at which point Mr. Oaf broke into a truly major tantrum. He desperately wanted, he proclaimed very loudly and belligerently to all assembled, to "see some titties." Apparently, that carnal impulse had been his motivation for instigating the whole episode to begin with. After my umpteenth refusal, he stormed out, sheepish, oil-begrimed minions in tow. He never spoke to me again, so at least something positive came out of the affair.

Life was not great, but I supposed it could have been worse. As it turned out, I supposed right.

7

NADIR

It was about that time that I moved into a house out in the country some miles north of Winona. Lest this sound like I'd suddenly come into some sort of unexpected inheritance, let me explain the true situation. I increasingly was feeling like a burden on my folks: they were housing and feeding me when I simply had no money to contribute to their own limited pool of funds. My horrible little Datsun didn't get good mileage, so even the tens of dollars I now was making weekly were mostly going into the gas tank. Having no money, I hadn't bought clothes since getting out of the Air Force, so I was raggedy in the extreme. I found a few of my old pre-military flannel shirts up in the attic room and wore one of them one night when an aunt took pity and invited me out to get a hamburger steak in Starkville, a small town about forty-five miles east of French Camp. As I ravenously shoveled gravy-drenched ground meat and greasy French fries into my gob, she kept staring at me in a very peculiar way. I assumed it was because of my appalling lack of table manners, so I slowed down a bit and pretended to chew. Then she pointed at my shirt collar and asked, "What's that?" in an incredulous tone. "That" turned out to be a dirt dauber's nest, a cylindrical, air-hardened mud tube no doubt full of the paralyzed spiders that momma daubers capture to feed their newly hatched larvae. I hurriedly plucked this earthy trophy of personal neglect off my person, face reddening in mortification. She thought it was hilarious, which didn't help. You can take the boy out of the country, but you can't scrape the country off the boy. This brings to mind one of my daughter's many classic sayings. Mississippi is known as the Hospitality State, she reasoned, because we are so hospitable, we let other things live on us.

The opportunity to move to Winona, thus relieving my parents of a burden, saving gas, and getting as far away as possible from my nefariously delighted aunt presented itself when my friend Doug (the one who tried to break the light barrier in his dad's Dodge) offered to let me stay, rent free, in an old abandoned house out in the country that was owned by his in-laws. All I had to do was pay the utilities, which still was more than I could afford, but I gratefully took him up on the offer. There was a bed, thankfully, a working electric stove and refrigerator, a rickety Formica-topped dining table, and a couch that had seen much better days. I obtained an abandoned TV from work and took the electronics out of the wooden cabinet, from which I made a small bookcase. I hauled some spare dishes over from French Camp, along with a single set of sheets, a blanket, and a lone towel that was about as threadbare as my pockets. That was pretty much it in terms of furnishings, except for my guitar. It was a desperately lonely existence. I couldn't afford the gas to head anywhere after work, so I sat up long hours into the night making up really bad, really sad songs about the futility of human existence, lost love, mortality, and any number of equally cheerful topics. I thought that I had pretty much hit rock bottom. The Loaf Bread Incident would show me just how wrong I was.

I could afford loaf bread because I finally found a real job; one that I quickly came to hate, but a real job, nonetheless. A few miles from the old house where I was living was a roofing company where Bennie had worked some years before. Bennie's work ethic and capacity for physical labor were simply astonishing; coupled with the innate geometric sense he'd inherited from Pop, those traits made him a very valuable employee in a profession where hard work and geometry matter. Bennie hadn't worked for the company for years, but he still was remembered there with great respect. It was on the basis of his performance that they agreed to take me on at a time when no one really was hiring. I was grateful. I knew nothing about roofing and could no more calculate how many squares of asphalt shingles it would take to top a house than I could repair ductwork on an alien space station. But I was desperate and readily jumped at the chance when one of the company's crew chiefs offered me the extraordinary sum of $7.00 an hour to come work for him.

The first week was a living hell. In fact, every week that I worked for the company was a living hell, but that first week was particularly toasty. The crew I'd joined was reroofing a church in Grenada. As was standard practice, they'd begun by tearing off the old shingles and underlying tar paper with large metal roofing forks, an awful process that jars your arm to the shoulder every time you slam the tines into a roofing nail, which is pretty much every time you thrust the fork down the roof. A wooden fence ran along one side of the church, making a narrow alleyway that was clogged head-high with roofing debris. The only way to remove the waste from such tight quarters was to load it by hand into an industrial-sized wheelbarrow, push that around to the drive and up a very steep ramp, and dump it into the back of a large truck. I did that delightful task eight hours a day for a solid week, while the crew kept sliding more grainy, grimy collages of shingle and felt fragments down the roof and onto the pile. (It was a very large church). While I had no technical skills, I must have impressed them with my willingness to take on odious, laborious tasks and work hard at them, because the next week I was hired away by another crew chief for an extra fifty cents an hour. And the next week. And the next. Three raises in three weeks! And while eight-fifty an hour still wasn't great, I could at least live on it as long as my car didn't die or some other stroke of bad fortune sought me out. Like Hantavirus, or rabies, or the plague, or psychopathy, all potential outcomes of the aforementioned Loaf Bread Incident.

With the proceeds of my first paycheck, I bought a coffee pot, coffee, some of that gross non-dairy "creamer," and some basic foodstuffs, including the cheapest family-sized loaf of gluey white bread I could find and a large jar of equally bottom-shelf peanut butter, figuring I could live on that fundamental carbohydrate and protein combo until the next check came in. I left the bread on the kitchen counter that evening and fell asleep, exhausted. When I got up at 5:00 the next morning to get ready for work, the bread was gone. Some heartless bastard had come into my hovel and stolen my meager provender! Or so I thought, until, with a true thrill of terror, I espied the empty bread wrapper on the floor. The end had been chewed away and the entire loaf—every last, single crumb of a family-sized loaf of bread—had been devoured. I had been sleeping alone in a rat-haunted building for weeks. Rats eat meat. Rats will, in fact, eat anything, as evidenced by a gruesome family tale. Mom and her two sisters, Benita and Jan, grew up in a little shotgun house in Clarksdale in the 1940s. Aunt Jan, the youngest, wrote: "There was a terrible rat problem in town for many years. In fact, the city had a crew that regularly went around and put out poison everywhere. Everyone had cats to help control them. I was probably about six when I woke up one night screaming – two big old rats were on my face and I was bitten twice – once on each cheek. Mother got a cat and I can't remember ever not having one in Clarksdale after that."[8]

Not having a cat, I went hungry that day, but after work I took my last few dollars and bought some very large, very powerful rattraps and another loaf of bread, some of which I used for bait. Not surprisingly, I did not sleep that night, but lay coiled up tight in bed with the cover pulled very, very tightly over my somewhat wasted but still tasty frame, hoping I didn't look too much like a particularly succulent burrito. In the middle of the night, I heard the sickening *thwack* as a trap was triggered, followed by an awful clacking cacophony that sounded like the death throes of a rabid allosaurid. I couldn't bear to face the awful spectacle that night so I waited till morning, when I found that I'd caught a rat, all right. While not the size of an allosaurus it was, quite literally, the size of a football. A corpulent, hairy football with needle-sharp teeth and a gross hairless tail, the base of which was as thick as my thumb. That night I caught *another* one of equal size. Then all seemed quiet, until a couple of days later when a disgusting smell emerged from my bedroom where another trap had been set. That one had gone off while I was at work, instantly turning an extraordinarily tiny

---

8   Janice Peters Roderick and Joye Peters Peacock, 1995, *Thanks for the Memories*, p. 54. Manuscript in possession of the author.

mouse into a hairy schmear of rodent pâté. Cleaning up that little mouse's remains somehow was even more revolting than disposing of the loathsome rat carcasses. Not surprisingly, I began to spend as much time as possible away from that place, which meant fishing or drinking, or both in combination. Coming "home" was like stepping into an Evil Dead movie. Life sucked.

Including work. Roofing, especially roofing in the Deep South, really does smack of Hell, especially when laying a "hot roof." I suspect that the technology is much improved these days, but back then one loaded obsidian-black blocks of solid asphalt into a "cooker," from which sludgy molten goo was pumped up a shuddering metal conduit to shoot out, all heat and steam and stink and glop, into large wheelbarrows on the roof. Those heavy, unwieldy contraptions were then pushed to some virgin patch of rooftop so that tar-speckled crew members could dip big mops into the goop, heave them up like harpoons bearing the putrescent heads of long-dead Medusas liberated from the La Brea tar pits, and liberally spread the unlovely stuff around in steaming, opaque brush strokes. Others stood by to shovel on gravel, which adhered to the bituminous surface left behind by the mops. The work was backbreaking, and breathing in the horrible fumes all day didn't help matters any. Especially in the summertime, when it might already be hovering around one hundred degrees in humidity that would drown an alligator gar, the heat rising from the melted tar was enough to make one feel faint. I worked with guys in their early thirties who looked sixty, their skin cooked from years of direct exposure to the harsh rays reflected from metal and glass and tar up on those wretched roofs. One guy about my age had been splattered with tar when the conduit broke. I simply cannot conceive of what it must have felt like as the steaming pitch bonded instantly to his skin. He was a mass of scar tissue all along one side of his body, including his face. He was still roofing.

While hot roofs were the worst, all roofing jobs were bad. Heat, dust, wasps, supremely unedifying conversation revolving almost entirely around women's reproductive parts: roofing had it all. Still, it was a job, one where I was treated fairly, and I greatly respected my coworkers for their technical acumen and ability to put in appallingly hard workdays in appallingly hard conditions, often while suffering from appallingly bad hangovers, with little complaint. While I never developed the technical skills that would have moved me any further up the metaphorical company ladder, I held a place of honor on the actual physical ladder, up which bundles of asphalt shingles had to be carried to crew members doing the nailing-on. As my body toned up from all the physical work and unaccustomed protein input, I became able to flop two bundles of roofing shingles, totaling about a hundred and forty pounds, onto my shoulder and carry them up together. And I could do that repeatedly, with no break other than for lunch, all day long. Such physical prowess earned me some respect, even if my feeble attempts to turn the conversation to something other than human reproductive anatomy did not. My compatriots thought Robert Frost was a villainous character in an animated Christmas TV special.

There was a lot to the job that I never mastered, including fabrication of sheet metal gutters and other architectural accoutrements that Pop or Bennie could have whipped out in their sleep. I also hated "roll roofing," where rolls of an asphalt-and-mineral grain-impregnated membrane were rolled out on low-pitch roofs, being glued down by roofing cement, gallon buckets of the same sort of infernal asphalt pitch that was the main ingredient of so many roofing products. That gunk was smeared onto the roof one handful at a time while the roofing gradually was unrolled behind the smearer. We wore gloves, of course (which had to be tossed afterwards), but there simply was no way to do that task without festooning your arms up to the elbows with sticky black oobleck. The stuff would not come off with soap and water, and even the most powerful commercially-available skin cleaners didn't work especially well. I discussed the topic one day with Bennie, who let me in on a trade secret he'd stumbled upon during his own time with the company. He swore that the grease from any chain-store fried-chicken entree would take roofing tar off one's skin in a flash. I tried it. To my dual amazement and horror, he was right. From that day forward, if we were doing roll roofing, I had drive-thru chicken for supper, following which I rubbed the greasy paper box liner down my arms, and presto! "Clean" arms that subsequently could be sanitized with soap and water! As if the job weren't gross enough already. I made especially sure to remove all traces of grease from my being when employing this trick. One never knew when the rats might be back.

The social scene in Winona did not relieve the daily drudgery of that supremely dire existence. I had just enough money to hang out and guzzle cheap beer at the local juke joints. Remarkably bad bands clanged out remarkably bad country music with monotonous predictability while people who knew one another all too well nonetheless tried to act like amorous strangers on the filthy dance floor. Parking one's beat-up piece of shit next to scores of other beat-up pieces of shit in the gravel parking lot. Pieces of human shit beating the shit out of one another in the same parking lot for no particularly good reason. Unhappy people trying to numb their unhappy brains with alcohol before driving off to their unhappy families, getting up the next day, heads pounding, to repeat the whole unhappy cycle. There was no future to any of that *danse macabre*; there was just an atonal, omnipresent "now," a depressing still life from some deranged cosmic artist's interminable Gray Period. Slowly, inevitably, the will to live diminished and, despite numberless attempts, happiness never was found like some golden placer deposit in the bottom of the sudsy glass. Some follow this appalling pattern for *their entire adult lives.* Ignorant as I was, at least I knew that the journey was leading nowhere that I was interested in going. But how to escape? I became so desperate that I even briefly considered going back into the military, where at least I would be assured of three to six square meals a day. Fortunately, before I did anything so rash, a miracle occurred.

He wasn't much to look at, as miracles go, but that fact detracted not at all from the unexpectedly positive outcome of our chance relationship. A relative of the man who owned the roofing company, the fellow in question was being groomed to take over the family business someday. For that purpose, he was enrolled part-time at Mississippi State University, a land-grant institution in Starkville. Up on a roof one sweltering summer day, in a rare interlude when something other than female genitalia was the topic of discussion, this worthy was complaining bitterly about the classes he was "having" to take at MSU. As the rising sun slowly burned the previous evening's alcohol fumes out of what was left of my brain, a thought began to form. A stubborn, tempting thought that wouldn't let go. This guy didn't know whether he was washing or hanging out, yet he was making it in college. Despite my best efforts at cell reduction, I still had at least some gray matter left. Could I...?

Whatever my other failings, I am at the end of the day a decisive creature. To think is to act! Accordingly, I took a day off shortly thereafter and visited MSU myself. I had realized what I didn't like about the military I'd fled as soon as possible; about the sham-glam music industry; about frying my fingers inside other people's home entertainment systems; and about my current blue-collar existence. I'd finally figured out what "proletariat" meant. It meant doing what someone else wanted you to do, for no reason other than to be able to purchase rat-bait bread and 3.2 beer while the tier above you dined on hamburger steak and white wine, and so on up the ladder to the insufferable elites who dined on Iranian Beluga caviar and Domaine Leroy Richebourg Grand Cru. I had no desire to further a career in chow hall abuse, flying saucer assembly, excruciatingly bad music video production, chicken grease-enabled tar removal, or what have you; for once, I wanted to do something because *I* wanted to do it, practicalities be damned. It was high time I tightened up. Accordingly, I visited the university with a plan to embark upon a really sensible vocation where I was sure to secure steady employment, a comfortable living, and the overweening admiration and respect of society in general.

I had decided that it was high time I become an archaeologist.

PART TWO

TAKING FLIGHT

THE APPARENTLY RASH DECISION TO PURSUE A CAREER IN ONE OF HUMAN-kind's more rarified fields came not out of a complete vacuum of knowledge, just a near-vacuum of knowledge. When I was in junior high school, my class did a "Career Day" tour during which we visited a garment factory in Ackerman, the ghastly denizens of which stared up at us from the tenebrous interior, expressionless and gimlet-eyed, like a legion of the undead hoping dimly for a bargain-basement exorcism. We then visited a grocery store where hapless middle-aged adults were packing groceries for minimum wage, looking at once embarrassed and pissed off as they studiously placed heavy jars of pickles on top of the eggs and left signature hand prints in billowy loafs of gluey white bread stuffed like vertical buttresses into brown paper sacks. If the school counselors were trying to drive up the teen suicide rate, they'd made a good start. To their credit, though, and perhaps to convince us that we could, in fact, take a different path, we also visited MSU. During our tour of the Biology building, a graduate student gave me a large, beautiful textbook that I treasured for many years. I understood the sanctity of books and I was extraordinarily flattered that someone in a different intellectual stratum had recognized and appreciated my interest in the broader world. As I stood on the lawn in front of that building, clutching my weighty treasure, I looked across the street and saw the Cobb Institute of Archaeology, a boxy edifice with ruined stone columns standing lonely sentinel on a raised stone platform in the front yard. I went in while the rest of the class was on break. The place seemed, appropriately enough, to be as empty as a tomb, but I did peer through the glass walls of the basement museum at cases of artifacts, a plaster sarcophagus, a replica of the Code of Hammu-rabi stele, and other marvels. The haunted figures of the garment factory faded in my mind. In their place rose up the haunted figures of the past.

I'd always had a bug for archaeology. When I was about ten years old, I found a remarkably ugly little stone arrow point in one of our gardens and was transported. Later, Andy and I dug some holes at the same old house site from which we'd hauled water back in the olden times. From one hole we dug up a silver Barber dime dating to the early 1900s. You can imagine how *that* fired the imagination of two young kids whose daily entertainment usually involved tar-geting each other's skulls with dirt clods and beeter-boppers. Even at that point in life, I had an intuitive understanding that indiscrim-inate digging was a destructive practice, so I never did that again, but I continued to pick up "arrowheads" (mostly spearpoints, as it turned out) wherever I found them. Some years later, a music teach-er at French Camp gifted me with a copy of George Vaillant's *Az-tecs of Mexico* for helping him disassemble and move a pipe organ from Tennessee down to the academy. I loved that book so much that I later acquired Prescott's *History of the Conquest of Mexico* and *History of the Conquest of Peru* and actually read the things. I picked up other books while in the military, on the ancient Romans and Greeks, the Maya, and other classic civilizations. I spent a lot of time with Toynbee's *Study of History*, a modern printing with lots of large color photographs. Nothing in my daily world came close to matching the romance inherent in those magnificent books.

Unfortunately, not all of the authority figures in my life were as encouraging as my music teacher. During my senior year of high school, students had to come up with a science fair project. I badly wanted to do something on archaeology, focused on that site where I'd found my first arrow point. My science teacher would not hear of it: "Archaeology isn't science," she sniffed disdainfully. This same teacher once told the class that coughing wasn't a natural function, but had only become a human condition with the introduction of smoking. So, while I didn't question her motives, I was suspicious of her characterization of the field. Archaeology seemed a pretty esoteric pursuit, to be sure, but *somebody* had to do it, right? And thus, on a hot summer day, the scent of roofing pitch still cloying my nostrils, I made my way to the university and stepped once again into the Cobb Institute, a place that was to become a focal point for much of my life.

I had an appointment to see the academic advisor for Anthropology, which turned out to be the umbrella discipline for archaeologists in the United States. I would not be just an archaeologist; I would be an *anthropologist*! About that larger discipline, I admittedly knew next to nothing. I had heard of Margaret Mead, but that was about it. Still, I was willing to give it a go, whatever it took. Two incidences of my initial contact with this seemingly arcane world turned out to be particularly fortuitous. First, I happened to be signing up just in time to participate in a summer field school, where I would get to go out and actually "do" archaeology right off the bat. Second, I immediately was smitten with the academic advisor, Janet. She was of serious mien, obviously very smart but also very nice, and she listened politely while I earnestly assured her that, while regrettably short on book-learnin', I wasn't afraid of hard work. She encouraged me to give it a go, and I left feeling a strange mix of elation and trepidation. I was entering unknown territory, but at least the local guides were welcoming enough.

That I was able to attend college at all was due to student loans, which were not nearly as rapacious in those days, and something called the Sumners Grant. A woman from the small community of Eupora, Mississippi, established this remarkable fund to honor her husband. They had run a timber business in the interior of the state, culminating in the sale of a very large area of timberland, the proceeds of which allowed them to create a private educational fund of twenty-two *million* dollars, money that then was invested so that the foundation's holdings rapidly grew even larger. The grant specifically provides tuition assistance for students from the hill counties of Choctaw, Attalla, Carroll, Montgomery, and Webster to attend college. I don't know how many thousands of backwoods bumpkins like myself have benefitted from that incredible act of kindness; I do know that I would not have been able to further my education without it. Mrs. Sumners passed away in 1987. I hope she left in full realization of all the good she did in the world.

So the stage was set, and in May 1984, I climbed down from my last roof, threw my guitar, raggedy clothing, and well-thumbed archaeology books into my horrible little yellow car, and bade Rathaven a most non-regretful goodbye. Mike, one of my coworkers who also happened to be one of my best friends from my Winona high school days, used the company card to buy me a trowel as a parting gift, so I was equipped for my first field school. I once more made the trek to MSU, where I milled about inside the coliseum with hundreds of others of the species, moving from table to table to fill out the requisite registration forms. At that point in time, all such stuff still was being done by hand, a process that took about half a day to complete. Nowadays, with the welcome aid of computers, it takes generally about twice as long.

My first task as part of the summer field class was to drive one of two trucks over to a rundown shed, out of which we loaded screens, shovels, water coolers, a crew-sized lunch cooler, wheelbarrows, a large gas-powered water pump, many yards of two and a half-inch-diameter rubber hose, and metal tool boxes containing measuring tapes, line levels, small root cutters, trowels, pencils, Sharpies, and a miscellany of other small tools and supplies. We also stocked big wooden Army surplus boxes with large root cutters, bow saws, stake hammers, rolls of black Visqueen, industrial-strength garbage bags, floppy sheaves of paper bags, cartons of tin foil, packages of metric graph paper, letter boards with bags of white plastic letters, and a variety of other field impedimenta. We then drove to the Cobb where, from an ill-lit basement room, we secured a dozen or so spring-covered metal folding beds (more Army surplus), some truly nasty single-bed mattresses, an alidade, a transit, their accompanying tripods, a stadia rod, and a couple of camera boxes loaded with everything you might expect to find in loaded camera boxes in the pre-digital days. All of that stuff eventually was piled into the two vehicles and lashed down until they looked like some cross between the Beverly Hillbillies' truck and the Grinch's overloaded sleigh. The odd thing was that this activity, which was carried out with the help of a few other students, was *fun*. Within fifteen minutes of hauling stuff out of the sweltering, spider-infested shed, I knew that, for the first time in my more-or-less adult life, I'd made the right choice. I'd always wanted to be an archaeologist. I was about to get my chance.

We headed down to Meridian, a small city in south-central Mississippi, from where we struck out into the highly dissected uplands. We were there to excavate at two sites: an ancient quarry that had been discovered up in the hills, and a stone tool production locus down in a stream valley, a site that had been systematically mined by a local artifact collector who obligingly hooked us up with a house where we could stay free of charge. We unloaded the trucks, set up the beds, laid the mattresses out for a badly needed airing, and spent the rest of the day repairing the screens that would be used to recover artifacts from the dirt as we dug. I scarcely could believe my good fortune, for the next day we arose early, ate a quick breakfast, reloaded the trucks, and hit the field to start excavating.

The first site we investigated was the quarry, which was indeed very high in the hills, up a winding, rutted red clay road through the pines. It was a fascinating place, because once you got your eyes adjusted to the play of the landscape, you could see large shallow depressions on the ridge top, remnants of pits dug by Native Americans at some time in the distant past. The pits had been dug to reach veins of a sugary-textured, semi-translucent rock called Tallahatta quartzite. How long ago that activity had transpired turned out to be difficult to ascertain, since the ancient quarry workers left little behind that could be dated. What they did leave behind in abundance was "debitage," a fancy word referring to all the waste products of stone tool production. "Flakes" is a more familiar term; the same stuff that many artifact collectors refer to as "chips." Whatever one calls it, an astonishing amount of very sharp pieces of broken rock had piled up on the hilltop over millennia of stone acquisition and preliminary flaking of tools. The debitage was hardily encased in red clay, so that pushing the sediment through the screens left one's hands quite lacerated by the end of the day. Once in a while a broken "preform," the rough, early stage of a stone spear point, would be found, but those were too general in shape to be diagnostic of any cultural period. So we knew we had a quarry and it was abundantly clear that it had been used intensively, probably for a very long time. But how long ago were we talking about?

The answer was found at the other site, which lay some miles away, back down the hill and on a low terrace overlooking a creek. That site basically was a spear point factory, where the preforms had been carried and worked into final shape by ancient craftsmen. Judging from the points that the collector had dug up and the ones that we found, that site, too, had been used for millennia. There still were flakes, of course; gazillions of them, especially smaller ones, reflecting the later stages of tool production. But there also were all the fragments of points that had broken in the production process, along with a few whole ones that had been lost or discarded as newly fashioned points were hafted onto spear shafts. Every day we recovered dozens of broken points from various stages of manufacturing, most dating between about 3,000 and 5,000 years ago. I knew a little about Pompeii, Chichén Itzá, Tenochtitlan, and Machu Pichu; I knew nothing about the prehistory of Mississippi except for some erroneous folklore that rapidly was dispensed with. One example: Native peoples lived beside creeks because they dripped cold creek water onto heated rocks as a way to flake their stone tools. Before I learned that this particular bit of "knowledge" was complete nonsense, I tried it once, very nearly putting my eye out when the rock exploded. Science!

We pushed at the stubborn clay-rich soil with flat bladed shovels, loading dirt into wheelbarrows and running them up ramps to be dumped into metal screens through which the dirt was washed using water pumped out of the creek. Artifacts were then retrieved and bagged, with informative tags for each "provenience" excavated. We filled out forms for each excavation level, taking photos as we went. I had the privilege of excavating one of the nicest artifacts of the dig, a beautiful little stone spearpoint some 9,000 years old, of a type traditionally called a "Big Sandy." That find pleased the instructor quite a bit. Eager to impress, I spent some of my extremely limited funds to purchase a book illustrating and describing such traditional point types. In order to memorize the lore, I recopied the entire book by hand, including the drawings. Soon I was able to spout names like "Big Sandy," "Benton," "Tombigbee Stemmed," "Bradley Spike," and the like with obnoxious pseudo-authority. While that parlor trick seemed to impress all the people I intended to impress at the time, it wasn't until much later in my career that I realized that such typological thinking was, in fact, an impediment, rather than an aid, to understanding. That realization was a real breakthrough, one that completely changed how I thought about archaeology in particular and the world in general. Indeed, it turned out to be an understanding that helped make me a better human being on all fronts, and one with the potential to have similarly good effect on all sentient bipeds on this planet, and perhaps even the semi-sentient ones. The belief that "types" exist to be discovered in nature is called essentialism, a philosophical stance that turns out to be pretty inappropriate where human beings are concerned. More on this epiphany in Chapter 14.

The excavation field school wrapped up after about a month. In addition to learning a lot over those weeks, I made many very good friends, including some who would become professional colleagues: Keith, David, Mary Evelyn, Ken. Bobby was a true kindred spirit, as evidenced by the fact that he brought a tiny little black and white TV to the field camp and woke early on Saturday mornings to watch cartoons. Besides a love of animation, Bobby and I shared a dangerous predilection for alcohol, although I admit that, for all my early tippling training, I was a rank amateur compared to him. Especially given that most of our limited funds went to Anheuser Busch stock, both of us were perennially desperately poor, so that our standard field fare provided nutritive value far below that recommended by government standards. Put more bluntly, we ate crap because crap was what we could afford. With the gallows humor that was another shared predilection, Bobby, Keith, and I spent many hours in dramatic lunchtime readings of the ingredient lists on tinned meat products. The cheapest brand, which of course is what we bought, was "Red Bird Imitation Vienna Sausages," a curious but convenient delicacy no longer in production. (I assume a papal bull was issued to achieve this state of affairs for the good of the flock). If you never have read the labels on such comestibles, I can't in good conscience recommend doing so unless your psyche is at least as strong as your stomach, or unless you have a particular fondness for spleen. We read even as we ingested, sharing a good laugh over it all, and passed on to other topics.

Or so I thought. At a departmental Christmas party, a couple of years later, I received a poorly wrapped, cylindrical present from Bobby. It was a can of Red Birds. Bobby gleefully suggested that we ingest them on the spot, but not being inebriated at the moment, I passed. The next year, I rewrapped the can and regifted it. It was on! The same can appeared in the mail many months later, battered and dirty; a birthday present from Bobby. I tossed the repulsive thing onto the dash of my car, where it rolled around in the sun gathering dust and photons for a year, at which point I rewrapped it and mailed it back. The next year it returned to me in the mail, in an even dingier state and sporting a partial coating of some sticky red melted plastic. I assumed Bobby had tossed the can into his car trunk along with what other dubious artifacts, God only knows. It resided for the following year in my tackle box, gently mellowing in the heat and degassing plastic worms, following which I sent it his way again. This questionable exchange went on for seventeen years, to the point where the essentially unreadable label maintained but a tenuous hold like a hanging chad on the can, which was swollen and bulging from the pressure of the unspeakable volatiles within. Finally, as I was once again packaging the thing to send to Bobby, the lid exploded. Not with a "boom," or a "wham." It went with a *"phaaank"*: the soft labial aspiration of a waterlogged zombie voicing heartfelt appreciation for finally being freed from its mushy grave in some time-forgotten swampland. It was only by great good fortune that the contents of the tin mostly vomited forth into the padded envelope I was holding. I had to look, of course, but immediately wished I hadn't. Nothing solid was left, the puerile pink meat tubules having dissolved into a greasy paste-colored liquid. Reeling from the unholy effluvium, it was a moment or two before I realized that not all of the can's contents had made it into the envelope. Some had splashed onto the bare skin of my arm, a realization engendered by another sensation altogether: the foul stuff burned horribly! Clearly, the beast within was trying to breach my body's biological defenses and assimilate my soul! I immediately ran to the bathroom and eventually managed to still the pain with cold water and lots of soap. The psychic scars remain. What sort of microbial witch's brew inadvertently had been concocted remains unknown to science; I suspect that it was some nondescript species of caustic archezoan, phylogenetically akin to the sulfur-eating bacteria of deep-sea thermal vents. I am not enough of a scientist to repeat the experiment to find out. And I never ate tinned meat products again.

Following the excavation field school, I embarked almost immediately upon another four and a half weeks of archaeology, this time doing "pedestrian survey," meaning that we were finding, recording, and collecting artifacts from previously undiscovered archaeological sites. Contrary to popular belief, most of the sites out there in the wide, wide world still haven't been discovered (at least not by archaeologists). We were doing "open field" survey, meaning that we would line up at the edge of an agricultural field, five rows apart, and, on cue, start walking and looking for artifacts of any kind. If one was spotted, be it a piece of prehistoric pottery, a flake, a projectile point, a piece of glass, a nail, or whatever, we would gather together and wander back and forth, making a good collection of the materials exposed on the plowed surface while marking out the boundaries of the site for measurement. I have done a lot of archaeology since that summer, but it remains the single most fascinating and instructive time of my life. That was archaeology I could *breathe*. Far more than digging in a square hole in the ground, survey really connects the material record of past peoples to the landscape where those materials are found. The scientific return on time invested is enormous. And it was incredibly fun. We must have found and recorded well over sixty sites that term, everything from ancient campsites thousands of years old, littered with stone tools and debitage, to Native villages boasting dense middens and thick accumulations of pottery and other artifacts, to Historic-period house sites marked by whiteware sherds, glass, and metal, with the occasional marble or pewter toy to enliven the experience. It really was fantastic.

Not least because Janet was the teacher. Although I have a limited sample of exactly one test case, and no control for verification, I nonetheless can testify with absolute certainty that there is such a thing as love at first sight. I know, because I was the test case. I'd felt it during our initial meeting, and the feeling only had grown stronger in the interim. I recognized that having a personal relationship with Janet was highly unlikely for several reasons. She was a faculty member in the program in which I'd just enrolled, and I didn't want to cause either of us any trouble in that regard. She was many years older than I, and she had two children, a bright, reserved lad of twelve and an equally bright, vivacious little girl of three. That was a daunting package. But love is a curious beast, always nosing around the edges of reason and, truth to tell, living more-or-less by convention hadn't really done a lot for me up to that point anyway. Janet was amazingly smart, highly principled, emphatically devoted to her calling, a wonderful parent, and extremely hard-working: I found her to be inspirational in all those regards. Plus, I thought she was physically very attractive, with long straight brunette hair, high cheekbones, and a lovely, not-quite-olive skin tone. So I was unavoidably tempted.

The amazing thing wasn't that I was attracted to Janet; what was amazing was the feeling that she was attracted to *me*. I am not what one would call a "looker." I am more of a "try not to look in case they look back" kind of hominid. I am short, at five feet, seven inches, but I have very broad shoulders, so that from behind I look like a third-string bull trying to push its way past the gate to see if there's anything left of the matador. My hair can only be described as lank, except for an annoyingly enthusiastic rooster tail that likes to gather atmospheric data as I perambulate throughout the day. My siblings and I are unwilling genetic recipients of what euphemistically are referred to as "the Peacock ears." "Weather vanes," "storm shutters," "jug handles," or "fruit-bat radar appendages" might be more accurate descriptors. So I never was confident of my looks, even though I knew I would be a loyal and supportive partner if ever I could get hooked up with someone willing to overlook my shortcomings. I was ready for that, even if I can't claim to have been ready for the responsibilities that would attend if Janet and I were to get together. In any case, the attraction between us remained unspoken that summer. Nonetheless, we had a glorious time, all of us, as we tramped the soybean fields of north-central Mississippi, recording and collecting sites that never before had been revealed to science. We stayed, free of charge, in a public school in the little town of Ingomar, with use of the showers, cooking facilities, and basketball court. Bobby brought his little black and white TV, so that we were not cartoon-deprived. What an incredible privilege it all was.

We wrapped up that inaugural field season with what became a treasured, if rather sticky and wasteful, ceremony: Bobby, Keith, and I each poured a can of beer over our respective heads. There was no particular reason for this silly *rite de passage*, which was reason enough for us to execute it. That end-of-fieldwork ritual would be repeated, often with other participants, for years to come. Relative to the awful faux-Vienna sausage affair, it was harmless enough, I suppose; at least it involved American swill-lager, so that actual beer wasn't being wasted.

Following field school, I spent a few weeks back at French Camp preparing for the big move into the dorm at college. There wasn't much to prepare, actually, except to rid myself of my horrible little car (I couldn't afford the gas, the repair bills, or the parking fees). My folks thought I was insane, of course. They approved of my seeking a college degree, but *anthropology*? To be an *archaeologist*? Earnestly, they suggested that I "keep my hand in" TV repair. Disingenuously, I assured them that I would. The fact that I have not yet electrocuted myself suggests that I followed the correct course of action.

In August I moved into a monastic cell in Hamlin Hall, one of the older dorms on campus. The plan had been for Bobby and me to share a dorm room. We were going to call it "Troll Town," after one of the lesser cartoons of the day. But life intervened to delay Bobby's return to school, so instead I found myself sharing a very small, very ugly room with a creature whom I will call "Jack," because that is a convenient nickname for "Jackass." Jack was everything that I aspired not to be as a human being. He was lawyer-spawn, which made me wonder why his rich dad didn't hook him up with better living accommodations, especially since Jack was gifted with an allowance of two hundred dollars *every week*. Perhaps Lawyer-Dad thought that rubbing shoulders with the unwashed masses would somehow transform his worthless son into something resembling an acceptable person. Apparently, I was not abrasive enough to sand off Jack's hidebound assholishness. On top of being an obnoxious cretin, he has some truly weird ways about him, the strangest being a seemingly uncontrollable need to abuse foreign students. Unfortunately for Jack, our dorm was referred to colloquially as "The Embassy," precisely because the Native:Foreign ratio was so low. To Jack, all foreigners, regardless of skin tone, hair shape, rhinal prominence, native tongue, or other phenotypic signifiers were "Chin Lees." Xenophobic Mississippians were nothing new to me, but Jack displayed his particular bias in a very peculiar way: he had a need to abuse Chin Lees with food. A few examples, from least to most weird: 1) he would slide empty, greasy pizza boxes under their doors when they were absent from the dorm; 2) he would make the rounds of the hallways at night, leaving individual slices of white bread impaled upon their doorknobs, creating a Dali-esque phallic effect that I would just as soon not analyze; and 3) he once burst into our room in a highly agitated state, shouting, *"Chin Lee!"* at the top of his reedy, lawyer-spawn voice. He yanked our little refrigerator open and grabbed an orange Tupperware bowl containing leftover tuna salad of some dubious vintage, then bolted out the door. Morbidly curious, I followed close behind. We emerged on the fourth-floor balcony, where Jack stood like Zeus, tuna salad container held aloft in his right hand while with his left he thrust an accusing finger toward a small compact car slowly passing by on the street. From what I could tell from our elevated vantage point, the driver looked to be of Asian extraction. Apparently, that was trigger enough for my lunatic dorm mate.

"*CHIN LEE!*" Jack screamed, as he let fly with the over-aged tuna bomb. It narrowly missed the car, exploding right in front of the vehicle to create what looked exactly—*exactly*—like the biggest pigeon squat in the universe. The startled driver yanked the car into a teeth-setting swerve, managing somehow to hold the thing on the road while looking upward to see if any more plastic-encapsulated seafood ballistoids were headed his way. While I couldn't begin to imagine what our (presumably) foreign friend thought was happening, I could begin to imagine revisiting my boarding options. Especially after I received my bank statement one week near the end of the semester to discover that Jack's ridiculous allowance apparently was insufficient to meet his liquid refreshment and Chin Lee abuse-supply needs. Admirable character that he was, Jack had found my checkbook and had forged my name on a number of checks written for a few dollars each, all of which were made out to a nearby convenience store where one could buy a variety of supremely unhealthy deep-fried chicken parts at any time of day or night. To a lawyer-spawn like Jack, a few dollars didn't mean anything. I, on the other hand, was living off student loans, Sumners grant, and a part-time minimum wage job at the university. To me, the purchase of cheap, supremely unhealthy, deep-fried chicken parts that could be obtained within walking distance was not a luxury; it was a *necessity*. I confronted him, of course, and he managed to talk me out of turning him in to the university, a decision I have regretted ever since. I let it go with him repaying me, especially since another boarding option had, in fact, presented itself. It had not been my imagination; she *was* interested. Janet and I hooked up.

The problems I'd imagined as a result of that momentous event mostly didn't materialize. The university had rules, which of course we followed and then some. I couldn't take classes from her, or work for her, or anything like that, which made perfect sense. They also told her that she couldn't be my academic advisor, a role she filled for other students in the department. That didn't make any sense, but we were in no position to argue. Despite following the rules, we had to endure a fair amount of pain along the way, primarily dished out by people who were violating the same rules left and right. *Amor vincit omnia*, with a few regrettable two-legged exceptions that a plumber couldn't expunge with industrial-strength drain cleaner. I also have no doubt that a large coterie of naysayers was convinced that my relationship with Janet wouldn't last. One scurrilous rotter even warned her that I was only after her money! (Which just goes to show how scurrilous rotters view the world). Before she passed, Janet and I had thirty-four incredible years together. Eat that, rotters.

My first semester in regular classes was hard. I was bound and determined to do well, but what I learned very quickly was that I never had learned how to learn, except for my brush with scholarship through Air Force training and encapsulating the decline and fall of the Roman Empire in doggerel verse. This was long before the push toward standardized testing that has so severely compromised our educational system, but the fact is that I cruised through public school without breaking a sweat, except for a disastrous run-in with algebra. I could have cruised through college with passing grades, but I didn't want just to pass: I needed to prove to myself that I wasn't just glib, silly, or useless, but that I had something positive to offer the world. I was ready to work for it, and work I did, extremely hard. Consequently, I finished that semester with good grades, except for speech class, of all things. I had won awards in high school for speechifying, but in college the professor and I were like oil and water. To me, she came off more like an overly effusive Mary Kay salesperson than someone who'd achieved the coveted milestone of independent thought. To her, I was some sort of radical troublemaker intent upon subverting truth, justice, and the American Way. My "persuasive" speech was an attempt to convince classmates that the U.S. military was overstaffed, a stance derived from my own experience, such as when we repeatedly were made to buff perfectly well-buffed floors on the many, many occasions when there was no real work for us to do. I still can close my eyes and smell the buffing liquid, which had the exact color and odor, if not the chunky consistency, of grade-school lunchroom puke.

As a visual aid for my speech, I displayed a comic book I'd rescued from a stack of discards at an Army base during a TDA in Germany. Entitled *PS: The Preventive Maintenance Monthly*, it actually is an interesting and beautiful piece of work, with colorful characters (the gruff sergeant; the buxom crew chief; the goofy private) who explain in layman's prose just how to install a fuel valve on a Jeep, clean a rifle, unclog an air duct, and so on. I thought that the magazine was very well done, and later in life I found out that no less a personage than the immortal Will Eisner, he of "The Spirit" fame, started this periodical! The two issues that I liberated were from the early 1980s and still clearly bore Eisner's influence. They were done by no lesser a light than Murphy Anderson, a Silver Age master who helped launch Hawkman, Zatanna, and the Atomic Knights, to list a few of his superb contributions to popular culture. Anderson also designed the way-cool costume of Adam Strange. That alone would have been service enough to his country and, indeed, the world, but such targeted use of a medium more often associated with incipient delinquency did suggest that perhaps the military recruiters weren't being overly picky in filling their quotas. That radical suggestion fell quite flat with the professor, who was visibly horrified by my unpatriotic, crypto-Marxist propagandizing. She was not, to put it mildly, "persuaded,' and from that time forward we were like same poles on different magnets. I saved my crowning blunder for my "instructional" speech, by means of which I had hoped to reestablish myself in her good graces. I chose the topic, "What is an Artifact?" On my way up to the front of the class, the professor attempted a bit of levity. "Oh, you're not going to talk about me, are you?" she asked. Alas, she tittered as she spoke. Alas, I never could abide tittering. Alas, my titter-conditioned response, which popped out before the rational side of my brain could apply the brakes, was, "No, ma'am; archaeologists don't study fossils." The room exploded in mirth. I got a C.

While college certainly was work, it also was enormous fun, due partly to the many characters I encountered. Kris was an excitable countrified gentleman from south-central Mississippi whose main ambition in life was to finish college with the bare minimum 2.0 needed for graduation, a goal he achieved with impressive precision. Despite being even shorter than I, and weighing considerably less, Kris had an awe-inspiring capacity for drink. I remember once when, having somehow made it to an 8:00 a.m. class with a few minutes to spare, he sat there, bleary eyed, hands cradling a plastic cup of coffee purchased from a dispenser in the hallway. Suddenly his head jerked up and his eyes opened wide. "Dang!" he said in a wondering tone to no one in particular. "I didn't get drunk last night!" On another occasion, Kris burst into the lab where several of us students hung out, shouting with a peculiar urgency, "Come on! Y'all come on! They got The Beast, six dollars a case!" As any eastern North American blue-collar stalwart can tell you, "The Beast" refers to Milwaukee's Best, a particularly cheap brand of American swill-lager that nonetheless does the trick if consumed in sufficient quantity. "They" were a local grocery store. We didn't see Kris again for about two weeks. When he reappeared, it was with less than exuberant mien due to the possum that had died somewhere in the understructure of his house trailer during his unholy tryst with The Beast. Fortified by copious doses of liquid courage, he'd pulled up the carpet and used a crowbar to rip up flooring until he found the putrid carcass. I think he was a little hurt that we hadn't accompanied him on that adventure in necrotic mammalogy. But, always glad to be providing a valuable service to his fellow sapients, he brightened up considerably as he beheld us all laughing until we cried after hearing of his marsupial misadventure.

There were many other fellow students I came to know and love. Greg, who went on to become a prolific author of science fiction and fantasy, never seemed to be taking anything too seriously, yet his mind was fantastic. He and I wrote a song together called, "Bambi's Got a Mohawk," in which Bambi: a) had a mohawk; b) wore chains; c) was something of a masochist; d) ate a very suspect mushroom; e) hired an assassin to take out his mother's killer; and f) threw up on Thumper when all of the excitement got to be too much. There was another Bobby, who was a real idealist, a real human being, and, unlike me, a real musician. After graduation, he played professionally for a while, following which he became a nursing home attendant, because, as he smilingly informed me, "Old people are cool." Todd had the distinction of being from a wealthy family, a most unusual trait in any anthropology cohort, and one he casually dismissed as we all fished and sang and guzzled beer together. He and I wrote a song called "Land Whale" that was pretty funny, if extremely politically incorrect by today's more enlightened standards. Pam was true-blue, pugnacious, and hard working. Eric never took jokes quite as far as I was willing to, especially if they were at his expense, but he put up with it all with gracious good humor. Like Kris, Jimmy was shorter than I, a trait I particularly admire in males of our species, but his outsized persona reflected both his rufescent hair and his upbringing in the Mississippi Delta, a world apart if ever there was one. Extraordinarily enough, Jimmy and I later would become colleagues in the same academic department at MSU.

Most of the classes I had at MSU were quite good, which made the few bad ones really stand out. Like the photography class where the teacher was so completely jaded and formulaic that he once repeated, *word for word*, an exquisitely boring, monotone lecture that we'd had just the week before. We were ourselves so jaded by that time that we didn't even bother to clue him in. A museology course was so lacking in substance that Jimmy and I sat in the back of the classroom dreaming up ever more outlandish displays to front a hypothetical museum. Mine was a giant, inflatable beer can of the type that, coincidentally enough, began to appear in front of country juke joints shortly thereafter. One instructor blithely informed us credulous students that pre-Contact Native inhabitants of Central America had gotten much of their protein from chili peppers. I was only disabused of that piece of complete nonsense a couple of years ago, thanks to my bemused daughter and her husband, both of whom are professional biologists. Not surprisingly, I remember more about the good classes. There was a gruff cultural anthropologist who put a lot of work into his job and whom I came to respect quite a bit, even if he, too, came across as rather jaded. On the first exam I took in his class on physical anthropology, I cockily provided a smart-ass answer to a question involving the conflict between science and Creationist dogma. It was the first and only exam I ever failed in college. In severely red ink, he scripted a response to let me know, in no uncertain terms, that such unprofessional behavior was not to be tolerated. I got the point, buckled down, worked *very* hard, and managed to salvage an A from the class. By the time I graduated, he and I were on very friendly terms, which I greatly appreciated after my initial *faux pas*. I got A's in all of my anthropology classes, and in most others, eventually graduating with a B.A. and a 3.83 average, ranking thirty-seventh out of a class of several hundred. In addition, I had the real distinction of having a couple of minor journal articles published, a most unusual accomplishment for an undergraduate, and I was the first-ever male recipient of the Lambda Alpha National Anthropological Honors Society Charles R. Jenkins Scholarship, an award that came with a modest little engraved plaque and an even more modest check. Not too bad for someone who still had to tie his shoes the kiddy way.

My academic efforts led to two of the greatest compliments I ever have received in life. Our son, David, had been more-or-less coasting along in school at the time when I moved in with Janet. Shortly thereafter, he became an A student and went on to get a PhD in astrophysics, as clear an indication of our lack of genetic connection as can be imagined. He told me years after the fact that it was seeing me work so hard in school that inspired him to kick things up a notch. I glowed. The other compliment came on our first joint visit to Janet's family in Washington State. Her mom, as original a piece of work as ever there was, made the following remark when Janet mentioned something about my academic achievements: "Oh, he's smart, too!" I could have hugged her. I think I did.

Life had become...*different*. Strange patterns kept manifesting. One of the more bizarre was that students kept puking on Janet. One infamous instance of this malodorous phenomenon, for which I fortunately was not present, took place when Janet was taking an illustrious visiting scholar on a tour of local archaeological sites. True to form, she invited a cohort of undergraduates to come along for the ride, a typical gesture of generosity and respect that she doubtless regretted when the student sitting behind her in the truck erupted like Vesuvius. Keith, who was sitting beside Janet, later described to me the unforgettable sensation of masticated canned peach remnants slithering like garden slugs down his bare neck. Once Janet even was puked upon *in absentia*. At an end-of-field-school party, the teaching assistant over-imbibed. The next day, Janet mercifully let him lie where he was sprawled on a metal bed frame, *sans* mattress, while the rest of us loaded up the truck for departure. He had the good sense to place a newspaper on the floor beside his head, an excellent preemptive measure soon put to good use. It was the local paper, which in that particular issue had run a story about the nice lady archaeologist conducting research in the area. By the time we were ready to leave, Janet's smiling head shot was festooned with morning-after bile. She took it all with amazingly good grace. At least he hadn't eaten peaches the night before.

DOMESTICATION

GETTING TO KNOW JANET AND THE KIDS, AND OUR LIFE TOGETHER OVER the next few decades, remains the single greatest adventure of my life. Janet really was one of a kind, a non-conformist in the most interesting ways. She was extremely smart—valedictorian in high school, Phi Beta Kappa, etc.—and her natural intelligence was augmented by an unquenchable spirit of principle and an exhausting work ethic channeled through quite an unassuming mien. There was nothing between Janet's inner self and the world; to this day, I never have met anyone with less affectation than she. Those qualities were so pronounced that many people persistently misperceived her as unidimensional, espousing real surprise when she broke what they thought of as her character. In high school, she stunned the locals on multiple occasions, such as when she openly challenged a loutish history teacher on his claim that you didn't want "coloreds" moving into your neighborhood because it would cause property values to drop. As a teenager, she earned money by driving a pea truck, a huge thing that she navigated out into the fields and back to the cannery, day and night. (I fell in love with her partly because of how well she could handle the department's field truck; a pretty clear indication of my roots). Janet loved rock and roll, and the list of classic concerts she saw in Seattle while a graduate student at the University of Washington was mind-blowing. She was a huge fan of the Clash, for many years wearing a "Cut the Crap" button to faculty meetings at MSU, leaving many an administrator nonplussed. Janet also was an extraordinarily dedicated teacher, with a rare ability to pull the best out of students who weren't necessarily the cream of the crop. She had a tendency to take on too much, especially since she gave everything her all. That was a trait that I would wind up imitating, although I could never give as much of myself as Janet did. She was magnificent.

It wasn't all work, of course. Janet loved people (especially her students), and she loved socializing with friends. In those days, cold beer could not be purchased in Starkville (Mississippi had some very strange blue laws), so we made many a cheery excursion to various beer joints across county lines. One such establishment I remember for its dim interior and its pool tables, which we put to good use in our own amateur fashion. Janet had a habit of hitting hot streaks, running in three or four balls in succession. It wasn't something she could do consistently, but I wished that it was because of the wryly triumphant grin she tried not at all to conceal. I also remember that particular place because it provided an unusual opportunity for artistic expression. The urination trough in the men's room was not hooked up to a water source; instead, the proprietor would nightly dump several bags of cubed ice into the thing, allowing melt water to carry away the waste. It was an awkward medium; ice sculptures nonetheless abounded.

I eventually moved in with Janet, David, and Nikki, beginning a different kind of life altogether. What does it mean to obtain a family of one's own? It means witnessing the slow accumulation of treasures: colorful books with bright, silly pictures, to be read in squeaky voices; rubber dinosaurs; plastic spacemen; flowers pressed in a wooden frame. It means waking up early on Christmas mornings to listen for the stealthy pattering of feet in the hallway, the delighted squeals as close siblings celebrated the irreverent uncloaking of their loot. It means having tablemates who know you will chide them for using the salt before even tasting their food, and who do so anyway, with amused smiles as you pretend to be perturbed. It means nicknames, and silly rituals, and funny drawings, and spontaneous dance moves that no one else will ever see. It means watchfulness, and care, and demonstrating by obliging example that breakfast is the most important meal of the day. It means worry, and hope, and comforting, and being comforted. It means making stories together. It means love.

We all bonded over many, many things: computer games, book readings, family trips, bad jokes, cheesy TV, long walks, canoeing adventures, and general silliness. I mostly contributed in the last category, which was, I think, a valuable element to add to the mix. Janet and I rapidly evolved into sex roles, something we never discussed but which just happened naturally. I did most of the cooking and all of the mopping and bathroom cleaning. She did the laundry, vacuumed, and mended clothes. By unspoken agreement, neither of us did much in the way of picking up or grounds maintenance. It's amazing how well we understood one another. If I had come in and said, "Hey, babe, guess what? I mowed the flower beds!", not only would she have realized that I was not kidding, but I would have been praised for my initiative. We did most things together, such as grocery shopping and taxes, although in the latter endeavor, she did the real work while I plugged numbers into a calculator at her direction while continually producing a blue string of rote invectives against the system. David and Nikki also had their chores, which provided them a weekly allowance, much of which went into their college funds, some to more immediate gratifications. Once, we split with them the cost of a floppy disk drive for our cheesy little computer by having them paint the entire backyard fence to count as their share. Janet assured them that such requirements would help "build character." As was almost always the case, she was right.

Cooking turned out be rather a revelation, because up to the time I began cohabitation, I hadn't really done it before. From the cheese-draped weenie delights of a Florida trailer park to the loaf bread glory days in Rathaven, it simply hadn't occurred to me to torture fresh victuals with hot skillets or boiling water when their tame brethren already had sacrificed themselves for science and waited, oh so conveniently packaged, for the loving touch of the can opener. My diet, if one would grace such a barbaric lack of palate with that loving word, had been limited and unhealthy in the extreme. The list of life forms I never had consumed, and to which Janet bemusedly introduced me, was an appreciable one: acorn squash, artichokes, asparagus, avocados, beet greens, leeks, fruit salad—yes, I said *fruit salad*—granola, yogurt (both of which are, I'm pretty sure, life forms of one kind or another); and the list goes on. I learned that such products, in proper combination, introduced to sufficient heat and a judicious sprinkling of cubic mineral crystals and minced plant leaves, could provide quite a delicious repast. And while recipes in books usually would guarantee a consistent outcome, where was the fun in *that*? I had a few false starts, including one particularly unfortunate campground episode when I magically transformed a Chinese noodle dish into an infernal witch paste that would have repelled even the most dedicated trash panda. Slowly, knowledge accumulated. Did you know that, when using pre-sliced deli squares for grilled cheese sandwiches, it's best to remove those little interstitial pieces of white paper *before* the completed ensemble hits the pan? And then there was the first time I ever tried to broil fish. With unwonted confidence, I put them in the oven; when I checked about fifteen minutes later, they hardly had cooked at all! I double-checked the temperature setting; all was right there. Fifteen minutes later, and they *still* weren't done. Eventually I pointed out this mystery to Janet who, with considerable amusement, informed me that that little compartment at the bottom of the oven where I'd placed our entrée was where one stores the baking pans.

The computer games were great. Early on, David and I developed a rivalry for high scores. It wasn't much of a rivalry, actually, given that he employed lightning reflexes, startling intuition, and supreme motor skills while I clumsily shoved the joystick around like a demented dentist trying to remove a circus giant's impacted third molar with a toothpick. Our competition was enjoined first on a Commodore Vic-20, on which we fought for the honors in "Omega Race." With a display of graphics hardly superior to those on a Pong console, two little spaceships (featureless triangles) thrust forward at command to bounce off the walls of the screen, which apparently constituted some sort of spatio-temporal barrier for featureless triangular spacecraft. I think it was the little arrows on the right side of the keyboard that allowed you to change flight direction, with the up arrow applying thrust. Little shots would come out of the top of the triangle when you held down the space bar; those would vaporize the abundant floating asteroids (featureless polygons). Some sort of rapidly spinning whatsit eventually would come whizzing onto the screen and destroy you upon contact if you didn't manage to blow it away first. This was, I believe, the only game where I ever managed to post a high score over David. He would have his revenge many, many times over. For example, he would, with admirable diligence, cajole me into playing "Ballblazer." That hellacious bit of programming was custom-designed to be a nexus of torture for those of us who lack any sort of directional sense. You basically had a first-person view of a checkered playing field that stretched into the distance with severe, nausea-inducing linear perspective. You were supposed to imagine yourself sitting in some sort of vehicle or chair. A ball would be released and your job was to catch it on the prow of your vehicle, pilot toward your opponent's goal, and hit a joystick button at just the right moment to fire the ball in, scoring a point. I never even knew where my *own* goal was, let alone how to grab the ball and move in any desired direction; David, on the other hand, could zip about the virtual plane with Tron-like precision. Why he enjoyed playing that game with me, I can't imagine: I never managed to score even a single goal in the many beat-down sessions I endured. I think he must have relished the consternation on my face and the futile invectives I hurled as, time after time, he would snatch the ball and run up unbelievable scores while my own tally remained a glaring "zero" and I grew increasingly motion-sick. I would have felt like a chicken under a clothes basket, had David not been having such a good time.

Nikki was three when first I met her, on the drill field on the MSU campus where a university open house was being held. I stole a large helium-filled balloon for her, which instantly won her admiration, even if the mode of acquisition was not demonstrative of desirable parenting skills. It was thanks to her that I got to witness a number of epochal events, such as the first day of school. Nikki was an incredibly accomplished little thing, picking up crocheting from her babysitter so well that she was featured in the local paper with the headline, "It's got to be seen to be believed." They got that right. She also was a great appreciator of the nonsensical, which I could readily supply with abundance. One Christmas season Janet and I snuck off to Arkansas to pick up a couple of aluminum canoes. We had a custom-built trailer hitch welded onto our Honda

Accord, and David and I constructed a frame on which we could hang the canoes from the trailer without bouncing them off onto the highway. We all paddled up many a muddy creek or shallow stream, Janet and David in one canoe, Nikki and I in the other. It was Nikki who named the two craft, "Air Biscuit" and "Gravy." We proudly, if unintentionally, rode Air Biscuit backward through each and every rapid we encountered during those most excellent years. We might not have been able to see where we were going, but we got a darn good look at where we'd been. It was quite a view.

Janet was the instigator of virtually all of our many adventures. Her suggestions would come seemingly out of the blue—"Let's drive up to Newfoundland for the thousandth anniversary of the Viking settlement at L'anse aux Meadows"—and always were met with the same response from me: "That's an *excellent* idea." She then would explain her reasoning, which might involve any combination of view-worthy archaeological phenomena, interesting cultural events, her parents out in Washington state, siblings Rob (younger brother) and Judy (still younger sister) and their families, hiking paths yet untaken, geological wonders, or just the desire for all of us to get out and do something together. To which I would reply, "Let's get packin'!" or some such homely affirmative, and before you knew it, we'd all be in the car, orbital entry craft of a carrier strapped up top, sometimes with canoes in tow, buzzing off into some unknown somewhere armed with little more than a battered road atlas, stale convenience-store sunflower seeds in the shell, and poor camp stove cooking skills.

Camping was always a riot. Setting up the tents, scrounging fire-wood, fighting to keep the camp stove lit in the wind, silly stories around the campfire, immolating marshmallows into something re-sembling sections of spent nuclear fuel rods, coffee or tea slurked out of cups that hadn't been properly cleaned in days, boiling one's fingers when trying to fill those cups from a cheap aluminum pot: camping had it all. It was a grimy, gritty, and immensely entertaining enterprise. But the mornings were tough. Crawling out of the sleep-ing bag after far too little actual sleep, body feeling like you'd been the tackle dummy at an NFL training camp, never really did it for me. Eventually, I convinced Janet that what we pain-prone grownups needed was an inflatable bed. We got one, a big one that came with a ludicrous little foot pump that produced about as much air per determined foot stomp as a consumptive chipmunk coyly blowing a sideways kiss. It literally took more than an hour to inflate the mattress. There were only two advantages to that exercise: building up thigh muscles and the fact that the other members of the expedition would eagerly volunteer to do any other chore. Eventually we bought a handy-dandy little electric pump that you plugged into the car's cigarette lighter socket, a technological leap forward into the deep abyss of mortification. That damned little unit produced an unbelievably loud noise, an excruciating, high-pitched, grinding shriek like an operatic pterodactyl with strep throat trying to hatch a live coal. We had to hold the car door nearly shut and stuff pillows into the remaining openings while the thing was running, and we still drew looks of astonished ire from every other camper within earshot. And it still took about 30 minutes to fill the mattress! When full, it approximated the size of your average midwestern state. That magnificent bedifice was inflated inside a small circular two-person tent, the bottom of which swelled out into four protruding corners like nylon buboes. The effect was appalling. We called it the "Lunar Turtle." Had Lewis and Clark camped in such splendor, Sacagawea would have scuttled the canoes out of embarrassment.

Our first real road trip together was a momentous one, coming at the end of a camping spree that took us across the continent, where her parents awaited in a house her Dad had built (with plenty of help from the fam; building houses builds character, and all that) on Camano Island, Washington. It's one thing to meet the parents for the first time; it's quite another to meet the parents when you are: a) not yet married to their offspring; b) considerably younger than your beloved; c) from altogether another cultural sphere; and d) scared out of your boots. Futilely, I practiced deep-breathing exercises as we drew close. When we got out of the car, Janet popped out and hugged her Dad, Bob (hugging is a Southern trait she'd acquired due to my dedicated instruction), while I dawdled, pretending the key was stuck in the ignition or something. When I did emerge, Bob gave me a piercing look over her shoulder that said, "Son, if you're trifling with my daughter's affections..." as loudly as if it had been shouted through a megaphone. I got the message. Once Bob and I discovered that we knew the same doggerel poetry by heart, things lightened up considerably. I always will remember swapping verses of "The Cremation of Sam McGee" with him as we worked around the farm. He and Gerry were quite a pair, a delightful mix of industriousness, humor, cantankerousness, intellect, and spark. He had been a state game biologist, she a public-school teacher. Every four years, they dutifully went down to the polling station and cancelled out each other's vote for President. He would tease her until she would punch him in the arm, *hard*, at which point he would beat a hasty retreat, chuckling mischievously. I quickly came to love them both very much, and I think they liked me OK, too, even if I did hug a lot.

While visiting Janet's siblings, I managed to distinguish myself in various ways. Once we visited Rob and his family in Broken Arrow, Oklahoma. Rob slapped some hotdogs on the grill, handed me a weird forceps-like implement, and asked me to bring 'em in when they were done. No pressure. I didn't have the gumption to tell him that I'd never grilled anything in my life. That particular gene was double-recessive in my case. Fortified by numerous samples from his excellent beer stock, I surveyed the situation. Turn 'em, don't burn 'em. Couldn't be too hard. I'd known many a Bubba who thought that a dangling participle was something a dermatologist could take care of with a judicious snip or two, but who could manipulate dead animal parts on a grill with casual aplomb. I gave a desultory poke with the forceps. As if they'd been training for the task since the moment their questionable innards had been stuffed into their mysterious casings, two franks immediately plunged into the glowing coal bed, hell salmon returning to the molten depths to spawn. Intrigued, I tried another poke. Another weenie took the plunge. Slowly, it dawned upon me that the cross-sectional radius of the meat tubes was, in fact, slightly smaller than the grate openings. Good science requires repeated verification. Poke. Drop. The rapidly charring mass was beginning to look a lot like a logjam on the river to Hell. My head cleared a bit as the stress of the situation took hold. "I like mine well done." That's what I'd say, I thought, as I gingerly used a stick to lift the grate, so as to insert the forceps and rescue the burn victims. As I performed this search and rescue operation, the other weenies rolled down the inclined plane, a few volunteering along the way to dive in and save their blackened brethren. Eventually, I fished them all out, wiped the worst of the carbon residue off on my tee shirt, and voila! Dinner was served! I think I got away with that one, but it might just have been Rob's beer stock talking.

Judy lived in eastern Washington State. Behind the beautiful house she'd built by hand was an imposing hill with a bare rock top. I'd never climbed anything like that before. "Mountains" in Mississippi are what one calls "hills," "hillocks," "hummocks," or "speed bumps" in other states. So, one fine summer day, feeling adventurish, up I went. I reached the top and stood proudly surveying the beautiful countryside, like Yertle high above his pond, until I saw a truly ominous thunderhead coming rapidly in my direction. I marveled at the raw power and impressive visual spectacle for a few moments, until it dawned upon me that I was the only thing sticking up on the whole top of the knob. "Lightning rod" striking me as possibly the worst epitaph ever, I did a quick visual survey for escape routes. The quickest way down was a talus-covered slope that precluded bipedal travel. It did not, however, preclude sliding down on one's butt. Pride goeth, and all that. I reached base level about the time both bottoms fell out. My butt was sore for a week.

We all have periods that we look back upon as the finest in our lives. Those first years of being a college student, of doing my first field archaeology, of getting to know Janet, David, and Nikki, and of having adventures together as a family will always be my favorite. Another chapter was about to begin for us all, this time on the other side of the Big Water.

PEACOCK

SABLE THREE PEACOCKS IN
THEIR PRIDE ARGENT
A CHIEF EMBATTLED

The Peacock family crest, drawn by a young lady tending a genealogy table at a county fair in England. The crest dates from 1668. Her peacocks look like parasailing turkey commandos.

An awesome photo of my father's family at their old home place in Choctaw County, circa 1931. Pop is the little blond lad in the front row; Grandpa Charlie and Grandma Dora are behind him.

My Mom's Mom, Inez Baldwin, with her two half-sisters, circa 1930. Inez was really beautiful, like a 1920s movie star.

Granddaddy and Inez at Sanatorium, Mississippi, where she was trying to recover from tuberculosis, 1942.

Granddaddy and Pop at the Vicksburg Military Park, 1954.

Granddaddy and his second wife, Jean who was not nearly so fond of us heathens as was Granddaddy.

Mom (center) with her two sisters, Jan (left) and Benita (right), in Clarksdale, 1946.

Mom (left) and a friend hanging out in Clarksdale in 1948. I love this picture. Mom had it going on.

Pop and Mom at about the time of their marriage. Not sure why I'm so aesthetically challenged given my progenitors.

My all-time favorite picture of me and my siblings, circa 1963. Bennie is on the left; I am the grubby little urchin on his lap. To the right are Robert, Hardy, Dennis, Andy, and Glenn. I think those are B-B guns but I wouldn't swear to it. In any case, I wouldn't have cared to be the photographer.

...p, that's me, about one year ...d. It was all downhill from ...ere.

...ight) The front of the old dog-...t cabin west of French Camp ...here I grew up, circa 1981. The ...tle red Volkswagen belonged to ...ennis who was home on leave ...m the Navy.

...re I am riding a little rocking ...se and holding a gun. Can't ...rt too early.

The back of the house after many, many years of piecemeal maintenance including replacement of the tin roof and removal of a non-functional chimney on the eastern side.

Pop's homemade shop in a typical state of creative disarray.

At the home place circa 1966. At that point the drive and the road still had dirt surfaces. Me, too.

Pop's forge. A lot of interesting experiments took place using this device.

A roof vent with weathervane that Pop made. He could do things like that in his sleep.

A sheet metal brake that Pop built.

Another pic of me with my brothers, circa 1968. Older boys in the back, little kids in front, and Glenn sandwiched in between.

rst grade, I think. *ɔe melancholy pression may flect a dawning alization that my ad was never ing to catch up my ears.*

Home schooling for all the wrong reasons, 1972. Clockwise from the back left are Glenn, Robert, me, and Andy. Check out Andy's boots.

bove) A hog killing. The metal drum d cauldron were used to douse the `cass with boiling water so that we uld scrape off the hair. That's our usin Dwight standing to the right of `rdy in the center. Pop is striking a tory pose so I assume that particular didn't escape.

A typical Peacock vehicle with Hardy behind the wheel.

Pop off to put some meat on the table.

Sometime in my early years. Either it was time for that pair of pants to be handed down to Andy or the forecast was for heavy floods.

(Right) Mom and Chico getting in some quality time. Not all Chihuahuas are created equal; Chico was the best.

(Below) If you don't like the Waldo game that's me lurking behind Sgt. Belcher's right shoulder.

SQUADRON 3704
FLIGHT 374
LACKLAND AFB
SAN ANTONIO TEX
JUNE 79

The eyes and ears—mostly ears—of America, 1979.

nd a buddy at Keesler Air Force
 in Biloxi, 1980. The picture isn't
·y; that's the hangover clouding
ir around us.

(Above) Hey, I won that one! An
Air Force bout at Lindsey Air
Station, Wiesbaden, Germany in
1980.

(Left) SIPTO training at Lindsey
Air Station.

(Below) Ricky, a fellow Southerner
who taught me how to play guitar.
They never could find a hat to fit
his head.

(Left) My good friend Danny at Lindsey. We saw
our first nude beach together while on assignment
in Italy. Neither of us was ever the same afterwards.

Janet in her element, 1982 B.C. That's "Before Claude."

My first archaeological field school, 1984. That is not OSHA-recommended field gar

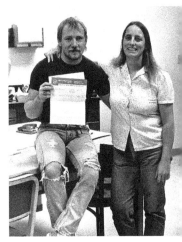

One of Janet's survey field schools out in the soybean fields of north Mississippi, 1985. This one had too few students enrolled for the class to make. Because they needed the experience, Janet taught it for free, a typically altruistic sacrifice of her time and energy that went grossly under-appreciated by the system. That's our puppy dog Hyper, who had the time of his life that summer.

Janet and me in my undergraduate days. We managed professional couplehood successfully despite having to make many adjustments to keep the system from freaking out. I'm holding a report she'd just gotten on radiocarbon dates demonstrating conclusively that a mound site in Union County, Mississippi, was about a thousand years older than previously believed. That was a good day. Plus, I was rockin' that mullet.

Another couplehood pic from my undergraduate days. Janet looks particularly fine here.

David, me, and Nikki, 1985. My main contribution to parenting was lunacy. That turned out to be a useful ingredient.

Out on one of our canoeing adventures. Not sure if the vessel shown is Air Biscuit or Gravy. (Insert) The "Lunar Turtle." Other campers mostly looked the other way.

(Above) Janet, her sister Judy, Gerry, and brother Rob. I married well.

Janet's Dad Bob, her Mom Gerry, and the rest of us at Cape Flattery, Washington State, 1994.

10

A MISSISSIPPI REDNECK IN
KING ARTHUR'S COURT

WITH BACHELOR'S DEGREE FIRMLY IN HAND, I HAD NO DOUBT ABOUT WHAT
I wanted to do next, which was to obtain a Master's degree. I considered applying to various academic programs in the United States,
but then I came across a brochure put out by the Department of
Archaeology and Prehistory at the University of Sheffield, England.
They were touting a number of programs, of which one in particular
caught my eye: a Master's of Science in Environmental Archaeology and Palaeoeconomy. That looked attractive for a number of
reasons. The program included study of a very wide range of topics—geomorphology, soil science, mollusks, pollen, animal bones,
plants, insects—which sounded useful, not to mention great fun.
Additionally, it was an "accelerated" master's, where one basically
went to school for eight hours a day for most of a year, following
which a dissertation had to be written. I could do the course work
in residence, and Janet and the kids could come with me, as she was
due a sabbatical. Plus, I figured that if I could learn to spell the program title, they'd have to give me a degree.

And thus it happened that late in the summer of 1988 we packed
far too many bags and headed off to take up residence in the green
hills of Yorkshire. We landed, jetlagged and weary, at London
Heathrow, where we rented a van and headed north. Driving on
the other side of the road was a bit of a harrowing experience, but I
thought I'd gotten the hang of it until we started coming into Sheffield and ran into—and almost through—the first roundabout I ever
had seen. I proceeded to break every traffic rule in the U.K., much
to the annoyance of the very many other people on the road who en-

thusiastically encouraged me to get a clue by the simple expedient of laying on their horns, cursing, and flipping me off in that endearing, two-fingered way one sees on British comedy shows. One of them yelled out that I was a "bloody prawn," which even in the terror of the moment I thought was a pretty cool invective. We eventually escaped alive, although it subsequently took a crowbar and several canisters of WD-40 to remove my fingers from the wheel.

We stayed in a YMCA for a few days while looking for a house to rent. We were lucky in that this boarding facility stood near the Wards brewery. "Wards Best" was a local brand of bitter, a robust, friendly brew that threw its arms around your shoulders and said, "No necktie needed here, son." The brewery was founded in 1837, ultimately taking its name from a rich partner who bailed the company out of a financial tight spot in 1868. His name, as befitted an alchemical wizard, was Septimus Ward! Take that, Harry Potter. The brewery survived three bombings in World War II, testament to the staying power of a good pint. It did not, however, survive a takeover imbroglio that closed the doors in 1999, and luxury apartments now desecrate the hallowed site by which we used to walk, taking in the delicious scent of hops and yeast on the morning air. Wards was just one of a host of deeply meaningful North Country breweries (Bentleys, Websters, Tetleys, Newcastle, Osset, etc.), and while a number of the most venerable establishments have closed, there has been a resurgence in the art in recent years. Anne Sexton said, "God has a brown voice, as soft and full as beer." I suspect that He has a Yorkshire accent to boot.

The place we eventually found and rented was a really cool old "semi-detached," a narrow, two-story house with a projecting three-faced bay window that likely had been a coal miner's residence back in the day. There was a beautifully etched glass pane in the front door that was invisible from the inside due to a wooden panel placed over the glass. I thought that was really strange, until our landlords pointed out that it was a blackout panel from World War II, which made it even cooler. The rooms were small, but we liked that. The kitchen was way small, but even that was ok, especially when we discovered the flamethrower function on the gas range. A little toaster tray sat on a wire rack underneath a hood extending over the top of the stove. Turn a knob, hold it down, and *whooosh*! Long jets of yellow-blue flame would shoot out like Saturn V exhaust over whatever treat you had on the tray. It didn't take us long to discover that crumpets smeared with butter, then covered with slabs of Double Gloucester cheese and toasted to near-immolation, were manna from the heavens. The butter would ooze out of the holes in the crumpets and run down one's chin, while the melted cheese made my moustache smell like melted cheese, both manna-ingesting consequences necessitating a face wash immediately following the excessive carb intake. As a result, I had a really clean beard and a more expansive waistline. Eccles cakes, very flakey biscuit-like things stuffed with raisins, also were amazing when broiled and buttered. And did I mention that such molten fare could be washed down with a pint of good Yorkshire bitter? I must have been an outstanding citizen in a former life.

We did most of our own cooking for two reasons: eating out was quite expensive, and the experience could be fairly gross. The European mainland has some fantastic cuisine; England, not so much. Fish and chips were fine, and pub grub always hit the spot. Even the "mushy peas," as apt a moniker as ever graced a putative foodstuff, were surprisingly tasty, if of a frightening lime-green hue. But pizza, a delectable staple in Europe, was in the U.K. a misnomer applied to tasteless, doughy rounds of bread made from stale flour bleached over-long in a neutron star, very lightly scolded with a recalcitrant tomato sauce that had taken holy vows to forego the cardinal sin of flavor, and topped with extraordinarily bland masses of some innocuous white cheese that went down like sticky gobs of sheet rock putty. How they managed to find bland cheese in England, only some deranged British pizza magnate could tell you. And that wasn't the worst of the horrors. I once stood in line at a local "sarnie" (sandwich) shop, planning on getting my usual cheese bap, when the customer in front of me ordered "dripping cake." Now, that sounds yummy, I thought, as I began to revisit my menu options. That revision came to an abrupt halt when he received his order. To my utter astonishment, "dripping cake" turned out to be a bread roll sliced in half and liberally slathered with *the viscous goop collected from the pan beneath the kebab meat rotisserie*. "Dripping cake" is a euphemism for a *grease sandwich*. Shudder.

So we cooked at home a lot, which was fine given the wonderfully fresh local produce that could be had at the markets, not to mention the unbelievably good bread cakes conveniently picked up at the corner bakery. Still, we missed the experience of eating out and were therefore excited when a Mexican restaurant opened up in Sheffield! We all loved Mexican food, and our salt-enculturated systems were starved for refried beans and picante sauce. What we got instead was a freakish mutation deserving of nothing so much as a quick burial, *sans* rites of any kind. Whatever it was they served us for far too many pound coins per plate was about as close to Mexican food as Danny DeVito has been to a GQ cover. There were crusty mashed-up beans that didn't taste like beans, imbued with some sort of mystery herb powerful enough to make a border collie lose its way. Some gluey rice maintained a stubborn outpost beside the cow flop of a leguminous entrée. Those already fell ingredients were doused with what I think was meant to be tomatillo sauce. "Tortoise squeezin's" more aptly describes both the flavor and the texture of that unfortunate embellishment. The whole mess was virtually inedible; we nonetheless ate it, if for no other reason than to eliminate the evidence at the scene of the unspeakable culinary crime.

I was not at that time a vegetarian. Janet had been for many years, and both David and Nikki were rather picky eaters. That led to a peculiar situation whenever, on our many trips out and about the country, we stayed at B and B's. The second "B" always included "bangers," a vaguely sexual euphemism for extremely fatty and quite delicious little sausages. Delicious they may have been, but Janet was having none of it, and neither were the kids. However, none of us thought it was right to waste food, and we were too shy to put in special orders, so the instant the host was out of sight, six additional bangers would be rolled onto my plate, making it look as though a Lincoln Log smokehouse had collapsed under its own greasy weight. I would shovel the things into my mouth as quickly as possible before our host came back to bear witness to my unbridled gluttony. One might assume that those generous donations were a long-term plot to be rid of me, save that: 1) to my knowledge, no insurance policy ever was taken out; and 2) Janet was encouraging when I did eventually convert to vegetarianism. The next time we lived in England, I took the lead in asking for veggie options, and of course the hosts were as accommodating as one might expect in a country full of friendly folk, many of whom are themselves vegetarians. They also make really good "veggie bangers," as it turns out, although I shy away from constructing euphemisms.

While we didn't often eat out at sit-down restaurants, there was a very convenient and quite reasonably priced alternative, which was take-out food. There was an excellent little Chinese place a few blocks away from our house, where you stood in line and watched an impressive family operation involving a constant stream of orders, flying handfuls of very fresh ingredients, and far too much open flame. We also liked Indian, which at the time one could hardly find in Mississippi at all. David liked his Indian food spicy, at least until he ordered something called a "Tindaloo" at our local take-out joint. The proprietor smiled knowingly when David ordered it spicy. What the proprietor knew that we did not is that "Tindaloo" is Bengali for "last will and testament." It was beyond hot; it was an infernal hell plasma. We couldn't eat it, but I'm pretty sure we set off a 3.5 Richter scale seismic event when a fiery gobbet dropped on the floor and rapidly ate its way into the planet's core. Where actual human food was concerned, we were most loyal to the "Proud Potato," a tiny little shop on the main drag that served enormous baked potatoes smothered with one's choice of a wide range of toppings. It was here that I discovered that cottage cheese is an excellent spud topper. Later in life, while visiting David where he worked in Leiden, a beautiful little town in the Netherlands, we discovered that Dutch beetroot salad on a baked potato is a foodstuff of cosmic significance.[9] The purple color is a little hard to get used to, but the flavor combination is superb.

9   An appropriate adjective, given that David was working at Leiden as an astrophysicist. I occasionally ply him with layman's questions concerning cosmology, questions that he more-or-less politely entertains. Once I proffered what I thought to be a clever little chestnut that I suspected no one ever had asked before: "What did the Big Bang smell like?" Without a second's hesitation, he replied, "Waffle House coffee at three a.m." One can only bow.

Adjacent to Yorkshire and the Humber on the south are the East Midlands, which one cannot visit without paying homage to the truly monumental Bakewell pudding. Bakewell is a picturesque little village in the Derbyshire Dales, not far south of Sheffield. It boasts a number of historically significant structures, including All Saints' Church, founded in A.D. 920, and a lovely multi-arched medieval bridge. As solid and tasteful as these works are, the eponymous pudding is even more so. According to local folklore, the Bakewell pudding (not to be confused with the Bakewell tart, another jam-filled pastry the name of which has been the bane of generations of local schoolgirls) was discovered by accident when a cook at a local inn laid an egg and almond paste mixture on top on a mass of jam rather than using it to create the pastry cradle into which the jam was supposed to have rested. Upon baking, the result was an alchemical miracle of which Newton would have been proud; the paste rose through the jam to form a heavy, custard-like mass with an atomic weight of infinity squared. Midlanders have been consuming these extraordinary accidents with gusto ever since. Depending on one's level of decadence, this weighty delight can be dusted with powdered sugar and—*pièce de résistance*—a generous dollop of fresh clotted cream! I don't know if it's possible to consume a Bakewell pudding without feeling one's arteries hardening with each bite, but I do know that the tradeoff is worth it, especially when one washes down the delectable desert with a slightly astringent cream tea. Some folks just know how to do it right.

We also liked the snacks available in England, particularly the crisps ("potato chips" to you Yanks), which come in a bewildering array of flavors, some enticing (malt vinegar, cheese and onion), some revolting (borscht, prawn cocktail, beef, roast chicken), some both (Worcestershire sauce and sun-dried tomato, marmite, pickled onion). When we went on our very frequent walking trips out in the glorious countryside of the Peak District, our packs were always well stocked with Double Gloucester cheese-in-breadcake sandwiches, crisps of various denominations, and a variety of candy bars reflecting our personal preferences. I particularly liked the "Aero" bars, which contained a lot of empty vesicles where gasses had escaped, and the "Yorkie," an immensely dense and correspondingly heavy ingot of lowered life expectancy. A popular ad of the time featuring that snack ran, "Yorkshire: where the men are hunky and the chocolate's chunky." The billboards displaying the ad featured a lot of North Country beefcake in various hyper-flexed, candy bar-consuming poses. I ate the things anyway. And many were the Kinder Eggs we opened while occupying table seats on the train. As if all that indulgence weren't decadent enough, it was not at all uncommon to top a hill while on a walk, spy a little village nestled between green hills, and hear the welcome jingle of the ice cream float as it caromed its way down the narrow residential streets. Regardless of how much unhealthy fare we'd already consumed, that little jingle triggered an irresistible Pavlovian response, and we would rush down to intercept the purveyor of a host of really, really excellent frozen treats. Janet's favorite was the "Triple Choc," the name of which pretty well conveys the allure of the whole experience. We never did understand how the English managed to stay ambulant, given their awful diets. It probably was due to necessity, given the relatively low level of car ownership. Whatever the medical explanation, I've seen English graduate students survive all-night drinking bouts and show up to class the next day capable of providing admirably coherent answers on any number of arcane academic topics, fueled only by a single serving of curry chips consumed several hours and pints earlier.

The English are endearingly fond of sports. Football (soccer) was one we never really got our heads around, and any inclination to do so ended on April 15, 1989, when helicopters came thundering over our little house en route to the nearby stadium in Hillsborough, where an awful crush of fans at the FA Cup semifinal between Liverpool and Nottingham Forest led to nearly one hundred deaths. The sports we favored were far more genteel, even if they also included copious alcohol consumption by the fans. And, in some cases, by the "athletes." Darts is a case in point. I'd been a fan ever since I'd been introduced to the game in Germany. I was myself a decent player, but I wasn't fit to stand in the same pub with the real monsters, those who routinely whipped out "one hundred and eighties!" with casual abandon. Darts tournaments were quite popular on the telly. That was great because, in their eagerness to achieve "action" shots, the camera operators would take up position below the players, shooting upward at an oblique angle to capture the full-body glory of the moment. Shooting upward at an oblique angle at your average darts professional is like photographing the Massif Central from ground level. The continental plate of the midriff provides both the physical anchor of stability needed for relentlessly *thwocking* small pointed missiles into a disk of abused cork from a distance of 1.73 meters and an unphotogenic roll of flesh that refuses to be corralled beneath the synthetic fibers of an equally abused polo shirt. Appalling aesthetics aside, those dudes could play! In 1999, we watched the Professional Darts Corporation World Darts Championship, when a corpulent upstart named Peter Manley, who practiced in the newsagent's shop he ostensibly was being paid to run during the workday, took on the world's best. He shocked the sport's elites and electrified inebriated television audiences around the U.K. by reaching the final against Phil Taylor, a giant of the game, if a giant uncharacteristically petite of tummy. Every time Manley toed the oche, a woman in the crowd held aloft a hand-painted sign proclaiming, "Oh, Peter, you're so manly!" Forthrightness compels me to point out that such was not the case. His insanely appropriate corporate sponsor was "Mr. Porky." I am not making this up. Taylor won the final in no uncertain terms, setting up a rivalry that became increasingly bitter and unsportsmanlike over the years, the bitter being mostly in glasses held by the audience members and the unsportsmanlike conduct being mostly on the part of Mr. Manley. Fans were taken aback when, in 2005, Manley changed his entrance tune from Chumbawumba's, "Tubthumping" to Tony Christie's, "Is this the Way to Amarillo?" One wonders whether they sell Mr. Porky products in Amarillo. One suspects that it would be a ready market.

Another sport to which we paid some attention is one that relatively few souls in America ever have witnessed: lawn bowling. We became aware of this peculiar pastime due to a lovely little bowling green located in Hillsborough. We had the good fortune to watch some locals playing there one day and it really was quite impressive, not least because of the players' snappy white attire, which they somehow managed to avoid staining with chlorophyll while rolling hard little balls along the manicured grass. The balls, or "bowls," are not round except for a little white one called, endearingly enough, the "kitty" (or the "jack"). The kitty is rolled down the green first to become the target; the "biased" bowls are then rolled with extraordinary precision to curl in toward the kitty. Points are tallied based on nearness of the bowls to the target. Having been thus introduced to the sport, we subsequently watched the World Bowls Championship on the telly. Lawn bowling might seem like a rather silly game to those of us who have been reared watching steroidal bipeds concussing one another in order to claim ownership of an inflated piece of pigskin, but it really is beautiful to watch. The control of the ball in terms of power, distance, and arc is incredible. Whether one could properly call the dapper practitioners "athletes" is a legitimate question, I suppose. They certainly are artists, and at least the oblique camera shots don't curdle the curry chips in one's stomach.

Another television favorite that we never would have seen in the U.S. was sumo wrestling. The wrestlers were magnificent juggernauts in embarrassing attire; the seemingly endless rituals before the typically brief bouts were quite anthropologically satisfying. The rankings were rather mysterious, but eventually we began to crack the code: Sekiwake! Ozeki! Yokozuna! A major revelation was that the wrestlers' professional nicknames translated into the most remarkable appellations: "The Fog"; "The Sea Slug"; "The Salt Shaker"; "Floppy Tits." Now admit it, how much better would WWA be if competitors had names like "Floppy Tits"?

Art, science, strategy, nerves, beer, snappy vests, and pasty northern Europeans all combined in our favorite sport to watch: snooker. Snooker is an incredibly challenging game that makes American billiards look ridiculously easy by comparison. The Scots always are a force to be reckoned with, probably something to do with lads perennially hanging about in pubs because their country has only eleven clear days in a good year. Our time at Sheffield coincided with the salad days of Ronnie Sullivan, John Higgins, and the immortal Stephen Hendry. Higgins was a family favorite, although we could understand only about every fourteenth word in his interviews due to his haggis-thick accent. To our great good fortune, it turned out that the World Snooker Championship is held each year at the Crucible Theatre in Sheffield! We bought tickets, entered the arena, and found ourselves sitting only a few feet from the most accomplished players in the world. The audience was fantastic; quiet as church mice during play, bursting out into appreciative applause when a particularly amazing shot was executed. And particularly amazing shots were the order of the day. We watched the final on the telly at home, in which Hendry won his record-breaking seventh world title.

Another spectacle we only could see in England was the Longshaw Sheep Dog Trials, an annual competition between trainers and their border collies, appropriately billed as "the wisest dogs in the world." It is an incredible event. The setting is beautiful; rolling green pastures with a somber stony prominence rising in the background, upon which rest the remains of an Iron Age hill fort. Three sheep are released from a pen in a field about four hundred yards from the viewing area; upon cue, a sheep dog shoots like a black and white meteor down to the milling ruminants. Guided by its master by a mysterious set of whistles, trillings, and odd calls (Come bye! Away! Walk on! That'll do!), the dog maneuvers the sheep through an intricate series of actions, from moving in a straight line toward the master to cutting one sheep out for the shedding ring, to finally penning all three animals in a small enclosure in front of the judges' stand. If those dogs aren't sentient, they are closer to that enviable state than many a Deep South politician.

David and Nikki were enrolled in the public schools, a situation they met with equal amounts of good grace and trepidation. There were some interesting moments as they adjusted to the culture. One day Nikki came home upset because she'd gotten into trouble when she and her classmates were coloring. As they were passing around a red crayon, they began to describe it to one another: "fiery red," "rose red," and so on, till Nikki suggested that it was "bloody red," an innocent contribution that unleashed pandemonium in the classroom and earned a stern rebuke from the teacher. How do you explain that to a young child? Bloody difficult.

We saw a lot of amazing things on the many family trips we took. One that was both astonishing and depressing was the wreck of the *Mary Rose*, one of Henry VIII's warships that went down north of the Isle of Wight during an attack on the French fleet in the year 1545. Astonishing because of the remarkable state of preservation; depressing because among the many thousands of artifacts recovered was a peculiar kind of canister shot loaded with razor-sharp flakes of flint, a horrible device for clearing the decks of enemy vessels. We took a trip to Stockholm where we saw the *Vasa*, an almost unbelievably intact Swedish warship that sank on its maiden voyage in cold Baltic waters in the year 1628. That mighty four-deck vessel boasted an outlandish number of guns for the time, but a design flaw led to its sinking only minutes after launching. One era's disaster is another's good fortune; by means of a complicated and dangerous series of lifts with pontoons and cables, the vessel was refloated in 1961 and now is the centerpiece of one of the most amazing museums in the world. My jaw literally dropped when we walked inside and beheld this stunning artifact from a bygone era. The *Vasa* has been preserved with a solution of polyethylene glycol sprayed over the entire vessel for years. As a result, the whole thing glows a rich amber-brown. The ship is incredibly ornate; even the posts used to tie it up in port boasted intricately-carved knightheads. And while the cannon and other pieces of equipment are impressive, what really seals the deal are all the everyday belongings of the sailors: whole chests full of clothing, games, money, provisions, etc. Archaeologists try hard to peer back in time; in the *Vasa*, one sails back into it.

An equally impressive artifact was Hadrian's Wall, upon which we trekked for many *milia passuum*. And castles! David had a particular fascination for the things, but we all liked them. Two in particular stood out to me. Dunstanburgh Castle is a massive ruined fourteenth-century edifice on the coast of Northumberland that eventually fell into "wonderfull great decaye," as the Warden of the Scottish Marches wrote a couple hundred years later. "Wonderful" and "decay" sum it up pretty well; it is the most romantic ruin imaginable. Caernarfon Castle in northwest Wales still exudes the majesty and power of King Edward I. From its walls one can look into the mystical womb of Snowdonia. But be warned; if you peer into that captivating snowy fastness, part of your heart will never come back. I would be there still, leaning on the cold stone walls of the mighty castle, staring into the bewitching mountains, if Janet hadn't lured me away with promises of a Triple Choc.

On a trip to Scandinavia, we stayed in a B&B in Amsterdam, where the proprietress took us under her wing and insisted that we rent bicycles as the only proper way to see the surrounding countryside. She pretty much took charge and arranged everything for us, displaying unusual pushiness for a northern European that turned out to be a great boon. We had a fantastic day cycling around the countryside, catching miniature ferries across canals, seeing "terps" (ancient midden accumulations) and other historic sites, eating like royalty at nice sidewalk cafes and generally having the time of our lives. The only drawback to that otherwise incredible day was the fact that the bikes were not sleek, aerodynamic vehicles engineered for grace, comfort, or speed. They were weighty clunkers of Precambrian manufacture, on which we bestowed names as the day progressed. Two, I remember: Nikki's, a light-green contraption she dubbed "The Tasty Olive," and my own perambulator, a horrifically heavy and uncomfortable conveyance I dubbed "Bunslayer." Before the day was done, I became painfully aware of body parts I didn't even know I'd possessed.

Our most ambitious trip was to Spain, which we hit on one of the longer university holidays. We spent most of our time in Basque country, which was fabulous until I got so horrifically sick that I wasn't even conscious of what hotel Janet checked us into until I could recover. Alien bugs aside, there were a number of mysteries we never really cracked about Spain. One involved breakfast, the hours and locations of which appeared to be state secrets, so that we wound up taking our morning fare at churros stands. "*Chocolate con churros*" is an extremely delectable dish of deep-fried sugared bread sticks dipped into molten chocolate. Delectable for the first several bites, that is, after which the unaccustomed palate tends to go into defense mode, like the first line of planetary satellites guarding against an alien invasion. By the time I finished a course, I literally would be shaking from the extreme richness of the fare. That unhappy state was not helped by witnessing locals finishing off their full complement of churros with gusto, following which they *tipped the trays up and drank the remaining chocolate.* One can only bow if one retains a waistline conducive to such callisthenic endeavors. Because we met very few people who spoke English on that trip, we relied far more than was advisable on my college Spanish, the high quality of which was on display when, at a restaurant in Madrid, I casually ordered orange juice for the kids. The mugs of hot milk that were delivered instead came with a side order of pandemonium.

I do remember some accommodations. One was a beautiful centuries-old farmhouse with glorious views of the countryside out the windows. Another was a cramped, horrible hotel with a communal shower that had a square sort of foot-bath in which one stood while lukewarm water dribbled tauntingly out of the showerhead. One stood, but one wished to levitate, as the bath hadn't been cleaned since approximately the middle of the fourteenth century, when the loathsome black encrustation riming the surfaces began to accumulate. I suspect that some really interesting crusader DNA remains encased in that icky biomineral deposit. We all took turns wearing my sandals as we rotated through our ablutions. The desire to take a flamethrower to them afterwards was a strong one.

The other main thing I remember from our trip to Spain is an impromptu walk we took in the mountains adjacent to Madrid. It was hellaciously hot, and perhaps we thought that the air at higher altitudes would be a relief. Whatever the reason, we set off, as we usually did, completely unprepared in every conceivable way. Our water ran out far before the halfway point, for example, causing me to suggest that we turn back. Janet and David were made of sterner stuff, and Nikki, young as she was, had the stamina of a marathon runner, so on we went. This was not a death-defying climb or anything; there was a perfectly safe and reasonable pathway leading up to the top of what really wasn't that tall a mountain. Perfectly safe and reasonable to anyone sufficiently hydrated, that is. The track seemed to go on forever, as the cruel sun beat down with supernova intensity, baking the already dry air. It was like being trapped in a gigantic convection oven. About the halfway point, the chemical balance in my brain somersaulted into freefall. I began to experience a horrific vertigo that threatened to pitch me off the mountainside and into the abyss if I didn't cling on to the rock face, which I did with a complete lack of pride. I could not look at David and Nikki standing near the edge without semi-hallucinating their demise, so I repeatedly and hoarsely demanded that they come back to safety. By the time we finally reached the top, we were all in pretty desperate straits, so much so that we violated one of the key tenets of outdoor safety by drinking from a spring in the middle of a meadow full of sheep. Fortunately, we took no intestinal passengers back with us. To this day, that remains the single sweetest draught I ever have imbibed.

Going to university in England was a real treat. I was one of a dozen students signed up for that particular degree that year, and we truly were a mixed lot. There were three Greek students, a Pakistani, a couple of Irish, and Brits from various parts of the isle. As the only representative of the United States, I was determined to stand out, a national trait the world could do with far less of. My classmates and teachers took my brashness with good spirit and patience, and slowly I learned to listen more than to talk. The only thing I didn't really like about the program was a strange pedagogical technique by which you had to do something wrong before they'd show you how to do it right. "Prepare a written description of this pig femur." "Wade out into the water, turn around, and draw a geological profile of the coastline." And so on. Once you handed in your feeble effort, the response would be, "Now let me show you how it's supposed to be done." I hated that technique, and never quite saw the point in it, but the practice was so widespread over there that it must have seen some success.

The academic program was very interesting, if intense. We went to school at least eight hours a day, barring holidays and weekends, our time being taken up with a mix of classes and laboratory assignments. Some of the latter sessions lasted well into the evening, owing to the fact that we had to do everything from analyzing snail shells to extracting insect remnants from soil samples taken at

Norse farmsteads in Iceland. The latter task was quite labor-intensive. From a walk-in refrigeration unit, each of us selected a plastic bag full of black reedy sediments. We were then instructed to dump our bags into large plastic buckets where the sediments were mixed with "paraffin." I was unclear as to what that meant; were we going to burn candles over the buckets? It turned out that what the English call paraffin, Americans call kerosene. The kerosene suffuses the chitinous insect remains so that, once mixed, water is added to the sediments and the remains float to the top, from where they can be poured off into screens. The resulting materials are then gently washed with detergent and water to remove the kerosene, following which they are transferred to glass containers that are capped after being filled with alcohol. That's when the real work of analysis begins. One can only imagine what some burly Norseman would have said had he seen us treating dirt from the floor of his hovel with such loving attention.

In the lab, we would sit at benches and transfer, bit by bit, the floating detritus from our entomological samples into Petri dishes filled with water. Peering through a microscope, we would sort out insect remains from vegetation, transferring pieces that looked like they belonged to the same species into individual labeled vials of alcohol. Following all that prep work, we finally would turn to a number of near-impenetrable taxonomic keys and a truly impressive comparative collection to try to identify what species we had. Everyone's favorite bits were the elytra, wing cases of beetles, which could be quite beautiful, many sporting bright colors of metallic sheen. Some beetles had long club-like proboscises, which helped me solve a long-lingering biological mystery dating from the days when we managed to watch "Sesame Street" behind Pop's back. Based on my work at Sheffield, I can pronounce with some confidence that Gonzo is a member of the order Coleoptera, of the family Curculionidae, most likely of the subfamily group Phanerognatha. In plain English, Gonzo is a weevil.

Some of the most memorable episodes in my Master's venture came during our class field trips. They were incredible. We got to crawl around in the attics of cathedrals, learning about their construction and seeing broken carpenter's tools lying where they had been left in the Middle Ages. We learned to identify a multitude of tree species out in the countryside. An enormous metal tube which we saw sticking up out of a mudflat turned out to be the remnants of a V-2 rocket. We visited Neolithic flint mines, where tunnels had been delved into the chalk bedrock with antler picks thousands of years ago. We crawled around on our bellies mapping caves with nothing more than strings, line levels, compasses, and measuring tapes. It all was enormously instructive and fun, not least because of the occasional unanticipated adventures. One evening we came into a town where we were to stay the night. A chip shop was still open just across the way, so I popped over to obtain a quick carbohydrate pick-me-up. As the bloke behind the counter was passing me my chips, he looked over my left shoulder and his eyes grew wide. I turned to look and found myself looking a dog in the face. I was standing up, and this dog was looking *straight into my eyes*. It was an Irish wolfhound; I could have saddled it and ridden it back to Sheffield. I offered my chips in the hopes that it wouldn't eat my face, but fortunately it was interested in neither.

The same good spirit shown by my associates' tolerance of my competitiveness was manifested in another very endearing trait. Unlike Americans, who are always judging and being judged, my fellow students, and indeed our instructors, would spontaneously, and quite unabashedly, break out in song, whether we were in a pub, in a van on a road trip, out in the field, or wherever. One of my major professors, in particular, had a truly excellent voice, and he treated us to a number of folk songs he'd picked up during his research travels in Greece. I loved those episodes. How much more fun life would be if we all could loosen up a little.

There was one area where, to my great surprise, I could not meaningfully compete: imbibing. The typical English capacity for alcohol truly is a marvel to behold. One night, Janet and I went to a pub where a rockabilly band featuring one of my classmates was playing. He wrapped duct tape around the first two fingers of his right hand and slapped away like a maniac at the strings of a battered old standup bass of Crimean War vintage. That was impressive, but the singer impressed us even more by drinking *seventeen bottles* of Newcastle Brown Ale while we watched. The more he drank, the better he got. His Elvis was liquid gold. He was still going strong when we left. One suspects that he was familiar with the sensation of *nausea vu*.

My time at Sheffield was valuable because, while we were required to read a lot of bewildering post-modern treatises, we also steeped ourselves in the basics of many fields relevant to scientific archaeology, including soil science, geomorphology, palynology, botany, and so on. Not that there weren't times when I wondered about the direction I was taking. Late one night I was working in the lab finishing off analysis of my assigned quota of Viking-period insects. I was so tired that my head was almost resting on the microscope as I pushed little black bits of chitin around in the water-filled Petri dish with a fine-tipped paintbrush. Suddenly a long, slightly curved object that looked sort of like a shiny black lacrosse stick came floating into view. Eventually, I managed to identify it as the genital armature of a coleopterid. To put it in layman's terms, I had just successfully retrieved and identified a Viking-era beetle prick. I rubbed my eyes wearily. A beetle prick. Hadn't I signed on to be an archaeologist?

My dissertation did not involve beetle pricks, fortunately, but it did involve snails; lots of them, from an interglacial deposit in eastern Lincolnshire. The snails were used to build a model of paleoenvironmental conditions in that part of the country. That, frankly, was more of an exercise than anything that would set the scientific community on its ear, especially as there were no actual archaeological remains in the deposit. I did, however, look at stone objects from another interglacial deposit, from an old gravel pit in a little town called Kirmington. Whether those objects were artifacts was another question; in fact, it was *the* question. Kirmington is one of a number of sites around the world where the beautifully named "eoliths," or "dawn stones," had been recovered back in the early twentieth century, when the race was on to find evidence of human ancestors as a point of national pride. For that part of my rather schizophrenic dissertation, I tackled the question of whether the objects from Kirmington were "real" artifacts, or whether they were stones that had been broken by other forces of nature (in a landslide, for example, or by rocks rolling in a stream bed, or by having a massively heavy, soil-freezing glacier settle over a gravel layer). Many people had tackled the "geofact" question before me, as a few have since, and it is fair to say that there is no definitive answer for individual objects: a flake of stone created by rocks knocking together in a river bed can look a heck of a lot like a flake of stone produced by an ancient flintknapper. But if one is looking at lots of objects, it isn't too hard to find quantitative differences between an archaeological site and a geological deposit. And once stone tool technology had evolved to the point where artifacts were taking on distinctive shapes, like the beautiful leaf-shaped handaxes of the Paleolithic period, the problem pretty much took care of itself. At the end of the day, I decided that the objects from Kirmington were artifacts, but I would not say that the question has been settled with certainty. Of more value was that I learned a lot from that project about the study of "lithics," as stone tools and tool-making debris are called. That knowledge has proved useful for my archaeological research ever since.

Janet's sabbatical time was put to good use, as she undertook a massive study of stone projectile points collected from north Mississippi during her field schools over the years. Using a classification she herself devised, and employing a powerful method called "seriation," she was able to order groups of points from different sites over time, allowing her to establish a chronological sequence spanning some ten thousand years. She then looked at features of the sites so ordered: how many different kinds of artifacts did they have? Did they show development of middens or other features of settled life? She was able to show with a high degree of certainty that people had begun settling down, or living at sites year-round, in her study area about two and a half millennia ago. That was at least a thousand years before agriculture! Janet was one of the first scholars to show that settled life was not an uncommon condition for hunter-gatherers in temperate environments. That was something one didn't find in the textbooks, because the hunter-gatherers who had been recorded ethnographically mostly lived in pretty extreme environments, like the Kalahari Desert of southern Africa, where sedentariness simply was not an option. Archaeologists influenced by cultural anthropology had nonetheless uncritically accepted mobility as a necessary condition of a hunting-gathering lifestyle. I was enormously proud that research done using archaeological remains from Mississippi helped us broaden our big-picture understanding of the human story, and that Janet was the one to figure it out. Getting to watch, and occasionally assist in, her research endeavors was superbly educational.

My time in the master's program at Sheffield was drawing to a close, so we returned to the States, where I finished writing my dissertation and undertook another pressing task: finding a job. Our foreign adventure had been at once incredibly enriching and severely pocketbook-depleting. In addition, we bought a house upon our return, which involved taking on a steep mortgage payment. The already strange path I had been walking was about to take an even stranger turn. I was about to torture wood for a living.

11

MECHANICAL BUTTS AND OTHER EPIPHANIES

IN 1990, I TOOK A JOB MAKING WOOD SCREAM.

Other than that, a lot of good things were happening. The Hubble Space Telescope was launched, the U.S. and Russia had begun eliminating chemical weapons stockpiles, Nelson Mandela was released from prison to become leader of the African National Congress, and East and West Germany were reunited. The Internet was about to be born, gas averaged $1.34 a gallon, Sinéad O'Conner was ripping hearts out with "Nothing Compares 2 U," while Billy Idol was Rockin' the Cradle of Love. Freddy Mercury was still with us and Desert Storm had yet to brew. Meanwhile, with five and a half years of higher education, two degrees, lots of field and lab experience, and a number of publications in refereed journals, I had no professional job prospects on the horizon. The problem wasn't that there were no archaeology jobs to be had; there just weren't any available within reasonable driving distance of Starkville. Especially because Janet had bankrolled our time in England and had done so on the half-pay of her sabbatical, I felt a pressing need to start pulling my share of the load. So I cast about for something approximating gainful employment, with three simple criteria for selection: 1) the job could not involve roofing; 2) roofs were in no way to be part of the equation; and 3) roofing was a non-starter. Surprisingly, that still left a lot of options.

One I tried that did not work out was to become an educator in our public-school system by way of the "alternative teaching certification" route. Social studies always had been my forte and with two college degrees under my belt I felt like I could make a meaningful contribution to society while bolstering my resume for an eventual job at a university. I looked into the possibility and it was pretty straightforward; take two tests, pass them, and become certified. One test was in the subject area, and I did very well on that. The other test, in "education," was comprised of the kind of stuff people are expected to learn when they actually obtain a degree in that field. I took the second test completely blind and missed passing it by the slimmest of margins, a result that struck me as pretty odd. I then read exactly one introductory textbook, took the test again, and passed it comfortably. That should not have been possible. The book was a jargon-laden mess. If our public-school teachers were allowed to spend more time on substance and less time on "effecting behavioral changes" and whatnot, the benefit to all concerned—which is to say, all—would be enormous.

Not that I got to challenge the system myself. Following certification, I applied for a job teaching social studies at a local high school. The application involved taking another test, this one a rather interesting exercise involving both subject matter and the tactical choices one faces in a classroom when resources for teaching support are limited. I think I did pretty well on the test, but I never found out for sure. I waited a few weeks and, having heard nothing from the school, called the principal to learn my fate. His answer? "I'm sorry, Mr. Peacock, but we really need someone who can coach." That particular requirement had not been in the ad. Some of my best teachers in high school taught history when they weren't in the gym, so I wasn't too upset, but they could have let me know. In any case, the one employment option that did work out paid pretty well *and* had benefits, a situation I hadn't experienced since the Air Force. It was a one-year position as a Research Assistant with the Forest Products Laboratory at MSU. The job involved developing acoustic emission technology applications for the wood industry. I had no particular qualifications beyond knowing: a) how to spell "acoustic," and b) that wood came from trees, but luckily enough, that was sufficient to get me hired.

Acoustic emissions, or AE, are waves produced when a solid material undergoes sudden structural changes due to stress. A piezoelectric sensor detects the stress waves and converts them into voltage. "Piezo" is a Greek word meaning "press," or "squeeze," which is what I was doing to my head a lot as I struggled to wrap my brain around all that stuff. The guy who hired me was interested in developing AE as a way of measuring the effectiveness of different wood preservatives at the cellular level. The system he'd worked out, and that I was hired to put into play, was a clever one. First, I would buy green boards of flat-grained southern yellow pine. Those boards were cut into long strips that were run through a planer to make them all exactly the same size. Then I would clean the sappy green-wood gunk off the planer to keep the shop boss happy. Next, I would cut the strips into little squares about an inch on a side and drill a small hole down through each block in the longitudinal direction, parallel with the tracheid cells. I would prepare a large number of such blocks from different boards and label them with an insoluble marker. The blocks were then placed in a vacuum oven until weighing showed that all the moisture had been removed, after which they were stored in a desiccator until ready for testing. Small-diameter solid waveguides with flat circular bases would then be adhered with high-density gel onto each of four sensors attached to the AE meter. When it was time for testing, the waveguides were inserted like mosquito proboscises, as quickly as possible, into a set of the dried, wooden blocks, which fairly quivered with pent-up drying stress. The blocks were then suspended in glass beakers that were filled all at once with equal amounts of deionized water. The "record" button was pushed on the meter. Several seconds of tense anticipation would pass, then...*crack*! An AE "event" would register though a speaker, a phenomenon signified simultaneously by the blink of a red LED light indicating that the minimum signal threshold had been exceeded. Then...*crack*! *Crack, crack*! *Crack-crackcrackcrackcrackcrackcrackcrackcrack*! The speaker chattered, red lights flashed, and a line graph on the computer screen shot up and down as stress waves leapt like spawning salmon up the waveguides, causing voltage to shoot from the sensors and into the machine! The tortured wood was screaming, and I was capturing its piteous lamentations in the name of science! Bwahahahahah!

That process was all sort of mad-sciency and fun for about the first twenty runs or so; I did it eight hours a day for several months. There is no telling what science would have recorded had one of the little waveguides been inserted into my own mentally desiccated, block-like head. That my stress waves regularly exceeded threshold, I doubt not. Press. Squeeze. *Crack*! I also was having some trouble adjusting to the culture of the place, which, being industry-oriented, was quite different from the iconoclastic milieu of an anthropology program. For example, we presented a poster on the screaming-wood research at a forest products conference in New Orleans. I had been to many archaeology conferences, which sometimes featured receptions with little dry squares of crusty orange cheese and maybe some stale cookies if you got there early. At the forest products conference, which boasted corporate sponsorship, they had smoked salmon and Champagne, both of which I consumed with immoderate gusto. My roommate for that conference was a fellow lab employee who is probably worth about ten times what I am now, but who never had had an anthropological experience in his life, so I suspect that I am the richer one, given a broader set of metrics. To give an example of his limited worldview, when it came time to hit town to get some dinner, he insisted we go to McDonalds. We were in New Orleans, one of the cuisine capitals of the world, and he wanted to hit the Golden Arches for every single meal! He particularly had a craving for chicken fajitas, popular fare at Micky D's at the time. He didn't know how to pronounce the second part of the menu item, though, and it took all of my limited diplomatic skills not to laugh out loud when he asked me, in all seriousness, what part of the chicken the "FADGE-ita" was. I was strongly inclined to tell him it was Spanish for preacher's beak. Eventually I persuaded him to accompany me to a German restaurant, which was as exotic as he could manage. He liked it, even if they didn't serve fadge-itas. Or maybe they did; my German had grown pretty rusty by that time.

My boss at the lab left before my year was up. I carried on the experiments in his absence, producing data that eventually were published in a German wood-physics journal, something I could at least put on my résumé. In his absence, though, I had to split my time with duties other than little square wooden-block abuse. Primarily, those additional duties involved working down in the furniture-testing lab with my good friend Bob. Furniture must meet federal standards for safety, hence the need for testing. Let's say you have a new design for a comfy chair. If a man weighing two hundred and seventy-five pounds sits in said comfy chair twenty-five times a day for ten years, is it still safe, or is the chair likely to collapse under his weight, sending a divine signal that sitting in a comfy chair twenty-five times a day between trips to the fridge is perhaps not the best way to insure a long and fruitful life? How does one even tackle a question like that?

By building a mechanical butt, of course, and rigging up an arcane conglomeration of pneumatic pistons, plastic tubes, pressure gauges, and electronic timers that cause the mechanical butt to sit in the chair at some particular pressure for some particular number of repetitions over some particular time span. Say, forty times a minute for an hour, at which point the infernal contraption is paused while Research Assistants clamber into the scaffolding like Charlie Chaplin in *Modern Times*, digital calipers in hand, to measure the amount of separation between various metal joints. Then, quick! Jump out of the way, a button is pressed, and FWOOSH, *creak*, SSSsshhhhh, *squeek*! FWOOSH, *creak*, SSSsshhhhh, *squeek*! Forty times a minute, with checks every hour, all day long! The "butt" itself was, in fact, sort of butt-shaped; a block of layered laminated wood cut into a wide curved surface with a little valley diving into the middle right where the plumber's crack would be.

That embarrassing facsimile of a human backside was just one of many different contraptions we built to automatically open and shut hide-a-beds, cause recliners to recline and unrecline, test the springiness of couches, and so on. I was a willing participant because I was being paid and because I was really tired of torturing wood. Also, while the work couldn't be described as exciting, it was nice to be associating with other human beings again, given that I had begun to talk to the little wooden blocks and I think they were on the verge of talking back. I occasionally contributed something useful to the design of those devilishly complicated furniture-testing apparatus, although most of my ideas, while workable, were of the Rube Goldberg variety. Mostly I took data and amused my coworkers by repeatedly forgetting that I was working in the midst of metal scaffolding, standing up too quickly and striking my head against the black steel bars with a resounding "bong!" that echoed through the basement lab like the rolling and the tolling of the bells. Bob, on the other hand, was really good at both design and implementation. With a background in mechanical engineering, he could visualize how all the pieces would fit together into a working whole and was undaunted in the face of the many technical problems that inevitably arose when we had to come up with a new setup. Plus, he said, "Yeesh" in good-natured tones every time I rang the bells. I'd never met anyone who said "Yeesh" before. Or since. Yeesh.

When I began the enterprise, I knew nothing about testing furniture except that, drawing upon my vast store of completely useless comics lore, I knew that Li'l Abner had been employed as a tester for the Stunned Ox mattress company, a job that required him to lie supine all day on their latest model. As I learned more about the actual business of furniture testing, I found that reality was scarcely less bizarre. Production of mechanical butts was, in fact, standard practice in the industry. The acknowledged masters of this arcane craft historically have been engineers of the American Seating Company of Grand Rapids, Michigan, who designed a special, heavily anthropomorphized device called "Squirmin' Irma." Irma started off in the early 1960s looking like an oversized kid's doll; her painted cheeks, mop of ropy hair, and long conical nose made her look like something Geppetto might have created as the lonely nights of interminable bachelorhood began to weigh. A description in the December 1960 issue of *Popular Science* mentions that, "Irma's job is to test seats manufactured for theaters, schools, and busses...She's designed to simulate the wear and tear caused to seats by people, particularly young people prone to wiggle." That's something I've always liked about young people. The name has since become oddly generic and is used to refer to any number of devices that drop or slam weights into seating. As weird as this all sounds, there are even weirder things out there. For example, a company named Evonik has an R&D center in Germany where they build mannequin torsos with no heads, arms, or lower legs but that otherwise accurately reflect the shape of adult human bodies. These things lie on cushions and, at set intervals, urinate fluids that are fed into their grotesque forms by a number of colored plastic tubes. The purpose of this carefully monitored, carefully controlled auto-urination is to test the absorbency of different polymers used in adult diapers. *Diapers that the mannequins are wearing*. Try putting *that* on your résumé.

I never had to undertake anything as bizarre as mannequin diaper assessment, fortunately, but there were other strange things afoot down in our basement at MSU. The coffin, for example, a sleek mid-range model that we were supposed to test for structural rigidity. In case someone wanted to get out? It never was explained to me. Or the pillows that I helped slash open so that we could hand-sort and weigh the contents to see how many actual feathers the pillow contained. Apparently, I was an ace pillow slasher/feather quantifier, because the ranking Research Associate offered me a substantial raise that day if I would sign up for another year of sticking knives into bedding. I thanked him, shook his hand, and went home to wash any remaining pillow dander off my hands. While I appreciated the offer, I simply could not fathom another year of that otherworldly existence. Instead, I began a different kind of otherworldly existence by taking my first official job as a professional archaeologist.

This job was in the field where most professional archaeologists—and there are far more of them than you might think—work, and that is something called cultural resource management, or CRM. If done right, CRM is an incredibly challenging profession. One not only needs to know how to do archaeology well—itself a major challenge—but one also must grapple with business practices, finances, laws, how to consult with Native Americans or other descendant groups, what to do if your truck breaks down out in the field, how to arrange for your crews to get their checks cashed, how to subcontract for artifact curation, radiocarbon dating, analysis of plant and animal remains, technical report production, etc., etc., etc., all while trying to keep the crews happy and functioning smoothly while simultaneously managing multiple jobs, all on strict deadlines and with stricter budgets. The challenge is what makes it fun, but it also can be very wearing on the psyche, especially if one is a born worrier such as I.

The job was with a company in Tuscaloosa, Alabama, necessitating a one-way commute of an hour and forty-five minutes over what at the time were some truly horrible roads. Get up way early; drive an hour and forty-five minutes in stress-inducing conditions; put in a ten-hour day so that Fridays could be spent at home; drive an hour and forty-five minutes back to Starkville. It was grueling, but my boss was a very reasonable fellow who kindly let me work from home when I was writing reports, which ranged in size from a few pages for smaller jobs to multi-volume extravaganzas for large excavations. All such work was driven primarily by the legal requirements of the National Historic Preservation Act (NHPA) of 1966, especially Section 106 of that Act, which states that federal agencies must "take into account" the effects of their actions on cultural resources, a general term that can refer to almost anything: an ancient Native American campsite, a Civil War battlefield, an antebellum plantation house, a shipwreck, an early twentieth-century bridge, or even traditional practices such as the gathering of wild plants by healers. Any such property or traditional cultural practice might be affected by management practices in any given project area. Obviously, one can't "take into account" the effects of management actions on historic properties unless one knows what historic properties are out there to be affected. And, thus, CRM was born.

The most common kinds of jobs in CRM are called "Phase I surveys," which basically refers to archaeologists going out to a proposed project area to see what's there. (The NHPA and other federal laws apply only to projects being undertaken on federal or tribal land, in cases where taxpayer money is being spent, or when government permits are required prior to ground disturbance. They do not apply to private development, although such is the case in many other countries). Archaeologists do this by pedestrian survey, either looking for artifacts on the ground surface if it's exposed (like the plowed agricultural fields we surveyed in my field school) or by digging small holes in the ground every so often and screening the dirt to see if artifacts—debitage, ancient pottery, glass, brick, nails, whatever—are present. If they are, then presto! You have a "site" which must then be evaluated for its potential to be listed on the National Register of Historic Places. I was extremely fortunate in having attended MSU, as it was one of the few schools in the country that offered a field school dedicated to archaeological survey, despite the obvious need for such training for anyone going into CRM.

Sites can be "significant" for a number of reasons, from scientific importance to association with historic persons or events, to the traditional meaning they carry for contemporary groups. Some sites are avoided even if they do not meet such criteria; cemeteries, for example, usually aren't listed on the NRHP but nonetheless are afforded consideration for obvious reasons. Interestingly, many cemeteries have been abandoned over the years, with the result that the locations of graves have been forgotten. I once worked on a project in Vicksburg, Mississippi, adjacent to the Mississippi River where a riverboat casino was going in. We knew that the project area contained a graveyard associated with an abandoned African-American church. I obtained the legal description of the cemetery before beginning fieldwork, during which another archaeologist and I literally crawled on our bellies through unspeakably thick privet, vines, and briars in hundred-degree heat, identifying unmarked graves in the cemetery plot by the sunken-in linear depressions marking where coffins had rotted underground. I was proud of our effort, and of the detailed map of grave locations that was part of our report, which would ensure that graves would not be disturbed when a parking lot for the casino was constructed. No sooner had construction commenced, however, than dark rectangular stains started showing up as the backhoe took swipes across the tops of narrow, eroded fingers of the heavily dissected loess bluff edge. Those stains, which were clear indications of grave shafts, were *outside* the boundaries of the cemetery, in an area where we consequently had not bothered to belly-crawl. It turned out that the legal boundaries of the cemetery were a convenient historical fiction. I learned two valuable lessons from that experience: 1) even when you look hard, look harder; and 2) never take historical records at face value. Dammit.

Phase I surveys can range in size from small sub-acre plots (where a borrow pit for highway fill dirt might be emplaced, or the foot pad of a cell tower, to give two examples) to corridors hundreds of miles long (as for a new highway or gas pipeline). It was on a Phase I survey that I found the weirdest artifact I have yet to find in my career; an entire prosthetic leg lying out in the woods behind a housing project in north Alabama. I really, really wanted to strap it to the bumper of the company truck and drive into our parking lot like a scene from *The Deer Hunter* but my work partner for the day wouldn't let me. Another Phase I we did was in northern Louisiana, on a game management area. We found a lot of sites, which was fun, but we also encountered one site that clearly was being looted. Shovel holes and discarded cigarette butts were everywhere, along with other signs typical of illicit digging. Because the site was on federal land, a law with real teeth called the Archaeological Resources Protection Act applied, meaning that if the perpetrators could be caught, an example useful for deterring future looting could be made. We carefully documented the evidence and turned it over to the appropriate officials. A few months later, I got a call at my office in Tuscaloosa telling me that they'd caught the criminals! My initial flush of righteous victory quickly segued into a blush of embarrassment when it turned out that the "criminals" were a grandmother and her grandson from the nearest rural community. The two of them would ride on a four-wheeler down a pipeline route to go and dig some arrowheads. Wisely, given the bad press that might have ensued, the agency admonished Granny, informed her that she was, in fact, breaking the law, and let her go. So much for my reputation as an archaeo-cop.

If a site is considered significant under the NHPA, damage to that site must be "mitigated" if a ground-disturbing project is to continue. This can mean just going around the site, or burying it, or otherwise preserving it; or, if those options aren't feasible, conducting scientific excavations of sufficient scale to save the information that makes the site important in the first place. These "Phase III" excavations can be quite large. The largest I oversaw involved two prehistoric Native American towns found underneath the present-day city of Nashville. The towns, which probably had several hundred inhabitants each about six hundred years ago, faced each other across the Cumberland River (they may, of course, have been parts of one larger settlement). The city was putting in a new bridge, the enormous footings of which were going to destroy large parts of both sites. Enter my CRM company; exit my mental wellbeing.

The reason for the near-loss of my marbles is that any CRM job can bring its complications: challenging working conditions, disaffected crew members, limited time and budget, bureaucratic tangles, unhappy descendant groups, technical problems, etc. This job had them all. For starters, I was charged with finding a house close to the project area that could be rented for a few months to house the crew. Given that we might have fifteen or more people working on the site at any one time, that was no small order. Ultimately, the only domicile I could find that was large enough, close enough, and available was an abandoned two-story house that last had served as a funeral parlor. Inside that somber building, we set up cots, hammocks, and whatever else we could cobble together for bedding. The guys slept in what had been the reposing room. The shower room was an enormous square thing tiled from floor to ceiling, with a huge drain right in the middle of the floor. We didn't like to think about what activities had taken place in there. The neighborhood looked rather seedy, but I paid little attention to that fact while I focused on getting things arranged. It was only at the end of the first day of moving in the crew, when everyone was hot, tired, and irritable, that I truly became aware of the questionable nature of our environs. I decided to spring for pizza for everyone, to reward them for a hard day's effort and to get our working relationship off on the right foot. When I gave the pizza guy our address over the phone, he said, "Sorry, chief. We don't deliver to that part of town." As he hung up, a blinking red light went on in my amygdala. What was illuminated was the beginning of one of the most difficult episodes in my life.

As we headed out to work the next day, I spied fresh syringes in the front yard, another clue that we were unlikely to meet Mr. Rogers taking his daily constitutional on our block. The sites themselves were fantastic; amazing archaeology, amazingly well-preserved underneath the more recent detritus of Nashville. There were thick middens, or layers of nutrient-enriched soil teeming with artifacts, the product of centuries of occupation by Native peoples. There were enormous hearth facilities, bathtub-shaped clay basins with flat floors, the soil around which had been scorched by the heat of the fires that had burned within. There were amazingly thick pieces of broken "salt pan" pottery, the remains of large shallow dishes used to boil off brine from the adjacent salt springs. There were stone-box graves, literally coffins made of slabs of limestone pried up out of the bed of the Cumberland, often containing more than one individual human skeleton. In short, the sites were easily among the most amazing, impressive archaeological deposits I ever had been involved with. And, within a couple of months, I almost didn't care.

It's not that my attitude was inherently sour; it's that my soul was shriveling under the multitudinous demands of the job, many facets of which were only nominally under my control. The sites were quite complex, which meant that the work was technically very demanding, and I had all I could do trying to make sure that everyone was doing a good job. As it turned out, I had to do more; much, much more. I was the only one allowed to run the brand-new total station surveying instrument, used for topographic mapping and laying out excavation units on our grid. I had to arrange for a place for us to store our equipment near the site, ultimately striking a deal with a local warehouse operator in exchange for an open invitation to every after-work beer-drinking bout we had. I had to monitor those portions of the sites we weren't excavating while a backhoe operator scraped away the soil to see if we'd missed any human burials or other important features. I had to find a place for the crew to cash their checks. I had to find a supplier of hose for our water pump. I had to identify and hire a security firm to help keep artifact looters away from the sites at night. I had to help our firm negotiate with the state, the city, the developers, and people who presented themselves as descendants of the site's inhabitants. That final group was an interesting bunch of folks. One of them, George, circled us with a bee smoker stuffed with burning sage. What he was burning was a plant native to the Mediterranean and northern

Africa, a ceremonial practice that I suspect would have left the site's original inhabitants at least as bemused as our reverential treatment of their broken pottery and other refuse. At least the smoke helped cut the smell of the nearby rendering plant that sat on the river upstream—and upwind—of our dig. At the end of the project, I gave George a large projectile point I'd fashioned out of beautiful white novaculite and he gave me a stick he'd carved with faces on the knots and decorated with beads and feathers. We parted friends, which was gratifying.

Nashville was not at that time a happy place, having a large number of homeless and a high crime rate, with both of which we gained personal experience. One homeless family, in particular, showed up at the dig one day in the most incredibly beat-up old station wagon imaginable. The dusty doors creaked open and out spilled a very large brood of equally dusty children. An impressively large, extremely hirsute man who looked for all the world like Earthquake McGoon (for all you vintage-comic fans) approached me, accompanied by an only slightly less hirsute woman whom I assumed was Mrs. McGoon. Jabbing a horny finger into my chest, he demanded to know, in a very threatening tone, if I had any problem with them "building their house" on the riverbank near our project area. I assured him that his housing concerns were not my responsibility. Before the day was done, he and his clan had erected a passable shelter using various bits of flotsam gathered from alongside the river. That shaky edifice stood for a few days until, while the family were out doing whatever it was homeless McGoons did all day, workers for the city came in and knocked it down with a backhoe. When the McGoons returned that afternoon, I had another grimy finger shoved into my chest, accompanied by a question I never had been asked before or since: "Where's my house?" I could only assert blamelessness, commiserate with his situation, curse "The Man" in a companionly way, and watch, relieved, as they loaded up and re-imbarked to find some other spot on the riverbank more welcoming to McGoon-kind.

My boss decreed that the crew would not receive per diem; rather, I had to find someone to cater our meals. After diligent searching, I finally found a local restaurant willing to take on the task, and to their credit they worked very hard to provide us with decent food. But per diem is a thing sacred to archaeological field crews, many members of which prefer to live on peanut butter and crackers while pocketing the extra cash. Instead, they had to eat whatever the caterers provided and, ironically, the greater the effort to create tasty, out-of-the-ordinary meals, the less it was appreciated. I could commiserate. There's something about coming in bone tired from a very strenuous day of field work that doesn't exactly prime one's palate for a nice hot bowl of "Autumn Bisque." Mac and cheese would have been more the thing. I tried to assuage the consequent hard feelings of the crew by constantly providing another staple of archaeological field projects—beer—out of my own pocket. That helped, but only to a limited extent. By the end of the project, I began to have desertions, which I could understand but which made my life even more difficult because I had a job to complete. I was sharing the crew's living, eating, and work situations, and in fact I was asking nothing of them that I did not undertake to do myself. There were, in fact, only two differences between us: 1) I was shouldered with enormous responsibilities that did not remotely end with the work day; and 2) I had a full-time, decent-paying job, whereas they were being paid much less for a temporary gig. Crew bosses in any business that is seasonal in nature know exactly what I am talking about. I confess that such worries were not something I'd anticipated when I stood in front of the Cobb Institute as a kid, dreaming about Egyptian tombs, Olmec pyramids, and Incan roads long untrodden.

As the long, long days went by, the problems multiplied. A crew member's car was stolen. Someone came into the house and, somehow managing to avoid the notice of the lab crew working there, stole a prized guitar. Deadlines loomed. Looters hit the sites, reflecting the less-than-sterling quality of our hired security. Lawyers abounded as parties with competing interests in the project clashed. And they still wouldn't deliver pizza to our funeral parlor. On top of all that, I simply couldn't stand being away from Janet and the kids for more than five days at a time, so every Friday, after an exhausting week's work, I would drive the five hours home, then reluctantly leave after lunch on Sundays to head back up to Nashville in time to prep for the next week.

Somehow, it all got done, but as things were wrapping up on that project, an unbelievably fortuitous event occurred: an archaeology job with the U.S. Forest Service opened up in Ackerman, Mississippi, only thirty miles west of Starkville! I applied, and I applied hard. To my immense relief, I got the job, and one of the more stressful chapters in my professional life ended. Commercial archaeology has evolved a lot since those days, and I have no qualms about recommending it as a career path for students. In fact, I like to recommend it, now that good practitioners are helping the business continue to evolve in positive ways. But for those in charge, there are few enterprises more challenging, especially if one tries to do the archaeology well. Good CRM archaeologists are easily among the best archaeologists in the world. I cannot say that I consistently managed to do a good job, but I can say that I tried. Along the way, I learned some extremely valuable lessons that, ultimately, I would carry into the classroom, making me a far better teacher than I would otherwise have been. But a penultimate stop came first; another stint in Federal service, only this time with a shovel instead of a soldering iron in my hand.

12

ON HOLEY GROUND

I WILL NEVER FORGET MY FIRST DAY ON THE JOB WITH THE U.S. FOREST Service. No sooner had I walked through the door of the headquarters of the Tombigbee National Forest than I found myself closeted in the District Ranger's office with that green-suited overlord and his two most highly-ranked minions, the Timber Management Assistant or TMA, and the Other Resources Assistant, or ORA. I swear I am not making that last one up. Let me explain the context of the conversation that ensued. Despite the fact that the NHPA had been signed into law in 1966, the Forest Service, like many federal agencies, had taken its sweet time in adjusting to the requirements of the legislation. This was particularly true in the Deep South for two simple reasons: there was relatively little "give a care" on the parts of the citizenry where environmentalism or historic preservation was concerned, and trees meant money. Part of the proceeds from each timber sale went to the host counties, which desperately needed the cash for schools, roads, etc. National Forests were created by the Weeks Act, signed into law by President Taft in 1911 to protect watersheds and promote fire control and conservation. Many such forests were created from horribly degraded agricultural lands. Later, millions of trees were planted by the Civilian Conservation Corp, one of the vanguard efforts of the New Deal legislation signed into law by Franklin D. Roosevelt. An explicit stipulation of the laws is that our National Forests exist partly to provide a steady source of timber. They definitely have served that purpose, sometimes at the expense of other resources.

Another pertinent piece of legislation is the National Environmental Policy Act, or NEPA, signed into law by Richard Nixon in 1970. NEPA is an extraordinary law, one that requires the federal government to publish its intent to carry out projects, to develop different alternatives for carrying out those projects, to solicit public comments on those alternatives, and to then take those comments into consideration before the agency reaches a decision on how to proceed. There are many cases, of course, where some government agency has paid only lip service to the law, receiving but ignoring public comment as it pushed to do things the way it wanted to in the first place. Not coincidentally, there also are many cases where some federal agency wound up in court as a result, where as often as not they lost the legal battle. Far more often, the process has resulted in a balanced approach and consequent wise management. Magna Carta, Shmagna Schmarta; NEPA is *real* democracy in action.

My colleagues were not thrilled that they had, by order of the Chief of the Forest Service at the time, finally been forced to hire the requisite number of archaeologists in Mississippi to meet the mandates of NHPA, NEPA, and other laws that directly or indirectly intersect with CRM. What, they demanded to know, as I sat there being grilled in the Ranger's office, was to be considered "significant"? If my fellow archaeologists had put them up to it, my new colleagues could not have asked a more difficult question. I knew very well that the answer most likely to piss them off would be "It depends," because they wanted immediate, unequivocal guidance on just how much trouble I was going to cause where their many other, equally important responsibilities were concerned. Steadying my nerves, I looked each of them in the face in turn, and gave them a straightforward and honest answer.

"It depends," I said.

How could it not depend? "Significance" always has been a fluid concept. Seventy years ago, few archaeologists bothered keeping wood charcoal recovered from their excavations. After all, we already knew that past peoples made fires, right? Then, in 1950 came radiocarbon dating, which happens to work very well on charred plant remains. Suddenly, all that stuff we'd been throwing out became very important indeed, such that the presence of charcoal at an otherwise poorly-dated site might be a reason for considering that site to be significant. On top of such ever-evolving scholarly contexts, it so happened that very little CRM work had been carried out on the National Forests where I would be working; they were pretty much blank spaces on the archaeological map. With a few notable exceptions, what little work had been done was not of especially good quality. Accordingly, until I had a better idea of what actually was out there, I had no basis for making decisions about what kinds of sites I would consider to be significant. My new colleagues weren't satisfied with such answers, of course, but there wasn't much they could do about it, since I was the resident expert. As I left the room, the TMA said in a semi-challenging tone, "I just hope you find enough to make all this worthwhile."

Be careful what you wish for.

Before I go further, it is important to note on my colleagues' behalf that they had little reason to believe that anything of archaeological interest would be found on the National Forests of north Mississippi. In fact, they had been told that was the case. *By archaeologists.* Over many years, a series of contractors, some holding Ph.D.s, ostensibly had examined areas where timber sales were to be held, or a land swap was to take place, or some other project necessitated hiring them. They consistently had failed to locate archaeological remains. They then had written up brief little reports with reassuring statements to the effect that "prehistoric activity in the hill country was seasonal and limited at best," and because the land had been logged, farmed, and eroded in the past, no sites were left anyway. "In any case, none remain to the present" is a typical example of the status quo of those times. So one can forgive my colleagues for being skeptical. (I should also note that the TMA eventually became my strongest advocate on the district, providing backing that was enormously useful and greatly appreciated. He recently moved back to Mississippi; we now are fishing buddies).

Although I, too, was a novice at looking for sites in wooded environments, I approached the job with a completely different attitude. I was working for the American taxpayer and I was charged with being the authority on finite, irreplaceable parts of our public heritage. There were two parts to my job: 1) if there were archaeological sites out there, find them; and 2) if I found any, do my best to evaluate their significance objectively, so that important ones could be avoided and thereby saved for the public, for all time. That was a weighty responsibility that I took very, very seriously. Put short, I was determined that the public was going to get its money's worth out of me. Fortunately for both me and the taxpayers, Sam Brookes, the ranking Forest Archaeologist in the Supervisor's Office in Jackson, shared that philosophy.

I had a lot to learn along the way, including coming to understand just how challenging it was to do a good job in the rugged environment that comprised my territory. A typical day went like this: drive to Ackerman in the little blue Toyota Tercel Janet and I had purchased as a commuter vehicle; pick up maps of project areas and equipment from the office; drive to some such project area, which might be, for example, a timber sale area consisting of several stands of trees and typically comprising a couple hundred acres or so which needed to be investigated; park the truck and suit up. Because I often worked alone, I had to carry everything I would need to be properly equipped for a day of archaeological survey in the dense woods. Heavy hiking boots? Check. Heavy, reinforced-fabric snake leggings? Check. Tough leather gloves? Check. Hardhat? Check. Shovel? Check. Wooden frame with wire mesh screen for sieving dirt? Check. Trowel, radio, compass? Check, check, check. From my belt hung two canteens full of water and a radio handset with all the transmitting power of an asthmatic cicada, which device I was required to carry for safety purposes. I suppose I could have thrown it at a wild animal in case of attack. I always donned an orange hunting vest, both for visibility in the gun-toting culture area I inhabited and for its carrying capacity. Into various pockets and pouches on the vest I would stuff a three-meter measuring tape, a thirty-meter reel tape, a metal clipboard with forms for recording sites, bug spray, plastic bags for holding artifacts, brightly-colored flagging tape for marking out sites, a camera, pencils and Sharpies, toilet paper, and lunch. As I found sites and collected artifacts by the bagful, that already heavy piece of apparel grew steadily heavier. I began to look askance at comics in which superheroes rely on artificial augmentation. Bug spray and gloves notwithstanding, my official alter ego, had I adopted one, would have been "Tick Boy" or "Poison Ivy Man."

On an average summer day, by the time I got geared up I already would be soaking wet with sweat. I learned early on to keep the project area map folded up in a sealed plastic bag to prevent it from disintegrating as first my shirt, and then my vest, became sodden with salty archaeologist exudate. The woods could be nice, open stands of timber with relatively little undergrowth, thanks to prescribed burns. As often than not, though, they were a vine-choked, briar-covered hellscape. To this day, my arms remain laced with pale scars, cursive dermatoglyphics bearing testament to the many unavoidable situations where I could only bull my way through the brush. The ticks seemed to have no particular habitat preference beyond archaeologists. While all ticks are bad, minute "seed ticks" are the worst, for if you happen to walk through a concentration of the little buggers, they happily will swarm through every available opening in your clothing and into every fold and collop of your body, no matter how private. I do not exaggerate when I say that there were days when I would find fifty or more of the insidious little creatures on me when I got home. Seed ticks are so small that days can pass before a persistent itch leads to discovery of an unwelcome hitchhiker. Even when detected, they are very difficult to get a grip on for removal. I purchased a specialized set of plastic tick pliers for the task, which helped. And, of course, there always is the danger of some tick-borne illness. In a typical bit of government lunacy, we were informed that we could not file for workman's compensation or make any other claims related to such diseases unless we could demonstrate with certainty that a tick found latched onto our body at the time of contraction carried the disease. We therefore were instructed to keep *every tick* we pulled from our bodies in individual jars labeled with date, time, and work location for that day. By a rough calculation, that would have amounted to more than five thousand ticks over the seven years I spent with the agency. I sometimes wish that I had, indeed, followed the instructions so that, upon leaving the job, I could have mailed five thousand gross little tick vials to the deskbound nimrod who had come up with that ingenious policy. A nimrod who, I am quite certain, never had actually set foot in the woods.

Besides ticks, I had to contend with spiders, who like to spread their webs just at face level along the paths that archaeologists take. Imagine holding a shovel in one hand and a screen in another while an enormous spider, whose web is masking your gaping features, does a little dance of arachnid panic on your face. There also were reptiles, of course. Mississippi is blessed with having all four of the poisonous snakes of North America: copperheads, moccasins, rattlesnakes, and coral snakes. I have seen all of those at one time or another in the woods and have come dangerously close to many in my lifetime. I once was surveying in a particularly horrible patch of woods in Chickasaw County, on a particularly hellacious summer day, when, stumbling and lurching my exhausted, sweat-blinded way back to the truck, I jumped over a narrow gully holding stagnant water choked with some bizarre, orange scum. As I jumped, I saw snake, and lots of it. I gained an extra foot or so clawing the air, then turned to look and saw something extraordinary. There were two moccasins in the drain, the largest of which was about the length of my arm and almost as thick. It had swallowed the entire head of another, slightly smaller moccasin, which had bitten the big one in the mouth, causing the head to swell up to the size of a softball. Both snakes were still faintly writhing. I was so freaked out by the scene that I hurried out of the woods to get home as fast as I could. In retrospect, I should have lifted the scaly torus up on my shovel and carried it out. It would have made a pretty cool display in a natural science museum.

Despite the very real dangers and the daily removal of blood-sucking vermin, all that time out alone in the woods reawakened a love for the outdoors that had gone rather quiescent during the years since I'd moved away from home. I saw a lot of wildlife, large and small. I don't know how many times my heart stopped when a nesting turkey exploded from the undergrowth right in front of me. Deer were common, of course, and snakes didn't really bother me as long as I wasn't jumping over them. I also really liked the micro-fauna. It's amazing what you can see if you just watch the ground in the woods, as I did every lunchtime. I once saw a tiny spider making its way along the forest floor, nimbly clambering over leaves and other detritus. Suddenly, a larger spider popped out from underneath a leaf and nabbed its smaller cousin! The cutest thing I ever saw was a roll of armadillo pups moving single file through the woods, sniffing at the ground with inquisitive, if befuddled, gazes. I stood still, watching, and to my amazement they came right up to me, each sniffing my boot in turn before heading off to complete whatever Mesozoic mission they were on.

One thing I was not burdened with for most of my time with the agency was a uniform. I did not have a uniform because I was that classic oxymoron, a "full-time temporary" employee. FTT was a status used a lot by the federal government at the time, and my initial letter informing me I'd gotten the job was indicative of the attitude of disposability that pervaded the system. It more or less read, "Dear Claude Peacock: As of [date], you will be employed as a Zone Archaeologist on the Tombigbee Ranger District. This is a full-time temporary position. It does not include benefits. You will not receive retirement. You will not receive a uniform stipend. This position may be terminated at any time. Welcome to the U.S. Forest Service."

Thanks; glad to be here.

They weren't kidding when they said that I could be terminated at any time. I was twice laid off during my time with the agency. Basically, I would work my ass off to get them all caught up on projects, they would lay me off and get way behind again, and the cycle would repeat. It really was a ridiculous way to do business. The second time I was laid off was the worst, because I didn't see it coming. The Forest Supervisor and his Deputy, the two highest-ranking agency officials in the state, came to our district office to give a talk at the monthly safety meeting. They spent some time degassing about nothing in particular, then they passed around a new organizational chart. My position wasn't on it. Every eye in the room turned to see my reaction. And that is what the bottom of a shoe feels like after its wearer has stepped in shit. I nonetheless worked very, very hard during those periods when I was employed, because I believed in what I was doing and because the obligation to the taxpayers is a real one. But I refused to accept the standing offer of a "loaner" uniform when we had public events down at the lake. If the Forest Service wanted me dressed in that fetching green ensemble, they could accord me the requisite status necessitating such sartorial suicide. My job eventually was advertised for real, and of course a veteran from a service period for which veteran status counts applied (mine did not). But someone at the Supervisor's Office (probably Sam, who constantly and fiercely defended both the resource and those hired to manage it) must have made a mighty case on my behalf, because they wound up hiring *both* of us, despite the fact that I'd already demonstrated that I could handle the job by myself. Strange days, indeed.

One way I was able to handle the job was by arranging with MSU to conduct survey field schools on my forests, then striking deals to hire a few of the best students to work with me the next summer. That was fantastic. I loved working with students; in almost all cases they were smart, earnest, and hardworking. I discovered that I had a knack for teaching that made me start thinking about whether I might climb yet another rung up the professional ladder. I think I impressed them positively in terms of taking the job seriously, while still making it fun. I know I impressed them one day when we were working near a lake on the Holly Springs National Forest. It was an oppressively hot day and tens of thousands of biting flies came swarming off the exposed mud of the partly evaporated lake, drawn by the enticing chemical cocktail of archaeologist effluvia. Those damn things *hurt*. Like a migrating caribou driven mad by voracious insects, I lashed out uncontrollably at the clouds of tormenting winged demons. The problem was, I had a screen in my left hand and a shovel in my right. My right hand is my fly-lashing hand. Missing my hardhat completely, I managed to strike myself in the forehead with the blade of the shovel, felling my own bad self where I stood. The students were, as I said, impressed. They were even more impressed when, a few days later, I did it *again*. Yeesh.

Not all of my experiences with students were of sterling nature, of course; many of them had not yet lived through the wild and wooly years at the interface between adolescence and adulthood. Lance, for example, was as happy-go-lucky a dude as ever I have encountered, but it's fair to say that life's more serious concerns had failed to take purchase upon his impenetrable skull. I tried to be a useful mentor, such as the time I cautioned him against eating the triangular sandwiches temptingly displayed in thin plastic containers at the convenience store where we stopped for ice each morning. Especially those sandwiches in which the ham displayed a greenish sheen. As all students of biology know, a greenish sheen on meat is Nature's way of saying, "Why, hello, friend; care to help reduce the surplus population?" Lance paid heed neither to Nature's visual cues nor my sage advice. The predictable result manifested itself the next day when he was gripped by a near-debilitating tsunami of diarrhea. I say "near" debilitating because, again in non-accordance with my advice, he insisted on coming out into the field. I admired his spirit and, against my better judgement, I yielded. I kept close watch on him throughout the day, fearing the worst as the sun and humidity rose. At lunchtime, Lance disappeared into the deep woods, rejoining our group some thirty minutes later. Now, even at that time in my young life I had been to a number of funerals; I had witnessed people's anguish upon the death of a pet; I had seen the look on my parents' faces when we were booted out of a house they'd believed we had been legally renting; I had seen my own face in a mirror after discovering I'd been living alone with giant hungry rats. But never, before or since, have I witnessed anything like the hangdog expression Lance had on his face as he plopped down on the ground, conspicuously far from his colleagues in the lunch circle. He looked ghastly; pale, shaking, and desperately, unutterably sad.

"Lance...what's the matter, mate?" I inquired, concerned.

Sheepishly, he replied, "I went into the woods to take a shit... and it smelled so bad, I threw up on my foot."

None of us were much good for the rest of the day.

My own diet in those days had regressed to something awful. I frequently accompanied my colleagues on lunch trips into Ackerman. Our choices of dinery were limited to two: deep-fried catfish sandwiches and greasy fries at a gas station or Pap's Place, "Where EVERYONE is special and Jesus Christ is LORD!" Pap's is hard to describe, although "surreal" is a legitimate adjective. Cherry, the waitress, was a creature of bubbling good spirit who would cheerfully banter with the customers in an accent as thick and raw as tobacco-flavored taffy. She once tried to enlist our aid in capturing a pregnant mouse that came scampering across the floor of the place. We declined, and continued to eat there anyway. The stainless-steel vats of waterlogged mac and cheese and overcooked weed greens were bad enough; the meat on offer looked like leftover freeze-dried wildebeest. Desserts contained enough sugar and shortening to seize up the circulatory system of a Titan. And all such doleful fare was washed down with huge plastic glasses of sweet—and I mean *sweet*—tea. Not surprisingly, the average waistline probably exceeded the average life span of the clientele. Pap's was locally famous for commercials featuring an anonymous biped in a mind-boggling homemade catfish suit standing next to Cherry, who flaunted a Minnie Pearl outfit while cheerfully belting out the official Pap's motto: "We don't rob you, we just fill yore belly!" Shirts for sale made this admirably direct exhortation even more elegant: "We don't rob you, we just FILL YOUR GUT." At least fair warning was given. Pap's continues to operate to this day. I highly recommend the experience.

For a while the Forest Service had an excellent deal called the Older American Program, which hired elderly local citizens to work part time answering phones, working in the shop, or otherwise providing a wealth of expertise. A lot of trans-generational wisdom was thus imparted, although the flow wasn't always two-way. Miss Hazel, who worked at the front desk, was nice enough on her good days, but she had little patience for smart-alecky whippersnappers. Once she asked me what was the oldest thing I'd ever found. Flattered by the attention, I launched into verbose description of an approximately nine-thousand-year-old spear point I'd recovered from a site not too far from the office. She cut me off before I could finish, asserting with a kind of spiteful triumph that "the Bible says that the world is only six thousand years old." Gently I disagreed, pointing out that I'd read the Bible, and nowhere in that Book is the age of the Earth stated. I explained the history of Bishop Ussher, and how he had calculated the date of Creation; how other scholars had come up with different dates; how it was that Ussher's particular read became dogma and began appearing as side notes in bibles, but that, again, the Book itself said no such thing. How radiocarbon, luminescence, uranium series, potassium-argon, electron spin resonance, amino acid racemization, fluoride, and a host of other physical and chemical dating methods demonstrate unequivocally that the Earth, and life upon it, existed far before 6:00 p.m. on October 22, 4004 B.C., as Ussher pegged it. Finally, I made her an offer: if she could show me where in the Bible the age of the Earth actually was given, I would donate five hundred dollars to her church. She didn't collect, and neither of us ever raised the topic again. Despite such differences, we got along famously, not least because I really respected her and wasn't afraid to show it. If everyone would stop trying to shove everyone else into a corner in this world, we could all share the middle of the room, which would allow us to look out the windows to see the bigger picture together. It's really a much nicer view.

Biblical matters did come up again, in the oddest way. I was working on the Holly Springs National Forest with Jim, a "Heritage Resource Technician" whose primary job was marking timber but who genuinely loved archaeology and was a real pleasure to work with. We were surveying in the high hill country north of the Talla-hatchie River and were finding an astonishing number of small sites. These were mostly scatterings of prehistoric pottery way, way up on the ridge tops. Why Native peoples had carried heavy pots up to those locales, about as far away from good water as one can get in the state, remains a mystery. Another mystery was that, now and again, instead of the usual thin, silty clay loam topsoil, we would hit pure sand in our shovel tests, and we never found artifacts in such a situation, even if the ridgetop we were testing looked exactly like the ones where sites were found. I tried to puzzle this out; had the vegetation been different in the past? Was the sandy soil too loose to support shelters? And so on. I had no real answers. Jim suggested that perhaps the sand was the result of the Biblical Flood, which had washed away some sites. Couldn't be, I reasoned, as the type of pot-tery we were finding was only about two thousand years old. That answer satisfied him, but the situation didn't. One day we found another sandy spot near the end of a ridge and, as usual, recovered nothing in our shovel tests, despite having found several sites in apparently similar physiographic settings that very morning. We dug several tests to be sure, then stopped for lunch. As I sat munching my cheese sandwich and failing to come up with any convincing scenarios that might explain the situation, Jim said, "Dang it, Evan, there's *got* to be something here!"

I dismissed the notion, given the amount of effort we'd already put in with negative results. Jim was insistent, and asked if he could dig a little deeper. I assented, then watched placidly as he deepened one of our standard, 30-centimeter-deep holes in the sand. Almost immediately, he let out a cry of triumph, holding up a very large piece of prehistoric pottery. And just like that, the lights went on. It wasn't that there weren't sites on the sandy soils; it was that the artifacts were deeper! We dug several more such deep tests and found the same thing over and over again; no artifacts for the first thirty centimeters or so, then lots of pottery, including many large pieces, then dwindling numbers of sherds down to depths of about seventy centimeters. Over the next few days, we revisited all of the apparently "sterile" sandy spots we'd tested before and found deeply hidden prehistoric sites on every single one of them. I launched into some serious study of upland geomorphology and ultimately ascertained that this was an expected pattern in sandy soils, as sites were "buried" by what is called bioturbation, the moving up of loose sediments by ants, worms, tree throws, and such. Beneath the culturally sterile "biomantle" was a "stone line," a concentration of artifacts marking the original ground surface at the time those artifacts were deposited about two thousand years ago. Below the stone line, artifacts had moved downward through root holes and insect burrows in the loose soil. The total effect was a "inverted tear drop" pattern of artifact frequency with vertical depth. Ordinarily, artifacts that are deeper in the ground are older. At our sites, they all were the same age, so one had to correct for that when trying to understand what the sites were all about. That was an important revelation, one that was published in a major journal in what remains one of my most-cited papers to this day. Our little prehistoric sites in a National Forest in north Mississippi thus played an important role in helping archaeologists to decipher the record of humankind, as a similar pattern in artifact distribution began to be recognized in sandy soils world-wide. All that return because Jim was too stubborn to listen to the cheese-sandwich-eating expert who was blinded by standard procedures. That was a valuable lesson.

Jim also did a lot of work setting fire to the woods. "Prescribed burning," as it is called, is an attempt to prevent fuel buildup of the type that has led to catastrophic forest fires ever since fire suppression became official government policy in the late nineteenth century. Properly controlled fires burn low, not too hot, and promote the growth of nutrient-rich plants for wildlife. Controlled burning is a tricky business, however, as many variables must be considered, including atmospheric conditions, locations and condition of firebreaks, humidity, amount of available fuel, and so on. The first thing that happens when conditions are right is setting the fire, which can be done by people walking through the woods with "drip torches," metal canisters from which flaming fuel drips out while one walks one's line. For big burns, a helicopter-mounted "heli-torch" (a.k.a., "hell torch") might be used, or a "Delayed Aerial Ignition Device," which basically dispenses ping pong balls filled with a substance called potassium permanganate. Ethylene glycol is injected into the balls, which starts a chemical reaction that ignites the helicopter-ejected "fireballs" or "dragon eggs" after they land on the ground. After a burn, it is common to find the melted ping pong balls scattered throughout the woods. I called them "fire oysters," which pretty well conveys their appearance. They did look like something a baby dragon might have flamed its way out of.

I had no practical experience with burning prior to my time with the Forest Service, unless one counts the multiple occasions when Pop, trying some controlled burning of his own, would set our property on fire and all of us would race out to cut cedar saplings which we frantically used to beat the flames out before they reached the house. My first experience with Forest Service burning wasn't much better. I was on my first survey for the agency, way, way out in the woods by myself in the Holly Springs National Forest, up near Tennessee. I hadn't been on the job more than a couple of weeks at that point, but already I had learned that the crappy handset I was required to carry wouldn't transmit a signal much farther than I could spit if I had a good tailwind behind me. It worked better as a receiver so I left it switched on just to hear the occasional human voice as I worked my way through the woods, plugging holes into the ground as I went. On that particular day there was an unusual amount of voice traffic. Through the staticky fuzz, I suddenly heard one very interesting phrase come through loud and clear, even over the top of the annoying helicopter racket that had been growing disturbingly loud for some time. "Looks like we're gettin' a good burn," the voice said. About the same time, I smelled smoke. And suddenly I realized that my colleagues were, in fact, setting fire to the very woods where I was surveying, apparently having forgotten that their new archaeologist was out there aerating the soil. Suddenly, the helicopter sounded *very* loud.

I ran.

A couple of hours later I walked into the district office, the musty smell of smoke and the sour expression on my face preceding me by a good ten meters. The TMA glanced up as I went by and I saw a little facial twitch of expression/amazement/ concern as some safety switch tardily went off in his head.

"Hey, you're working out in Compartment 38, aren't you? You might want to be careful; we're having a burn out there."

"Thanks," I said, "for the tip."

I eventually became fire-certified myself, which was interesting. I learned a lot about "ladder fuels," "mixing heights," and other topics useful for individuals who get paid to set the woods on fire. I learned that, as a last resort, firefighters battling forest fires carry an aluminum sleeve into which they can crawl and wait, if trapped, while the fire passes over them. I learned that people taking refuge in those devices are called "baked potatoes," a bit of gallows humor that I found to be pretty depressing. I tried to read Norman McClean's *Young Men and Fire*, but found it to be even more depressing. The whole forest fire thing is an industry, one occasionally promoted by local arsonists who get hired to work on the fire crews. Each summer, legions of Forest Service employees go on detail to help fight blazes out West, where pronounced elevation changes, dry fuels, and low humidity can combine to promote truly terrifying conflagrations, infernos so hot that mature trees literally explode and topsoil is sterilized to lunar standards. I gained great respect for folks who undertake the job in those conditions and there was tremendous peer pressure for me to go along. Janet was very much against the idea, and because her happiness always outweighed other considerations, I stayed back at the District Office and helped take care of daily business during everyone else's absence. Just as well, really, since the only time I helped with a prescribed burn on the district the smoke gave me a migraine so bad that I had to stop on the way home to throw up, and then had to confine myself to a dark room for two solid days. Not the kind of help you need in a situation where the slightest error in judgement can mean death.

An interesting thing about our National Forests is that they are favored locales for any number of illegal activities. Dumping of garbage is common, and usually takes place beside secondary blacktop roads. Whenever I came across bags of garbage, I immediately would notify our Law Enforcement Official, or LEO. He and I would then search through the bags for information that would identify the culprit. We almost always found something: a bit of mail, a prescription bottle, etc. He then would place a call and offer the perpetrator a deal: come and clean it up, or pay a hefty fine. Usually they chose the former course, and we would stand and watch while they picked up the mess, typically blaming their offspring all the while. I once found a very weird dump scene. I was surveying an isolated sliver of National Forest land located beside a small country church and came across a long gully nearly filled with all kinds of plastic cemetery furniture: wreaths, little metal wreath stands, flower baskets, faded plastic flowers, etc. Turned out that for decades the church's groundskeeper had simply been dumping the stuff on public land rather than hauling it away. For an archaeologist, it was the ultimate ceremonial site. Another weird crime scene I encountered was at the head of a dirt logging road. I stopped the truck and got out, only to notice that I'd parked in some sort of viscous, squidgy, lichen-gray sludge. Turned out that a local "port-a-john" operator was stopping to empty the things on public land rather than taking them to a sanctioned disposal facility. I informed our LEO; they put out some cameras and caught the guy in the act, at which point, appropriately enough, he found himself in a world of shit.

Another illicit activity is the cultivation of marijuana. I came to realize that fact when I returned from the woods one day to find the LEO waiting for me at the back door of the office, with nothing like a happy look on his face. Whenever I found an archaeological site that I thought might be significant, I would mark it with brightly colored flagging tape so that it could be avoided during subsequent logging operations. On that day, I'd found a really nice prehistoric habitation site approximately a quarter of an acre in size, and I'd left a nice, bright, highly visible boundary to mark it. I was so intent on my job that I didn't notice when I flagged my way through a patch of pot, much to the chagrin of the LEO, who was having the place monitored, and, I assume, much to the relief of the perpetrator who doubtless appreciated the inadvertent warning.

Speaking of crimes, it was during my time with the Forest Service that I had one of the most embarrassing moments of my career. I was shovel-testing through a horribly tangled, chokingly dense stand of woods and undergrowth beside a highway in north-central Mississippi, on a horribly hot and humid day. As usual, I was by myself. Near the end of a day spent fighting my way through the vegetation in truly punishing conditions, I heaved the dirt from a shovel test into my screen, pushed it through with weary arms, and saw nothing except for a piece of bone about the size and shape of a golf ball. It was the ball joint from a mammal femur. It did not look old, so I shook it, along with the roots and such, out of the screen and started forcing my way forward toward the next test locale. Then I stopped. A mammal bone? I went back and lightly scraped the ground with my shovel. It immediately became apparent that other bones were there, just below the leaf litter. Whether it was because I was in a state of physical and mental exhaustion or because I had accidentally inhaled some sort of hallucinogenic spores from that haunted ground, the context of those bones suddenly struck me as very peculiar. Lots of pretty large mammal bones, deposited relatively recently, but long enough ago that a humus layer had formed over them. Bones in an incredibly dense, almost never-visited patch of woods. A patch of woods beside a lonely highway running through a sparsely populated part of rural Mississippi. All of those facts coalesced into three words that leapt to the front of my brain and raised a bright, terrifying flag of warning: *civil rights worker*.

While that unpleasant notion may seem farfetched, it or some similarly nefarious event was not out of the question, and consequently I was presented with a quandary. Should I scratch around some more, to see if the bones were, in fact, human? If I did so, wouldn't I be further disturbing a crime scene? Eventually I decided to leave the spot alone and take the bone I'd dug up to a specialist, which I did the next day. The specialist, an expert in human osteology, agreed that the bone was suspicious, although given its size and condition nothing could be said for certain. At that point I felt I had no choice but to alert the authorities, including the District Ranger, the Forest Archaeologist down in Jackson, and the local County Sheriff. Those august souls, along with a variety of other interested bodies, met with me out in the woods the next day, where the osteologist and I carefully cleared vegetable mold off of what were, indeed, many bones over an area a few square meters in size. It very quickly became apparent that the bones were not human. No sooner had I breathed a sigh of relief than the ridicule began, ribbing (pun intended) that continued when we got back to the office, where loud mooing echoed through the building for the rest of the day. "Oinking" would have been more appropriate, as it turned out that my suspected crime scene was, in fact, the remains of a very large pig. Regardless of the actual species involved, a new one was born that day: *Homo tombigbeensis*, "Tombigbee Man." I put up with the bad jokes for a week or so until we had our next safety meeting, at which occasion I pointed out to the assembled crowd that, with some sixty thousand acres under our purview, there was no way that people had not been buried in our forests. That it was only a matter of time before bones would be found that would turn out to be human. And that, if such possibilities were ignored, we would be in violation of our public trust and legal obligation to pay attention to such remains. The teasing stopped, albeit grudgingly. But my district colleagues had the last laugh when, upon my leaving the agency some years later, they presented me with a cow skull nicely mounted on a wooden plaque, their signatures standing out like petroglyphs in black Sharpie against the pallid bone. That ghastly thing held a place of dishonor in my office at the university until it eventually fell apart, at which point I gladly added it to the archaeological record. I trust the next archaeologist to dig it up will be better at bone identification than I.

In order to liven things up a bit, one summer I hosted three archaeology student interns from England, with housing arranged in a dorm at MSU. This well-meaning gambit turned out to be something of a disaster, due to the fact that none of the young women could drive and public transport in Starkville was essentially non-existent at the time. What with trying to pay proper attention to my own family life, I had very little time to spare for them outside of regular work hours. I did haul them down to the Choctaw Indian reservation in central Mississippi once, where they were refused entry into the casino because the brain-dead miscreant minding the door had never heard of an international student ID card. The work situation didn't help, either. I took advantage of their presence to do small-scale excavations at some prehistoric sites far up in the hills of north Mississippi, work that turned up very little of interest. The interns did, however, become intimately familiar with poison ivy, ticks, chiggers, and impetigo, none of which exactly endeared them to the state. Toward the end of their stay, an opportunity arose to excavate where a comfort station was to go in at a thousand-year-old mound site partly owned by the Forest Service. That was more fun, although we didn't really find much; at least some cars passed by occasionally, so the girls got to meet some locals. One day I was down in our excavation unit when a farmer went by on a horse-drawn wagon. Eager to capture this authentic bit of backwoods Mississippiana, the interns grabbed their cameras and rushed over. The farmer stopped, and shortly thereafter I heard him ask, in a thick drawl, "You married, little darlin'?" His impromptu proposal meeting with little interest, he eventually flicked the reins and went about his way. I wish I could have been a fly on the pub wall when the interns related their experiences back in England.

Being a government employee in the hill country of Mississippi, where the political stripe is as red as the iron-rich clay subsoil, was another interesting experience. There never was tension such as one finds out West, where my archaeologist colleagues have been known to survey in their civvies because it makes them less of an obvious target, but tension does exist. I found myself continually puzzled by the communication wall that stood between our government centers and the populace at large, a tradition of long standing in the area. To give one example, the mound site mentioned above had been partly excavated by a state archaeologist back in the mid-1930s. When he was done with his dig, a bulldozer was used to push up dirt to fill in his trenches and "shape up" the largest mound at the site. Despite such loving ministrations, work done at the site by MSU in the 1990s showed that the five mounds were, by and large, very well preserved, with remnant house floors and other structural features, small pits filled with charred corn cobs (called "smudge pits" because of the smoke they would have produced), and of course artifacts such as broken pieces of pottery and flakes from stone tools. In addition, one of the trenches from the 1930s that bisected a mound was found and cleaned out, and at the bottom of the trench was found a bottle containing a note from the excavator! Despite such finds, many locals remain convinced that "the government" built the mounds back in the Thirties. Why the government would pay people to build fake Indian mounds apparently wasn't a consideration; what matters is that someone told that story, it caught on, and the story remains reality for many folks, all evidence to the contrary notwithstanding.

One benefit of working with the Forest Service was training, of which I received a great deal. Training on NHPA, NEPA, informed consent, and so on. All of that training turned out to be extremely useful, especially when I later had the responsibility of teaching about laws that affect archaeological practice. Useful, but at times pretty dry, and it always was nice to socialize with my green-suited colleagues during the breaks. Sometimes the conversation took unexpected turns. One day a group of us were chatting together in the hallway and the fact that I'd been to school in England came up. One of the staff members at the Supervisor's Office in Jackson apparently was impressed by this fact. At least, she was motivated to ask me, "What language do they speak over there?" "English," I replied, quickly passing on to another topic to save her embarrassment. But I wish—oh, how I wish!—that what I'd said was, "American...but they speak it with a funny accent."

Mom was working in the cafeteria at French Camp Elementary School in those days, which was nice because I got to see her more often. Always a very hard worker, she quickly rose to be manager of the operation. I was very proud of her, even if I could not resist pressing her to reveal the closely guarded secret behind "mystery meat." She insisted in rather offended tones that there was no such thing in *her* cafeteria. But I could have sworn she once whispered, "hound dog spleen" as she turned to go.

I was sitting at my desk one spring day in 1993, working on a report, when the phone rang. It was Mom, calling to tell me that Pop had fallen, hit his head, and would not wake up. It turned out to be a case of alcohol poisoning, or at least poisoned alcohol, obtained from a bootlegger and consumed in what turned out to be lethal quantity. The fact that we still had bootleggers operating in rural Mississippi at that date was ludicrous; that Pop met his end that way, at only sixty-four years of age, was even more so. Pop was at heart a very kind soul, a hard worker, a creature of great native intellect and curiosity, and a fierce defender of family honor. He was in practice a troubled man whose dalliance with the bottle caused a lot of pain for all of us, Mom especially. I didn't realize how much I loved him until he was gone. Rest in peace, Daddy.

After seven years of off-and-on again employment, innumerable scratches and insect bites, untold gallons of sweat and the discovery of one new hominid species, I had, with the help of Heritage Resource Technicians and the MSU crews, recorded about one thousand previously unknown sites on the National Forests of north Mississippi. Few archaeologists ever are so lucky. Like the kudzu I sometimes surveyed through, though, there still were areas of the discipline I wanted to cover. With honorary shovel and autographed cow skull in hand, I bid farewell to federal service and set out to spread my tendrils higher.

13

CREEPING UP THE TOWER

HAVING SCALED MORE RUNGS THAN I MIGHT HAVE IMAGINED POSSIBLE, one more step up the ladder beckoned. That was to get a Ph.D. and enter Academia, that rarified grove where ideas are currency and deficit spending ostensibly is frowned upon. A soil scientist I knew in the Forest Service was being allowed to get a Ph.D. while being paid and having her tuition covered by the agency. That sounded like a good deal, so I floated the idea past my District Ranger, who obligingly took it to the higher-ups. He brought back a memo from one of those higher-ups stating that it was "obvious that this person is not going to stay in the Forest Service, so why support his request?" That is what one calls a self-fulfilling prophecy, which I obligingly adhered to by applying and being accepted into the archaeology doctoral program at Sheffield.

England was just as glorious the second time around, except that this time I wasn't part of a cohort. Rather, I tutored a couple of classes and reported directly to my co-major professors on a more-or-less weekly basis to update them on my research progress. My thesis work was an attempt to quantify pre-Columbian human environmental impact by charting changes in freshwater mussel communities in the southeastern United States over the last six thousand years. Freshwater mussels were a staple food source for Native peoples for millennia, so there are large numbers of shells at archaeological sites to be examined. I found that those species most sensitive to siltation in waterways today began to decline about five thousand years ago, with the rate of decline increasing when plants first began to be domesticated, increasing again when people settled down, and increasing yet again when people first became maize farmers. Clearly, human actions have been affecting the landscape in measurable ways for a very, very long time. We are the inheritors of a human-modified environment; we also are the bequeathers, so thinking about things environmental from a long-term perspective is healthy if we want our descendants to be able to make a go of it.

Upon receiving my degree, I applied for a number of academic jobs, including one that, astonishingly, had opened up at MSU, in the same department where Janet worked! Things got weird as a result of my decision to apply for that one, despite the fact that Janet immediately recused herself from the process, to the extent that she didn't even know who else had applied. Regardless of that action on her part, insinuators insinuated, as insinuators do, and the interviewing atmosphere accordingly was very strange. Ultimately, I came in second for the job, but I also interviewed at Georgia State University, where things went very well indeed, so that I was waiting by the phone for GSU to call with an offer when, to my surprise, MSU called first. The person who'd beaten me out for the MSU position, who had *accepted* their position, nevertheless had continued looking and had, against all professional norms, accepted a subsequent offer from another university, leaving MSU in the lurch. Consequently, the Department Head was obliged to call me up as Number Two on the list. Given the likelihood that insinuations would continue, I had to think about the offer, but not for very long, considering that moving would have disrupted Janet's career, which was in many ways at its apogee. She and I talked; I made the return call; and we wound up spending many productive years together as professional colleagues.

My first faculty meeting was a strange experience. I was in a joint department—Sociology, Anthropology, and Social Work—so the conference room in Bowen Hall was pretty crowded. It was daunting to sit there in the midst of all those prehensile egos. Did I really belong? Had the government cheese and peanut butter spoons of my youth been fuel enough for Academia-scale neural networks to form? Was my remnant backwoods accent still too thick for the erudite to take me seriously? Scientists have a term for this feeling: "imposter syndrome," which psychologist Ellen Hendricksen described for *Scientific American* as "a pervasive feeling of self-doubt, insecurity, or fraudulence despite often overwhelming evidence to the contrary. It strikes smart, successful individuals. It often rears its head after an especially notable accomplishment, like admission to a prestigious university, public acclaim, winning an award, or earning a promotion." Wordy, but accurate. Wisely, I kept pretty quiet at first, taking cues for action from more experienced souls (although it must be admitted that it didn't take long for my own prehensile ego to manifest). Janet and my other colleagues in Anthropology were dauntless: smart, prepared, hard-working, and willing to hold their collective ground on points of principle, which was necessary in a joint department with consequent competition for attention and resources. I learned a lot from all of them, and Janet continued to be my mentor for the rest of her life.

Not that it was easy for her, or my other female colleagues; quite the contrary. Something that I observed firsthand was the unequal treatment of women in Academia. An alarming number of my male colleagues couldn't seem to stand it if a woman voiced her opinion in any sort of formal context. In most cases, the best that could be said was that those guys weren't conscious of their own behavior. Of course, if that's the best that can be said, it doesn't reflect too well on an environment where people ostensibly are paid to be critical thinkers. At worst, it was overt sexism. Some of it was downright ridiculous. To give an example, Janet once applied for a National Science Foundation grant for which she had to have letters of support from peers. She made the mistake of asking a male counterpart at our institute to provide a letter. He did so, summing up his assessment of Janet's scholarly record with the phrase, "…and she has a hint of shyness that is becoming." I remember him showing her a copy of that letter—after the original had been sent, unfortunately—and how proud of himself he was, standing there waiting to be praised for having rendered such notable service. One wonders how he would have described a male colleague: "He has a boyish insouciance and fills out his slacks nicely"? Janet should have brained him, although it would have taken a lot of whacks to get through his thick skull. I can't imagine what the NSF reviewers thought. More nefarious was the holding down of women who were trying to work their way up the career ladder. I sat on a number of promotion and tenure committees at various levels, and I can tell you that it was not, at that time, a level playing field. Women were denied promotion who had records at least as good as men who sailed through the process. It is fair to say that things improved during my time in the tower, but it also is fair to say that more improvement is needed.

One of the most daunting things I was involved in at MSU was the creation of a new master's program in Applied Anthropology. That effort entailed crafting a proposal that had to go through numerous stages of review, including by the Board of Trustees of the State Institutions of Higher Learning, who traditionally have been reticent to create new structures within the academic system. The proposal had to include a fully worked-out curriculum, complete with course proposals, course cycles, degree requirements, etc., as well as a detailed comparison of our proposed program to existing ones within the state and region. Rather to the surprise of our colleagues in Sociology and Social Work, we succeeded, and the new program began in the Fall of 2001 with the five students needed to fill the arbitrary minimum number set for graduate-level class enrollments. To this day, I am not sure how we managed to pull it off. While the university had gotten behind the effort, a chilling caveat was that the program had to be undertaken "without additional resources." While the Anthropology faculty took that to mean "no additional hires," the Department Head and the Dean at the time of the program's inception were more literal in their interpretations. The initial years of the program thus were particularly difficult ones. All student research assistantships had to be externally funded via grants or contracts; no teaching assistantships were forthcoming; no funds were provided for renovating space for students, and so on. In addition, our teaching loads remained at three courses per semester, despite a college workload policy that specified a reduced load in order to deal with the many additional duties a master's program entails. Basically, we had much, much more to do, with no additional help whatsoever. It was a brutally hard, truly Sisyphean arrangement. We'd asked for it, but Lord, how we worked!

In the Fall of 2008, we joined with faculty who were Near Eastern archaeologists, long housed in the Department of Philosophy and Religion, to form a new department, Anthropology & Middle Eastern Cultures. At first, we were going to call it Anthropology and Near Eastern Studies, until someone wisely pointed out that the resulting acronym would be aurally problematic. Slowly, the gamble began to pay off. By the time I retired, we had doubled the number of faculty, brought in huge amounts of grant and contract money, and were attracting large numbers of really excellent graduate students from around the country and abroad. All such gains earned us the respect of the administration, with consequent loosening of the resources belt (and, finally, the correct teaching loads!). The greatest reward has been the extremely high rate of student job placement in CRM, government agencies, museums, non-governmental organiztions, and many other outlets, including acceptance into high-quality Ph.D. programs. I am very proud that MSU offers such an excellent Master's degree, and beyond proud that Janet and I got to help bring it into being.

Generally speaking, university faculty operate in three spheres: service, teaching, and research. Service tends to be the least enviable of the lot. Some tasks, like advising students, serving on a wide variety of committees, revising curricula, etc. just go on and on, like a stream of graywater that threatens to rise above one's snorkel if ever you slacken in your stroke. There also is service outside the university, such as serving on professional boards, filling offices in professional societies, reviewing manuscript drafts and grant proposals, giving public talks, and basically trying to be a good professional and public citizen. That sort of thing simply has to be done, so one simply does it. Some of it can be quite rewarding.

One obligation that I always took very seriously and usually enjoyed quite a bit was to answer queries from members of the general public, whether they came by phone or email, or in person. We made a lot of valuable contacts that way, including with artifact collectors who often were willing to share valuable information about their finds. To give one example, a collector friend once called up to tell me of a site that was being destroyed by a contractor excavating fill dirt for highway construction. Because the highway department was involved, the area should have been surveyed by an archaeologist prior to any ground disturbance. Turns out that it *had* been surveyed; it also turns out that not all archaeologists are created equal. The surveyor in this case had inspected the area, seen a few artifacts, and written the site off as "not significant." I contacted the landowner and received permission to take a look myself. I immediately knew that the contractor had a problem, especially after I spied pieces of human skull lying on the ground surface. The situation rapidly became a mess. The contractor, not surprisingly given that he'd followed legal procedures and hired a professional to investigate the area, was pissed. I think I learned five or six new swear words when I met him at the site to discuss the situation. Eventually, personnel with the state Department of Archives and History did salvage work at the site, uncovering several human burials, posthole patterns marking spots where houses had stood about 2,000 years ago, and a number of other important features. Due to circumstances, the work was done too quickly, and no report has yet been generated, but it still was better than nothing. Without my friend's sharp eyes and willingness to communicate, that irreplaceable part of Mississippi's story would have disappeared under the bulldozer and been lost for all time.

Of course, not all interactions with the public at large were so useful. We received a large number of calls or visits each year that ranged from harmless to downright surreal. Many are the rocks I have looked at that were brought in by enthusiastic seekers of knowledge convinced that they could see ancient writing, or dramatic scenes of battles or buffalo hunts, in the coarsely-textured surfaces of what were just stones. One gentleman told me in all earnestness that he'd found on his land an ancient manuscript in some sort of mysterious cursive script. That would have been pretty amazing, given that Native groups in the Southeast did not have written language prior to arrival of Europeans. I watched with some anticipation as he pulled from a large plastic container a curved brown object about two feet long. It took my practiced eye no time at all to determine that the object was a piece of pine bark, which he dramatically flipped over to show me—drum roll, please—bark beetle tracks. Needless to say, I was unable to provide a meaningful translation. On another occasion, a woman called me from her farm in Alabama where, she assured me, she and her husband had observed a creature new to science that was killing their goats. She piqued my interest when she mentioned that they'd found a skeleton of one of the creatures and had it hanging up in their barn. Upon request, she obligingly sent me a photograph of sufficient quality to allow me to determine that it was, in fact, an animal quite well known to science: to wit, a goat. It could have been a vampire goat, or perhaps a zombie goat, but being neither a biologist nor a necromancer, I hesitated to proffer either hypothesis. Another day the phone rang, and with no introduction or preamble whatsoever, a woman on the other end of the line informed me that she and her sister were having an argument they wanted me to settle: did rats just chew holes in walls or did they also drill them out with their tails? Politely, I informed her that I was an archaeologist, not a mammologist, but that I was pretty sure that teeth were the tools of choice. She didn't believe me, but at least she never called back.

The best (or worst) example of this sort of thing that I ever heard comes from a dear friend who also is an archaeologist. While he was sitting at a display table at a public event, a man brought over a cigar box full of objects, which included the usual stone projectile points, pieces of pottery, etc. But nestled among the ancient artifacts was, as my friend described it, a "brown object ...obviously organic...roughly three inches long and an inch and a quarter in diameter...oval in cross section and rounded on both ends. There was a faint line around the middle and the top part was plain, and maybe a little rough textured. The bottom was a different texture and color, smooth with a slight purple tint." It reminded him, he said, of a small eggplant. After guessing that it was "some sort of seedpod," he was informed by the leering owner that it was his wife's gall bladder.

One day the phone rang and I found myself talking to a woman whose son recently had been killed in Iraq. While going through his belongings sent back by the military, she discovered part of a cuneiform tablet. The scientific value of such an artifact is incalculable, and whether it was simply picked up or purchased it is very likely that one or more laws had been broken, something she suspected and which made the conversation difficult. She wanted to do the right thing but did not want to tarnish her son's memory. She could only just control her voice as she asked me what she should do. Immensely moved, I commiserated with her loss, thanked her for doing the right thing, and, following some rapid on-line searching, put her in touch with the proper authorities to deal with the situation. Service comes in many forms, but that was one I never expected.

Teaching was awesome. Despite the often-crushing workload, I loved it, especially the introductory level classes, as it was a real privilege to introduce students to a wider world. Many of our Anthropology students were simply superb, and it has been one of the great joys of my life to see so many of them going on to become professionals in many fields, proud parents, and outstanding citizens. Many professors choose to maintain a strict status wall between themselves and their students, insisting on being called "Dr. So-and-So," for example. That is a perfectly understandable stance, and indeed may be the better one where pedagogy is concerned. I never liked it, personally, and freely invited students to call me by my given name. Most did, although, being in the South, many students preferred to invoke the honorific title. My pointing out that "Dr. Peacock" sounds like a backup character in Clue sometimes helped. Especially since my retirement, I have become very good friends with many former students, which is both great fun and a significant honor. To any out there who may be reading this book, thanks for making teaching such a positive experience. I am very proud of you all.

Not that it was easy. Even for those individuals with a natural flair for teaching, that first semester usually is a very tough one. Many students these days are in college for the express purpose of getting a degree that qualifies them for employment. Fair enough; goodness knows, a lot of sacrifice is required to get that all-important piece of paper in the Land of the Free, the Brave, and the Student Loan. But that attitude often means that introducing them to abstract ideas and otherwise trying to broaden their horizons may not be appreciated, which is regrettable. The whole idea of a general liberal arts education—that glorious mix of science, physics, history, language, poetry, art—was one that our Founding Fathers embraced as a recipe for elevating the human condition, thus making for better, more responsible citizens. That laudable ideal has been grossly compromised by a number of destructive elements in recent decades, including the imposition of a business model on university operations, the corrupting influence of corporate research support, related (and relentless) cuts in public funding for higher education, self-serving accreditation processes, and disparagement of the whole intellectual enterprise by dogmatists who are afraid their kids might actually learn something. Teaching in the face of that kind of intransigence is hard. It would be much easier to roll over and submit to such forces, never teaching anything challenging, but that would be a hideous disservice, especially at a time when ignorance explicitly is being touted as a *virtue*. Once, Janet and I were driving through the panhandle of north Florida, on a blacktop road way out in the country, when we passed a small church. The inspirational message of the week, proclaimed in tall black letters on a sign next to the road, was, "An open mind is an open gate to Hell." Years later, sitting on the second-floor balcony of a bar in downtown Starkville, I espied at a distance the sign in front of another church, which read, "If you open your mind, you let the Devil in." I am not a preachy person, but one thing of which I am absolutely positive is that ignorance is *not* a virtue; it is an illness, for which there is a ready cure. I know, having made at least some medical progress along that line myself.

Challenging students to expand their understanding can be a punishing enterprise. Even getting to a point where you can begin challenging them in such a manner can be difficult. A surprising number of students enter college with poor writing skills, for example. If one cares about such basics, one will spend an inordinate amount of time correcting such errors when one's time would be better spent on substantive issues. That pressure, along with ever-increasing class sizes (a necessity given that public funding is being cut and tuition has to take up the slack), drives many professors to adopt "Scantron"-type tests, by means of which substantive feedback is sacrificed for speed (and sanity). I hate that. When I was a student, I always felt insulted by the generic, anonymous return on multiple choice tests. In all of our combined sixty years or so in Academia, neither Janet nor I ever gave a multiple-choice test. *Ever.* Even when we had classes of sixty or more students, all of our exams were of the short answer and/or essay type, and we graded each by hand, spilling copious amounts of red (undergraduate) or black (graduate) ink as we wrote detailed corrections so as to give personal, one-on-one feedback to every student, in every class, that we ever taught. I cannot adequately convey how long that took, or describe the many, many nights when one or both of us sat up till midnight or later scribbling away on exams or the research papers we routinely required even in the large introductory classes. It was brutally hard, but students sacrifice a lot to go to college, and we saw it as our job to make sure to give them their money's worth. Not sure what a pound of flesh is worth on the open market, but I like to think that we succeeded.

As the Hard Copy Age was yielding reluctantly to the Electronic Age, all of us in Academia faced an interesting question. How to accommodate the tidal wave of information that had become available via the Internet? Should students be allowed to cite online sources? Cite them they certainly did, and cite them they certainly did not, as plagiarism violations shot through the roof. It always amazed me when a student turned in a paper that very clearly had been written by someone else, a condition usually signified by consistent subject-verb agreements, proper syntactical structure, structured critical analysis, and other such overt clues. Of course, it was just as easy for us to find what was being plagiarized as it was for the students who were doing the plagiarizing in the first place. It was during an online search for such a document when the scales fell from my eyes, as I discovered the many web sites where one could purchase a term paper on pretty much any given subject. "Cheaters com," and so on. That was one major advantage of the subjective approach Janet and I took; no for-purchase website was going to have material matching the questions we set.

Not that students didn't try, of course. One assignment Janet developed for her Intro to Archaeology class was a net-based project whereby students would find the website of a dig somewhere in the world and answer a series of questions about the project. I remember her pausing in her grading late one night to ask me a strange question: "Do you remember playing 'Gabriel Knight: Sins of the Fathers?'" She was referring to a computer game involving a sort-of writer (voiced by Tim Curry!) pursuing Voodoo-invoking bad guys, mummies, and various other ghoulish entities through the back alleys of New Orleans, Germany, and Benin. It was a great game, very advanced for its time. Apparently, the student whose paper Janet was reading was also a fan, as his site description was of a Gabriel Knight locus, taken directly from the game manual! To give another example, a nephew once asked my advice on a school paper about Mesoamerican archaeology. According to one Internet site he was using, the Aztecs had developed quite a daunting treatment for war captives, which was to sew a live chihuahua into their chest cavities. That might have been an interesting element in a Gabriel Knight sequel but as scholarship, it left a wee something to be desired.

The hardest day of teaching I ever had was September 11, 2001. None of us really knew what was going on that horrible day, but I had classes to teach, so off I went to teach them. The students were, as you might imagine, distracted; there was fear in the air and I had to settle things down before I could lecture. I forget what I said, but it was something generic along the lines of, "If we panic, they win." We all got through it together, but it was not an experience I would care to repeat. More fear was in the air after a spate of shootings took place on campuses across the nation in the mid-2000s. There was one such scare at MSU, when an "active shooter" alert fortunately turned out to be a false alarm. We were trained to deal with such situations, which was pretty depressing in its own right. Inevitably, following such events we had politicians pushing for guns to be *allowed* on campuses across the country; *concealed* guns, at that. Having seen the panicked reaction that occurred when the false alarm was raised on our campus, I cannot begin to express what a bad idea that would be. I thought the university administration and campus police handled the whole situation very well, which was some considerable comfort. But none of this made teaching any easier.

Research always feels like the reward for doing all the other chores. Research chops are of paramount importance in Academia, with applicants being chosen for jobs largely on the strength of their research profiles. Ironically, finding time to actually *do* research once a job is landed becomes very, very difficult given all the other demands placed on faculty. But research is fun, and personally fulfilling, and important not just for the research results themselves but also because those results feed directly into teaching. If there is one problem with how research is evaluated in an academic setting, it has to do with rate of publications (that darn business model). If a scholar takes three years to produce a masterpiece, surely that should count as much as when another scholar cranks out three lesser works per year? It does not work that way, alas. Quality is a consideration, but how that is determined is often rather cryptic.

In addition to publishing like crazy, academics also are expected to help fund their own research, and to financially support graduate students, in particular, by getting research grants from government agencies, private foundations, or pretty much anywhere opportunities might lie. Getting grants is a difficult enterprise, to put it mildly. I managed to obtain four National Science Foundation grants during my time at MSU, which was pretty good by anyone's standards. At least one of those grants became the topic of a Mississippi radio talk show, the host of which disparaged my successful effort as a waste of taxpayer money. What said host failed to understand is that, in these days of reduced state funding, universities are in fierce competition for students (and their tuition dollars) and in poor states like Mississippi, getting a high-level grant greatly raises the prestige of an academic program, allowing that program to compete more successfully for students from around the world. Those students, who might otherwise not give our dear old Magnolia State the time of day, significantly boost the state's economy, providing a particularly excellent return on taxpayer investment in the NSF and other scientific funding bodies. They also leave with a positive appreciation for the state, which doesn't hurt. And all that is on top of the actual research results stemming from funded projects. So grants are great investments that give back to the states in many ways, and they are especially helpful in relatively poor states like Mississippi. Not that the talk show host would have cared. Regardless of political stripe, an ideologue is a mentally constipated individual for whom raw data provide no roughage.

I was able to get my doctoral work published, which got me off to a good start in my academic post. Over subsequent years, I came up with some pretty good ideas, some of which actually worked. Perhaps the best was an idea for sourcing shell-tempered pottery, which was produced in different times and places around much of the world. "Temper" is something added to clay when making pottery; for example, bone china is so called because crushed bone is used as an additive. Pottery tempered with the crushed shells of river mussels became widespread in eastern North America around a thousand years ago. As I learned more about freshwater mussels, I realized that the bits of shell temper might serve to tell us where such pottery was made and how it was moved around via human migrations, trade, etc. This is because mussels take up elements from the waters they inhabit, building a chemical signature into their shells. To test that idea, I collaborated with some other folks, including a chemist. We put sherds (broken pieces of pottery) into a machine that shot a laser beam into the little shell bits, sending the resultant "ablated" material into a spectrometer where the elemental composition could be determined. There still are some bugs to work out, but the method seems to work very well and with the very welcome aid of some excellent colleagues, good progress is being made. If I am remembered for anything in the field, I think it will be this one. I would prefer that to *Homo tombigbeensis*.

In addition to lab work, archaeologists must go into the field to obtain materials for research. I described my own survey and excavation field schools earlier in this book. While still a student at MSU, I also got to work at an impressive "tell" site in Israel, an eighteenth-century cotton plantation in the Bahamas, and the magnificent, circa 2,000-year-old Ingomar Mounds site in Union County, Mississippi. While working at the university, I led or participated in many field projects, including excavations at a large, palisaded, thirteenth-to seventeenth-century Native village site near Starkville; at the approximately 3,400-year-old Poverty Point World Heritage Site in Louisiana; and at what is still the oldest known mound in Mississippi, an earthen monument in Lincoln County built more than five thousand years ago. Looking back over it all and remembering that first arrowhead on the family farm, the book about the Aztecs my music teacher gave me, and gazing as a high schooler into the dimly lit museum of the Cobb Institute, I remain astonished that the fanciful dreams of a Mississippi hill-country boy turned out not to be so fanciful after all.

*ur first rental house in England, on Middle-
ood Road in Sheffield. Ours was the second
d bay window. These houses were built as
sidences for coal miners back in the day.*

*Right) A riverboat tour on the Thames, 1988.
hat's Kingston Bridge in the background.*

*ut and about in England. That is the Royal
order Bridge at Berwick-upon-Tweed, a
pically endearing place name. The bridge
is opened by Queen Victoria in 1850.*

*Tower Bridge in London. Nikki was
in her pink-and-blue phase. No idea
why I wasn't wearing socks.*

Big brother and little sister on a footpath in the English country-side.

Traveling via public transport in England. "Pizzaland" was best passed by unless one had a taste for oven-baked sheetrock putty.

(Left) Learning how to map caves in England. That actually was pretty hard, as I am claustrophobic, but I had to rep the Stars and Stripes so in I went.

My Master's cohort at the University of Sheffield. Grinding work but enormous fun. We were studying up on animal bones that day, a part of the program that apparently didn't take too well as I later misidentified a pig bone as human. Can't win 'em all.

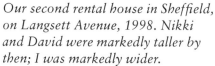

Out and about in the Netherlands, specifically a dockyard in Monnickendam, 1998.

Our second rental house in Sheffield, on Langsett Avenue, 1998. Nikki and David were markedly taller by then; I was markedly wider.

Crossing a stone wall in the Peak District, No. 547 of a series.

Crossing a stone wall in the Peak District, No. 764 of a series.

(Right) Conwy Castle in typically balmy north Wales weather. David's knowing smile is signifying that we were going to look at every damned rock in the place. Nikki's knowing expression is signifying resignation to that fate.

(Left) Out and about in Australia. This is on the awesome beach at Cape Woolamai on Phillip Island southeast of Melbourne.

(Above) On a beach in western Washington I think I dropped our lunch down there.

(Left) Janet screening dirt at the Tell Halif archaeological site in Israel, 1987.

(Below) Out and about in the Smoky Mountains.

Spooning at the Roman aqueduct at Caesarea Maritima, Israel, 1987.

)ut and about at Teotihuacan, Mexico, 2006.

Right) A winter expedition in Ferry County,
Vashington. The one and only time this
eacock has ever worn snow shoes…

…Janet styled them better.

irt of my wood-
rturing apparatus at
e Forest Products Lab,
iss. State University.

e made wood scream
id we had graphs to
ove it. Aside: I bought
at tweed jacket in 1985
d wore it to every
ofessional function for
e next 35 years.

Cultural Resource Management archaeology on the Cumberland
River in Nashville, early 1990s.

(Above right) Getting ready to go out on a survey on the Tombigbee National Forest. I was required to wear a hardhat in case a tree fell on my head.

(Right) Breaking more OSHA regulations while photographing an excavation on the Tombigbee National Forest.

(Below) Being an archaeo-pirate on an MSU field project. Janet is rethinking her mating options.

A pretty typical Anthropology display for a public day at MSU. I was making stone projectile points, which may yet prove to be marketable skill.

lping Nikki take data on penguin chicks in zentina, 2002. One such chick shat on me, ich I considered an honor.

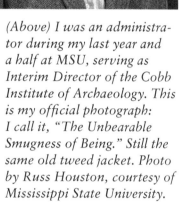

(Above) I was an administrator during my last year and a half at MSU, serving as Interim Director of the Cobb Institute of Archaeology. This is my official photograph: I call it, "The Unbearable Smugness of Being." Still the same old tweed jacket. Photo by Russ Houston, courtesy of Mississippi State University.

(Above left) My brothers circa 1990. From left to right: Bennie, Robert, Dennis, Hardy, Glenn, and Andy. Andy rarely wore a shirt when the cameras came out. I like how we're all about the same height and share a complete lack of fashion sense.

An irreverent moment with Mom. Only Robert would have the temerity to pinch her butt.

Mom during her days as mavin of the lunch room at French Camp Elementary School. She refused to reveal the dark secrets of mystery meat.

Just a really nice photo of Mom and Pop.

14

LESSONS LEARNED

AND SO THE LONG DAYS AND LONGER NIGHTS OF ACADEMIA DRIFTED BY. Janet retired in 2014 for two typically altruistic reasons: to give someone else a shot at a job, and to be able to devote more of her time to complete research projects that had backlogged over the years. It was a difficult transition, which was not surprising considering how much of herself she'd given to the job over thirty-seven long years. Janet being Janet, she eschewed the usual pat-on-the-back, rocking-chair kind of ceremony that sees many faculty members out the door. That sort of thing just wasn't her style. But she did not leave uncelebrated. With the help of some awesome former students, over the course of a year I secretly arranged for a surprise gathering of Anthropology graduates at what Janet thought was simply the annual picnic on the Cobb lawn, held to celebrate the end of each academic year. About a hundred people from all over the country attended, many of whom had launched their professional careers under Janet's tutelage. Plus, unbeknownst to Janet, Nikki had flown in from Arizona, where she was working on a post-doc in ecology. Janet and I arrived at the Cobb and exited our car. As we walked toward the building, a wave of applause and happy shouts came rolling towards us. For a moment, Janet was taken aback. Then she looked at me and said, "This is for me, isn't it?" Score one for the home team! The day was great, full of reminiscence and catching up, topped off with drinks at the outside court of a nearby bar. It was very much like a family reunion.

There were some sad losses during those years. Mom suffered a series of strokes that seriously compromised her ability to function, a situation that ultimately landed her in a nursing home where she passed away in 2002 at the age of 69. Hardy died in late 2012. Such losses inevitably make one think of one's own mortality and lead one belatedly to pay more attention to one's own health. The basic lifestyle of an academic archaeologist is not a particularly healthy one, consisting of long periods of sedentary desk-bound existence followed by field sessions during which one works like a galley slave. As we aged, both Janet and I developed sciatica, doubtless a result of heaving buckets and wheelbarrows full of dirt around like we were amped-up teenagers on a construction site. Her case became severe, so much so that for a while she had real trouble standing or walking. True to form, she didn't let that stop her. I never will forget the day when, at her insistence, I drove over the sidewalk to get her to the lawn in front of the Cobb. There I helped her out, where she lay on the grass until I could get the car parked. With the help of some friends, I then wheeled her into the building on a rolling chair, from which she spent the day laboring away, as usual. Anyone who thinks that academics are shiftless never witnessed Janet double-pumping the clutch. On August 24th, 2018, she passed away after a long, typically valiant, struggle against cancer. True to form, she remained in control and calling the shots until about six hours before her death, mustering her strength at the end to console *me*. The last full sentence she managed was, "The four of us had some good times." Yes, we did, my baby; yes, we did.

With Janet's passing, my heart went out of my academic endeavors. Somewhat to the astonishment of my peers, I retired that December to pursue other activities, including finishing this book. Here's a weird thing that all retirees endure; once your intentions are announced, people immediately begin to ask, "What are you going to do now?" I had prepared a stock answer that, with practice, I was able to deliver with a straight face. My plan, I earnestly assured such inquisitors, was to open up a really, really low-end barbeque joint called "Gristlin' Dixie," the signature dish of which would be something called "chicken-fried stank." That usually stopped their gobs for a moment or two.

Somewhat unexpectedly, I found myself returning to my country roots. I bought some land in Webster County and an old pickup truck to drive around out in the woods. I named it "Vader's

Helmet" because of the horrific murky-black custom paint job. My dogs love it when I put collars on them and they take up positions about where the Sith Lord's cerebellum would be. I named the land "The Roost," because, you know, Peacocks and all that. A friend set up motion cameras out at The Roost and recorded deer, turkey, racoons, squirrels, quail, and an enormous bobcat that I named "Sparky." And there are two fishing ponds! Life is good. I even found myself eating at Pap's again, thanks to the only high school reunion I ever have attended. I showed up in Ackerman early one night for the gala event, hoping that disco wouldn't be part of the evening's proceedings. Spotting a group of elderly folks congregated around the front door, I stopped to ask them if they knew where my party was meeting. Turned out that they were my party. Ouch!

One positive outcome of my changed life status is that I reconnected with my siblings and their families in ways that were long overdue. One weekend I reconnected in ways that might very well have led to an early demise. Glenn asked me to accompany him on a trip to Milton, Florida, where our cousin Ted had an old deck in his yard which needed to be dismantled. If Glenn and I would help with the dismantling, Glenn would get the lumber, which he planned to use for a deck at his house, free of charge. Having lurked in near-seclusion for months due to the coronavirus outbreak, I was more than ready for an adventure. Knowing Glenn and Ted, I strongly suspected that misadventure was to be a more likely outcome. I was righter than I knew.

We left Glenn's house early one morning in his battered old Ford pickup, a vehicle distinguished by a lack of air conditioning and a set of bull's horns prominently affixed to the hood. An equally battered twelve-foot trailer bounced along behind us. Somewhat to my surprise, we got to Milton without mishap and spent the next day working furiously, drenched with sweat in the early September humidity of the Panhandle. The lumber was quite weathered, so screw heads instantly stripped when we tried to back them out with a drill. Instead, we had to pull things apart using a combination of hammers, crowbars, brute strength, and a Sawzall when we could fit the blade between members. Once dismantling was complete, we had to use a jack and chain to pull the four-by-four posts out of the ground, after which the encasing concrete had to be busted from post bases with a sledgehammer. Finally, all of the encrusting hardware (joist brackets, squirrel feeders, etc.) had to be wrenched off and the lumber loaded onto the trailer. We also loaded up an old motorcycle and some kind of enormous tractor part, so the combined weight of the payload was considerable. It was a long day, but great fun, and the cold beer went down very well that evening. We went to bed weary, satisfied, and in eager anticipation of the all-day fishing trip planned for the morrow.

We got up very early the next morning, intending to hit the water by first light. Ted, that generous soul, had bought lots of bait the previous afternoon: frozen fish, packaged squid, and live shrimp. We stopped at a gas station for final supplies and headed out, arriving at the launch on the Blackwater River right on schedule. Ted's wife Star, Glenn, and I took our places on the boat, one of those really large double-pontoon things with a nice canopied deck. Ted expertly backed it into the water. Having little draft, the boat floated easily off the trailer, and Ted went to park the truck. The plan was for Star to ease the craft over to a dock where Ted could come aboard. It was a good plan, contingent upon only one key factor: the motor starting. When that failed, a premonition began to grow that the uncustomary smoothness of the operation up to that point was bait that Fate had used to lure us into a bleak oblivion. Ted strolled down to the water and asked what the problem was. Star, her voice growing louder and more strained as we receded, explained the situation, which all of us pondered as the boat picked up speed in the strong current, our captain and the dock growing smaller by the minute. There was nothing else for it. Off came my shirt and shoes, out came my wallet and cell phone, and into the water I went. I gripped a rope in one hand and swam as best I could against an insistent current with a very large boat in tow. I finally reached the dock, blowing like a lovestruck manatee. I caught my breath while Glenn and Ted diagnosed the situation: a dead battery. Glenn and I fished from the dock while Ted and Star went off to buy a replacement. About an hour later the new battery was installed, the motor cranked easily, and we belatedly headed downstream toward Pensacola Bay.

The day was glorious; warm but overcast, biting flies the only distraction as we slowly cruised down the river and into the beautiful bay. I hooked something big on a trolling line; it tossed the lure before we could get a look at it, but we took it as a good omen. We made our way to first one bridge then another, stopping at each to drop lines. We caught a number of small bullhead catfish, but no specks, snook, snapper, or other desirable species were to be had, probably due to our complete lack of knowledge where fishing in brackish water was concerned. It didn't matter, especially since one o'clock p.m. was officially the start of Happy Hour. We eventually made our way to the mouth of the bay, where we docked to use the facilities at a restaurant and where I discovered that I had no idea about how to tie a large boat to a wooden post in choppy water. I ignominiously hugged the post till the others returned, then went to take my turn. Rest stop completed, we headed back upstream.

The day had grown long and Ted remembered that an open bridge we'd passed was soon to be closed, blocking access for the evening, so he told us to hang on, and opened 'er up. That boat could move! We clung to the siderails, laughing and enjoying life as only slightly buzzed grownups can, until, somewhere around the interface of East and Blackwater Bays, the engine cut off. The gas gauge read full, which was odd given that we'd been out all day. It became even odder when Ted mentioned that he'd not put any gas in that morning because of the gauge reading. It became odder still when we learned that he'd had the boat out a couple weeks before, for eight hours. We might reasonably have ascertained that two full days of boating should have dropped the fuel load by some detectable level, but with the gauge reassuringly indicating otherwise, like the loaves and fishes, the collective assumption was that we were good to go. That such was not the case became pressingly apparent as we began to drift back toward the Gulf of Mexico.

What to do? Our first gambit was to grab phones and search the internet for a boat towing company, although business hours had come and gone. We finally found a number that answered. Ted asked if they could bring us some gas. "Sure, sport," the miscreant on the other end of the phone answered. "For eight hundred dollars." Stunned, we looked at each other as the seriousness of the situation sank in. About that time, we saw a small ski boat with a single occupant heading in the direction we needed to go. Several loud whistles and exaggerated gesticulations later, he came over and gaped in astonishment as we explained our predicament, while the shore slipped slowly by and the sun nipped at the trees. After some consideration, it was decided that he would give us a tow, given that he'd put in at the same landing as we had. Relieved, we tossed him our mooring rope. As we did so, Star perspicaciously noted the rope's thin circumference and aged state. Within twenty yards, it broke. Fishing around, she found a ski rope in some recess and we hooked up again. It worked! Our benefactor turned his craft north and off we went!

For a bit, anyway. We had miles to go, and twilight was upon us. The small ski boat was laboring mightily, but we were making only about two knots. Smoke began to pour from our benefactor's motor and the transom of his craft kept dipping dangerously low into the water, which lapped hungrily at the gunnels. The futility of the effort quickly became obvious, and when a tiny boat ramp was spotted on the western bank, we headed that direction. As we neared the ramp, the water became so shallow that even the ski boat was hitting bottom. A new plan was hatched: we disengaged the towing rope and tossed out our anchor. Glenn and I stayed on board while Ted and Star clambered down onto the ski boat. They took positions on a flat platform near the bow, the skipper passed them both a beer, and hope dawned. Then he opened 'er up, and they took off upstream, Ted and Star bouncing on the platform like ping pong balls, beer and river water spraying into their faces. Ted, I should mention, was recovering from a major hernia operation, and the blood drained from my face as we watched them clinging on for dear life, jostling like kids on a used carnival ride. Hoping that his innards would make it back intact, Glenn and I cast out our fishing lines, trying to relax with a bit more recreation before the light faded completely.

Which happened more quickly than anticipated, due to the enormous, terrifying storm that came hurtling out of the east like some gigantic harbinger of doom, a rolling black cloud bank sporadically illuminated by lightning that flashed and crackled across a front, stretching in either direction as far as the eye could see.

"Might get some weather soon," Glenn remarked casually as he flung his line out again. The words hadn't even left his mouth when an incredibly cold blast of air hit us directly in our faces, a startling sensation given the heavy, humid atmosphere that had been blanketing us all day. In a strained voice, I suggested that perhaps we might consider reeling in our lines and taking at least nominal cover beneath the canopy, which was looking more and more dubious as shelter. Grudgingly, Glenn complied, and not a moment too soon. The storm hit us like a freight train, sheets of heavy rain driven almost sideways by powerful winds. The surface of the estuary looked like something from the Roaring Forties, all choppy waves and foam. And although the canopy did offer some protection, the wind splattered us with rain in random gusts, so that we both were thoroughly soaked in no time. I kept my hand over the pocket that held my cell phone while trying to make nonchalant remarks as the storm grew ever more intense. Glenn made some less-than-nonchalant remarks when his side of the canopy suddenly folded, sending a generous freshet of water right down the back of his shirt.

It was fortunate for us that the wind was blowing west instead of south, since I had no interest in visiting Guantanamo Bay and the anchor was proving hopelessly inadequate under the conditions. The pontoon boat was bucking up and down as we were driven toward shore, straight toward the riprap lining the little concrete boat ramp. Fortunately for the boat, the wind veered southwest at the last minute, so that we just missed the rocks and instead found ourselves beached on a parcel of land festooned with "No Trespassing" signs. I waded through the surf and urinated against one such marked tree, figuring that the rain would quickly eliminate any evidence of my crime. Then we sat on the boat and waited. And waited. And waited. Ted and Star couldn't find us, and the storm was so bad that they couldn't get sufficient signal to do an internet search for the landing location. When they finally could, the landing, minor cultural feature that it was, did not show up. They got through to us eventually, and I waded out again to discern and relay the closest street names. By the time they rolled up in the truck, it was far too late to attempt loading the boat onto the trailer. Ted knocked on the door of the house standing on the property where I had peed, which turned out to belong to a completely understanding and sympathetic woman who graciously allowed us to leave the boat there for the night. Exhausted, we roped the craft to a power pole and drove the considerable distance back home to peel off our soaked clothing and crawl into welcoming beds.

The next morning, we were at the landing early, and fortunately the tide was in, so that the boat was floating. Ted and Glenn waded out to the boat and poured a couple of gallons of gas into the tank. It cranked right up and Ted was able to back the trailer far enough down the miniscule ramp to allow us to load. We were back home at a respectable hour, which was fortunate, since the coolers still held bait fish, long-dead shrimp, and tasty squid bits floating around with packages of pallid cheese, half-drunk bottles of water, and a remnant beer or two that looked oddly enticing despite the early hour and the clinging bio-slime. The stench was appalling. All of the fishing rods were hopelessly tangled together and the paper garbage bags had melted, but at least the gas gauge still read full. With inordinate cheerfulness, we cleaned up the whole mess and spent the remainder of the evening devouring delectable grilled fish and vegetables Star whipped up, drinking nominally de-slimed beer and shooting the breeze inside a back-yard tent as more heavy rain settled in. Life was good!

The next day, Glenn and I loaded up our belongings early and started on the long journey back to Mississippi. About half an hour down the road, I realized that I'd left my car keys behind, so back we went. That detour wasn't helpful, given that the rain was growing heavier still, the leading edge of Hurricane Sally churning her way up the Gulf. The consequent low visibility added considerable danger to the enterprise, because, of course, the trailer lights did not work. An hour or so north of Milton the skies cleared, everything on the trailer was holding well, and the tension slowly drained from my body. We could go only about fifty miles an hour with our heavy load, but as long as nothing went wrong, we would make it back to Glenn's place well in advance of the hurricane. We both grinned as we passed the Mississippi state line and turned north. Homeward bound!

Until about thirty miles south of Meridian, when, traveling up Interstate Highway 45, a rear tire blew out on my side of the truck. Never a good thing when you're hauling a large heavily-loaded trailer, particularly on a highway notorious for eighteen-wheelers. Ever unflappable, Glenn managed to slow us down and get the truck and trailer just off the highway, onto a tiny patch of asphalt where we could set a jack. We first tried a 20-ton hydraulic unit that Ted had loaned to Glenn. The truck began to lift...and then settled back with a sigh as the ram descended into the cylindrical body while oil, or hydraulic fluid, or something else I didn't want to touch squirted out of what I assumed was the jack's mating orifice. We then set a frighteningly gracile scissors jack beneath the rear axle. I grabbed the ridiculously long sproingy crank handle, not wanting Glenn to undertake the operation considering that he already had undergone a number of previous operations; eleven hip surgeries, to be precise. I cranked and cranked, and slowly, *slowly*, the truck began to rise.

I was astonished at how weak I seemed to be, until I belatedly realized that I wasn't just raising the truck; I was raising both the truck and the attached, heavily-loaded trailer. The spare tire was beneath the bed, trapped beneath some overly complicated mechanism that had to be manually unscrewed, which meant that Glenn had to get underneath the truck. The overworked primary instrument had begun to bow out ominously on one side, so he wisely placed a second one at the rear of the vehicle. By that time, we both were soaked with sweat, the only physical relief coming from the snatching winds that sucked at our clothing each time an eighteen-wheeler thundered past. I held my breath until Glenn finally got the tire free. He then tied the holding mechanism to some point beneath the bed with a piece of rope. Once he was clear, I set the spare tire in place and threaded lug nuts back onto the waiting bolts. I eased off on the jack, the truck came down... and the spare immediately went almost completely flat. I cursed and punched some air. Glenn just chuckled as he rummaged around in the tool box, where he found a remarkably small air compressor that looked like it might have seen duty at Verdun. He plugged it into the cigarette lighter and flipped the switch. It didn't work. He slapped it. It still didn't work. I began to feel panicky, but Glenn remained cheerfully unperturbed. He slapped it again and, grudgingly, with an aggrieved whine, it came to life. Waiting for the tire to inflate was like watching corn grow, but after about thirty minutes it held enough air that we considered it safe to head to the nearest town and buy another spare for the journey home. The station attendant whipped a used tire onto the rim in record time. Glenn gave him a pocket knife as a tip.

At that point, I was determined that we should travel on back roads rather than the interstate, which was dangerous at the best of times and downright terrifying given the load we were pulling and the questionable reliability of our conveyance. I would rely on Google Maps™ to navigate. That worked fine for a while, until my phone ran out of juice and I discovered that the charging cable coming out of the dash didn't fit the phone's receptacle. No problem. Glenn barked commands into his own phone, which obligingly began to issue directions. That would have worked well except for two complicating factors: 1) it was hot, and without air conditioning we had to ride with the windows down; and 2) Glenn is as deaf as a post without his hearing aid, and possibly deafer than a post when, with hearing aid in, the rushing air coming into a vehicle blankets his aural receptors with an unbreachable wall of white noise. "Turn right on the next road," the phone helpfully suggested. Past the next road we went. "Make a U-turn and then take your next left," our electronic guide remonstrated in an accusatory tone. On we sailed. I had the pleasure of viewing parts of the state I'd never seen before ere we finally, finally pulled into Glenn's yard, tired, hungry, but whole, with never a lost board or tractor part. Despite—or because of—the misadventures, the whole trip was enormous fun. What stories lie around the next bend in the road, I can't imagine.

And so time passes. Grandkids very much make my world go round, despite my lack of genetic contribution to the human experiment. I broke down and hired someone to mow the lawn on a regular schedule, much to the astonished gratification of the neighbors. The guy does a great job and will even mow the flower beds if I ask him to. I knew that I had achieved the American Dream the day I realized that my dogs have more toys than I did as a kid. And, slowly, the research bug began to bite again, so that once more I am immersed in archaeology, which I love. I alternate between fishing and inhaling sherd dust from my analysis tray. Can't really ask for much more than that.

My friends and I are all now at least two bites onto the far side of the apple, and it won't be overly long before we work our way down to the core. Thinking about such things I realized that, once the older of my two dogs passes, I have enough remaining life span to take proper care of just one more. I grasped about in vain for a suitable name for this next-and-last canine, until I mentioned it to Glenn, who immediately suggested "Omega." Exactly what I was looking for! Omega and I are going to be good buddies.

There is a difference between growing older and maturing, of course. We are all doomed to the first, while some never manage the second, as often is evidenced by the way we treat one another. My innate optimism and faith in humanity have been greatly strained by the reemergence in recent times of overt racism. This is, of course, the first topic that springs to mind when most people think of Mississippi, and there is, of course, legitimate historical justification for such perception. Racism was an omnipresent fact of life when I was growing up, one of which I became cognizant at a very early age. Like all behavioral codes, one learned the boundaries by observation, mimicry, and experience. My first memory in this regard is of an incident that took place when I was about five years old. We had visited some relatives in the Delta and were driving back home past the endless flat fields reeking of herbicides, rows seeming to stretch out to infinity. I was riding in the back of the pickup. As we drove past one field, I saw an African-American boy about my age playing some lonely game out there amidst the young cotton plants. Our eyes met, and some action seemed called for. Motivated by programming and expectations that I felt without understanding, I raised my little fist in a threatening gesture. A look of angry defiance immediately clouded his childish features and he raised his own small fist in mute but eloquent reply. And thus we parted, his brown form dwindling as he receded into the distance. I remember that moment very clearly because I felt quite bothered, both by my own action and by his response. I remember telling Mom about what I'd done, and while I don't remember receiving praise, neither do I remember any admonitions. And so I was left to wonder: had I done right?

I remained troubled at heart as I grew older, even as the expectations of the code became clearer (and more rigid). I remember one day when an aunt and uncle came up into our drive, ordinarily a joyous occasion. But there was no joy that day as my aunt emerged, stern-faced, from the car to announce in an outraged tone that "They just shot our next president." She was talking about George Wallace. I had only a vague notion of what was going on; I only knew that "they" had hurt "us" and that an angry sense of injustice was the expected response. Not long after, integration took place. I remember that as being a very strange time. New words like "busing" were part of an alien lexicon in which adults conversed worriedly. One day we all piled into the truck and went for a drive far into the countryside to where a group of earnest citizens were taking matters in hand by building a school that, as I understood it, we kids might be attending. It was going to be called "We Care Academy." I remember the tone of defiant righteousness in the voices of the adults as they proudly discussed the project with my parents. I remember being afraid. How could a young child *not* be afraid when the grownups were going to such lengths to protect us?

We did not attend that academy, although I don't remember why. Instead, we were pulled out of school and taught at home by Mom for a year. That was weird. We had textbooks and homework, and Mom worked very hard on our lessons. Twice a day she called a short break during which we were required to run down to Cowboy Land and back to get some exercise equivalent to recess. How on earth she managed to homeschool us on top of everything else she had to deal with, I have no idea. Eventually, we were re-enrolled into public school in Mathiston. We had to take tests to assess whether we were prepared to enter the appropriate grades and I remember how proud Mom was of all of us (and of herself, no doubt) when we passed with flying colors. Why Mathiston, I don't know; nor do I know why we ultimately returned to school at French Camp. But I do remember that for the first term, Andy and I were instructed to walk downtown to our Aunt Gerry's house to have lunch, so that we would not have to "eat with them." "They" included a set of black teachers who were assigned positions at the school, a situation I remember being discussed with great disdain by the grownups in our increasingly confused world. And through all of the confusion, I remember the feeling of aggrieved resentment that permeated the atmosphere, a smoldering outrage that something unwanted was being forced upon us. How the little black kids and their grownup counterparts felt about the whole deal, I still can't imagine, but it must have been terrifying to leave their schools to enter a new, potentially quite hostile, environment.

And then, something amazing happened. It was all *fine*. "They" were just kids, like us. I liked some of the new kids, like Brenda, a smart, feisty girl in my class, a great deal. The new teachers were just that: teachers. Mr. Pittman, a truly gifted history teacher, rapidly became one of my favorites. There were no fights; no gangs formed; nothing burned down. We were all just people, doing what people do. I was relieved and puzzled at the same time. What on Earth had all the fuss been about? Why on Earth would anyone care about "eating with them" or any other social interactions with other human beings?

What the fuss was about, of course, was fear: fear of the existential kind, which is as incredibly powerful a motivating force as those who seek to manipulate others could hope to find. Or manufacture. Upon routine encounter, the "other" isn't; without such encounter, "otherness" is an extremely powerful tool for demagogues and rabble-rousers. It is depressingly obvious these days that racism still is prevalent in American society, astonishingly so, given the decades that have passed since the Civil Rights Act and integration. Sadly, about the best that can be said is that much of this disease remains unexpressed (at least publicly) until there is a trigger. I recall one occasion when I reported for work at a U.S. Forest Service office only to find the staff all abuzz about a couple that had been spotted "parking" in a car on the road to a recreation area. Apparently, more recreation was to be found inside the car. I could understand why such PDA, carried out on a public road in broad daylight, might be gossip-worthy on a slow day, and made some casual remark to that effect. I quickly was given to understand what the buzz really was about: they were a *mixed* couple. He was *black*. She was *white*. I laughed out loud upon hearing that bombshell report. It was the late nineties, for heaven's sake—the *nineteen* nineties. Why on Earth did it matter what color their respective skins were? To my utter astonishment, it turned out that I was definitely in the minority, which at least gave me a fleeting sense of kinship with the gentleman in the car (assuming that he was, in fact, a gentleman). One of the office staff, a woman about ten years my senior, was particularly biting in her criticism. I knew her pretty well, or so I thought, including the fact that she overtly self-professed to be a Christian. Impulsively, I put the question to her: If all people are part of God's creation, why does the color of someone's skin matter?

To my surprise, she had a ready answer; so ready, that it was clear that she had *thought* about that very question. A beatific mask dropped down upon her features, frown lines smoothing as though she'd just received a megadose of Botox. Her eyes shone like a little child's as she said, in reverential tone, "I believe that, in Heaven, we won't be able to tell the difference."

My follow-up question was the obvious one: If it is a Christian's duty to act as heavenly as possible while on Earth, why make such a big deal out of the "difference" here?

Instantly, the beatific mask was replaced by an outraged scowl. The color rose in her face; her eyes narrowed, and through pursed lips she hissed a terse phrase right out of the *eighteen* nineties: "I think they should be horse-whipped."

Yikes! I could have argued the point further, but I never am good in a debate when rational arguments fail, nor am I particularly adept at defusing confrontational anger. Plus, pushing people on their religious beliefs when I am not myself religious feels hypocritical, so I let the matter drop. I'm sure that neither she nor I ever looked at the other the same way again. I could not help but see an unrepentant racist who harbored poisonous bile in her heart while espousing the doctrine of brotherly love on Sundays (but not *that* kind of brother, apparently). She, I presume, saw a godless, bleeding-heart liberal who no doubt wanted to raise her taxes and hand her grandchildren over to a socialist creche for proper absorption into the hive. How very strange that we held such different viewpoints despite having been raised in basically the same blue-collar environment in rural Mississippi!

The history of racism in Mississippi is particularly convoluted and it certainly isn't limited to the binary opposition of black and white, although that sternest of racial codes at least initially conditioned all others. The river towns of the lower Delta once were home to a large, thriving Jewish merchant class before an overt campaign of racism on the part of their "Christian" competitors—a campaign invoking the deleterious social consequences of those merchants selling liquor to "darkies"— led to an exodus. Following the Civil War, Chinese immigrants actively were sought by large landowners in the Delta looking for a cheap (and docile) replacement labor force. The consequent introduction of the "Coolies" led to some astonishing contortions by local power structures. For a time, some Delta towns maintained *three* of everything: white, black, and yellow churches, schools, theaters, etc. With considerable savvy, those immigrants quickly moved out of the fields and into towns where they successfully exploited a new unfilled niche, selling stuff to newly-freed blacks with whom white merchants preferred not to do business. As a consequence, what became a Delta institution, the "Chinese store," was born. The gradual accumulation of wealth allowed for subsequent generations of Chinese Americans to take their places on, or at least very near, the top rung of Delta society.[10] As this example demonstrates, just as biological species change over time, so, too, do social races. Mississippi's unique trajectory in this regard has much of value for the rest of the world to consider.

---

10   James W. Loewen, *The Mississippi Chinese: Between Black and White.*

As noted in Chapter 8, the belief that pure forms of entities exist to be discovered in nature is called essentialism. Essentialism actually works quite well for some pursuits: physics, say, where there certainly is such a "thing" as a hydrogen atom. But it is a poor "ism" where life, including culture, is concerned. Life (including culture) always is in the process of *becoming*. To be successful, life *must* be variable, else we'd all be wiped out by some flu strain. Sameness is a recipe for disaster should the environment change in such a way as to be deleterious to some particular form (think: potato famine). Consequently, there is no one essential form of any organism, including people. As has often been remarked, there are no discrete human "races" in any meaningful biological sense. As described in that fount of eternal knowledge, Wikipedia:[11]

> *In biological taxonomy, race is an informal rank in the taxonomic hierarchy, below the level of subspecies. It has been used as a higher rank than strain, with several strains making up one race. Various definitions exist. Races may be genetically distinct populations of individuals within the same species, or they may be defined in other ways, e.g. geographically, or physiologically. Genetic isolation between races is not complete, but genetic differences may have accumulated that are not (yet) sufficient to separate species. The term is recognized by some, but not governed by any, of the formal codes of biological nomenclature.*

Notice the ambivalence? This isn't politically correct waffling; it is an accurate assessment of the fact that biological "race" is *not* a fact. It is not even a particularly useful concept. Scientists (including anthropologists) were quite confused about this matter for a long time, with extremely regrettable consequences, such as the empowerment of those who sought to profit by perceived racial divisions (think: National Socialism). The extraordinary thing is that many

---

11 En.wikipedia.org, accessed January 19, 2019.

scientists *still* are confused about this matter, and their confused notions becomes accepted as fact when reported by a surficial press. For example, one can hardly call up news on the Internet today without seeing yet another story about the discovery of a new "kind" of fossil human. In the same stories it will be revealed in marveling tones that those different "kinds" of humans interbred with "modern" humans at some point! If creatures can breed and produce viable offspring, they are the same species. What is being witnessed in the fossils are morphological adaptations to specific, local-scale environmental conditions, which is a guaranteed evolutionary outcome that explains a lot of things: why Neanderthals had relatively robust skeletons (useful in the difficult northern climes); why skin tones are darker around the equator and lighter toward the poles (regulation of Vitamin D production upon exposure to sunlight); why sickle cell anemia is more common in people who live in equatorial zones and their descendants (it provides some protection against the malaria parasite); and so on. It's not that these differences don't matter; they matter a great deal as we seek to understand disease histories, human migration histories, and other topics of importance. But there are no hard edges to any of these phenomena; all such traits blend into other traits across space. There are no sides to the boxes, because there are no boxes.

The human eye is capable of detecting only a very small part of the electromagnetic spectrum. It was only with the development of suitable technologies that other parts of that spectrum became known (think: X-rays). Our cultural perceptions of race similarly have been limited by the lenses of our upbringing, our social environments. The broader perspective that allows us to perceive humankind as a whole, in all its diversity, may be enabled by a growing public consciousness of genetics, although powers that profit from division doubtless will continue to try to mold that consciousness to promote perceptions of genetic divisions rather than the genetic whole that is our species' inheritance (and the larger genetic whole that is life itself, of which we are only a very small part). Our individual behaviors are not genetically determined, of course; although there are genetic predispositions, our particular life histories, including social and environmental influences, strongly influence behavioral outcomes. And there is the highly pertinent fact that we all are sentient beings: we can *choose* to accept the reality of holism, or we can choose to reject it, just as many choose to reject the realities of human-influenced climate change, or evolution, or pollution, or social injustice, or whatever. We do not have to wait for further shared consciousness of genomic realities to make such choices; the exercise of free will always is an option and one that is, in fact, an American ideal and a cornerstone of Christian beliefs. In a Christian framework, the price exacted for choosing incorrectly is eternal damnation and torment. At the risk of once again treading into a space where I have no real right to be, I still am compelled to ask those who are Believers: which choices are more likely to bring the reward of eternal bliss promised by an all-loving Creator? Those that divide His children, or those that unite them? Those that harm His creation, or those that nurture it?

Allow me to offer a local example of the losses that accrue from xenophobia. Once, I was driving home from my job in Ackerman when, in dire need of a haircut, I stopped at a small beauty parlor beside the highway to see if they also cut men's hair. Curtains were drawn across the windows, including the small window in the door. I tried the handle; the door was locked. Assuming that the business was closed, I was turning to go when suddenly the door was yanked open, an arm shot out, and I literally was dragged inside. The elderly matron who had a surprisingly strong grip on my wrist maintained it while she deftly shut and locked the door with her other hand. After one last peek behind the curtain, she shoved me quite forcefully into a chair, paying no heed to my attempts to communicate my desired state of coiffage as she rummaged around in a cabinet drawer and came up with a sinister-looking pair of scissors.

"It's *them*," she growled, as if that explained her odd behavior.

"Them?" I responded nervously, visions of Sweeney Todd flitting through my brain.

"*Them*," she affirmed. "I have to keep the door locked or *they* come in." She carried on in such cryptic terms as, without soliciting anything like directions, she began clipping furiously away at my lank locks. Intrigued, and rather more able to focus as the flashing blades remained reassuringly north of my jugular, I listened, eventually ascertaining that she was talking about Hispanic migrant workers. The confirmatory tipoff came when, with a particularly nasty growl, she said, "They sit there in the chairs, talking to each other in that…that *language* of theirs!"

"Spanish?" I ventured.

She paid no heed but carried on snipping and sniping with equal vigor. Eventually, she dropped the scissors, took the money from my hand without counting it, and shoved me out the door. I heard the lock click before I was on the first step. And that is what racism is: it is building walls against perceived "others" until you yourself are boxed in. What a sad condition. Life is *short*. What a waste to live it in fear, to wall yourself off from the cultural differences that make it interesting!

Once biological race is understood to be the fallacy that it is, it is a short step to start recognizing the other, equally arbitrary boxes that we tend to let control our lives. Perhaps we ultimately will find common ground through the increasingly pervasive outreach of social media and mass entertainment (although the former platform seems to be having the opposite effect at the moment). We are very good, in all cultures, at anthropomorphizing the most astonishing range of things: frogs, pigs, rabbits, fish, candlesticks, alarm clocks…even watercraft (long live Boaty McBoatface!). Here's a radical thought: why don't we try anthropomorphizing our fellow human beings?

I had the great benefit of formal anthropological training to help me understand why, in logical terms, racism simply makes no sense, a gratifying marriage of moral certainty and well-established facts. My brothers got there by a variety of paths; I hope that someday they will share their own stories. I was too chicken to ever talk to Pop about such matters. I suspect that I was doing him a disservice. Mom came a long, long way, which was to be expected given the goodness of her heart. It was a sign of the times that her funeral was attended by an African-American woman who'd worked with her in the lunchroom. It was a sign of the times that such attendance was still unusual. It was a sign of the times that the shared sense of loss manifested as a desire to offer comfort; as a moment of connection; as warm welcome to a fellow grieving soul. That reassuring reaction has been on display over and over again in the face of far too many national tragedies even as the frantic promoters of discord mount their respective soapboxes to try, yet again, to keep us divided. Ultimately, they will fail, because ultimately, people are better than that.

Each of us, at one time or another, has thought about what we might have done differently in life. What problems could we have avoided? What if we'd made different decisions at this point or that? How might our lives and the lives of those we know have been changed? What if we could go back in time and change one—but only one—thing in our lives? I thought about such matters a lot while writing this book and I have my answer to that final question. It would be that summer day so long ago, when I bounced along in the bed of a battered pickup truck leaving its contrail of dust along a lonely country road. There, alone in the distance-devouring cotton field, I would see him: the dark-skinned little boy playing some solitary game under the immense blue sky of the Mississippi Delta.

I would again raise my hand. This time not in a fist, but in a wave.

THANKS

My heartfelt thanks to David, Nikki, Dennis, Bennie, Glenn, Robert, Andy, Rob, and Judy for letting me share something of their stories; to Dennis, Glenn, and Kathy for family photos; to Aggie for the author's pic; to David for photo improvement; to Billy, Bobby, Sam, and Ian for early reads and wise counsel; to Judy for the lovely cover art; to Julie for genealogical information; to Carole Byars for copyediting; to Ian "E.N." Brown for doing me the extraordinary honor of writing the foreword; and to Easty and Ian for being generally awesome.

A NOTE ON THE TYPE

The text of this book was set in **Sabon** which is an old-style serif typeface designed by the German-born typographer and designer Jan Tschichold (1902–1974) in the period 1964–1967. The chapter heads are set in **EVELETH**, a premium high-resolution letterpress family with exceptional realism and vintage charm produced by Ryan Martinson of Yellow Design Studio in 2014.

CPSIA information can be obtained
at www.ICGtesting.com
Printed in the USA
LVHW072223030921
696875LV00010B/161